Nuclear contamination of water resources

Proceedings of the conference *Water resource consequences of a nuclear event*, organized by the Institution of Civil Engineers and held in Glasgow on 7–8 September 1989

Thomas Telford, London

Conference organized by the Institution of Civil Engineers, and co-sponsored by the Commission of the European Communities and the National Radiological Protection Board

Organizing Committee: Professor G. Fleming (Chairman), B. Alexander, R. C. Clayton, J. L. Gray, Dr A. D. Horrill, Dr M. Jones, A. Knight, S. Newstead, Dr A. D. Wrixon

British Library Cataloguing in Publication Data
Nuclear contamination of water resources.
    1. Water. Pollutants. Radioisotopes
    I. Title
    628. 1685

ISBN 0-7277-1527-5

First published 1990

Published for the Institution of Civil Engineers by Thomas Telford Ltd, Telford House, 1 Heron Quay, London E14 9XF.

Printed and bound in Great Britain by Mackays of Chatham.

Contents

Opening address

R. McGILLIVRAY, Chief Engineer, Scottish Development
Department, Edinburgh, UK

The fact that this important conference is taking place, and has attracted
Authors from so many countries, is a measure of the widespread concern
that arose following the accident at Chernobyl; and of the seriousness
with which we all view its effects and implications.

For those unfamiliar with the organization of water supply in
Scotland, here is a brief description. Unlike England and Wales, there
are no plans to privatize water supplies, and the provision, management
and operation of this basic service is a local authority function carried
out by the nine regional and three islands councils. At the centre, the
Secretary of State for Scotland has responsibility for the overall national
policy as well as a duty, under our water legislation, to promote the
conservation of water resources. Both sides work closely together.
When they collaborated over 18 years ago to carry out a comprehensive
survey of developed water sources in Scotland, the report published by
the Scottish Development Department revealed ample resources to meet
all requirements in the foreseeable future; it was aptly titled 'A measure
of plenty'.

Nearly all of Scotland's water is drawn from surface sources, over
80% of it from upland catchments. When the major problems in water
supply in Glasgow had to be resolved almost a century and a half ago,
the city looked to an upland source - Loch Katrine some 60 kilometres to
the north. The loch provided substantial quantities of pure and
wholesome water which required no treatment. Engineers were rightly
proud of this major scheme. Other cities and towns followed this
example. As a result, the inhabitants of Scotland have grown to believe,
and to expect, that we have more than sufficient public supplies of good
quality water. It was at a later stage in the history of these water
schemes that the following was realized: chlorination was needed; much
of the water was soft and plumbosolvent; other issues were involved;
these works were no longer the province of the civil engineer, but that
chemists and scientists were equally important in their operation and
that very close collaboration of the various disciplines was essential.

It was comparatively late in this long history before radioactivity
came into our consideration. I think it is fair to say that many of us in
the UK were not familiar with its units of measurement. The Chernobyl
accident changed all that. We had to learn, virtually overnight, a new

Nuclear contamination of water resources. Thomas Telford, London, 1990.

language containing becquerels and millisieverts. The general public has a dread of radioactivity. Suddenly it was necessary to reassure people that water supplies, which hitherto had had their confidence, had not become dangerously contaminated. Another close relationship sprang up - between those in the water industry and radio-chemical scientists.

Earlier monitoring of radioactivity in the environment, including surface waters, had taken place in the 1950s and 1960s; but this was related to the testing of nuclear weapons. When these tests stopped, the need for such monitoring passed. Plans drawn up afterwards related to specific areas around nuclear installations, and were local or national. It was not envisaged that there could be a nuclear event of such magnitude that it would significantly transcend national boundaries.

Nuclear accidents had occurred, but none with such international impact as that at Chernobyl. That one event brought home to us the lack of real preparedness in the water industry. Nevertheless, advice was given and action taken quickly, even if on a crisis management basis and even if it did come in for some criticism after the event. Water authority personnel generally had no previous experience of sampling and analysis for radioactivity. Procedures had to be set up very quickly to ascertain whether there was any indication of significant contamination of water supplies. The sampling and reporting arrangements became more concrete as time went by, but fortunately it quickly became clear that there was no cause for concern. Perhaps one of the greatest difficulties for water engineers, as I have suggested, was in coming to grips with concepts and units of measurement which were strange to them, and to us, and in convincing local consumers that their water supplies were safe to drink.

In Scotland, the effects of the Chernobyl accident on water supplies were minimal. However, Paper 1 describes the situation at the other end of the scale: the situation that arose for the water industry in the Kiev area, close to the accident site. The spectre of large-scale contamination of water supply sources strikes dread into the hearts of those responsible for the provision of water services, and their efforts are directed at preventing it. As we all know, water is essential to life. While it may be possible to prevent the consumption of, say, milk or specific foodstuffs, this cannot be done with water. Surface water sources are vulnerable to airborne contamination, both directly and by run-off from a contaminated catchment area. There is nothing that can be done to protect a large reservoir, river or catchment from such contamination. It is fortunate, therefore, that, except in the most extreme cases such as in the immediate vicinity of an accident site, it is unlikely that the levels of radioactivity in water supplied to the public would be so great as to make it unsafe to drink. The volume of a reservoir, or the size of a catchment, is normally such that radioactivity deposited on the surface is likely to be heavily diluted; in fact, the highest concentration recorded in a Scottish source following Chernobyl was 21 Bq/l for iodine 131. This was exceptional and less than 1% of the level at which action to restrict consumption would have been required.

There are, of course, exceptions but public supplies in general have a number of natural safeguards - time and volume, rainfall patterns, the effect of treatment - all of which tend to reduce the likelihood that the public in general will receive hazardous doses of radioactivity from its drinking water. I will not dwell on this, as the Papers themselves give details of radiological standards for drinking water and monitoring requirements, and of the consequences and management of a nuclear event for water resources. The Authors may disagree with the views I have expressed, but, whatever our views, we must not be complacent nor suggest that planning against a future event of international proportions could exclude consideration of water supplies.

What has been done in the UK since Chernobyl? The Government has taken serious note of the event and of the fact that national contingency plans for such an occurrence did not then exist. The main action was to set up the National Response Plan for Nuclear Accidents Overseas, the first phase of which is now in place. Another early action was to enter international agreements to ensure wide notification between countries of any incident involving a significant release of radioactivity to the environment.

Locally, a scheme was set up to carry out a programme of routine monitoring for radioactivity of Scottish public water supplies. This was begun early in 1987 and covered a variety of types of water source throughout Scotland. The aim was twofold: firstly, to confirm that there were no remaining effects from the Chernobyl accident; secondly, to provide an indication of the normal background levels of activity to be found in water supply sources. This second aim was to satisfy one of the first, and most widely asked, questions at the time of Chernobyl when initial results of water analyses began to be reported: 'How do these figures compare with normal levels?' At the time, this seemed to us, as civil engineers, a reasonable question, but we could not answer it with any real conviction. The response had to be that the results showed very low levels of activity, far below levels at which action to restrict use of water supplies would need to be considered.

Later, we learned from the radio-chemical experts that the question had little relevance in an emergency situation and that levels of radioactivity in water could not be looked at in quite the same light as, say, concentrations of some chemical substance. The important consideration is what a particular level of activity represents in terms of long-term dose to the consumer. The levels of activity found in water supplies immediately after Chernobyl were insignificant in that respect. In our subsequent monitoring programme - which is continuing - it has proved virtually impossible to obtain measurable results. The initial 14 month programme produced only three results which were marginally above detection limits; and this out of some 100 analyses. One of them related to naturally occurring activity. Thereafter, the sampling and analysis procedures were modified to try to obtain positive measurements. However, even the more rigorous approach now adopted has produced only a few results slightly above the detection limit.

It is clear, then, that water resources in Scotland, which were only marginally affected at the time, have not suffered any longer term effect from the Chernobyl disaster. It must be remembered, however, that we were several thousand kilometres from that occurrence and that when the radiation plume was passing over, rain fell on only parts of the country. In other places, and other weather conditions, the picture was no doubt quite different.

I know that in Scotland, and in the UK as a whole, we have all learned lessons and are now better prepared to deal with a terrible event of this kind. It is my earnest hope that the main result, or lesson, to emerge from Chernobyl is that of a world-wide re-examination of safety measures so that we may be confident that everything has been done to remove the likelihood of a future accident.

Special address

Academician A. ISHLINSKY, President, World Federation
of Engineering Organizations, Moscow, USSR

It is my belief that the subject of the present conference is not only of
extreme importance and interest but that consideration of it is a matter of
great urgency in our nuclear age. More and more often these days the
demand is heard that all operational nuclear power stations should be
closed and development of nuclear power stopped altogether. Is that
right? Can humankind do without nuclear power stations? I personally
doubt it very much.

Certainly, energy from the sun, the wind and 'geothermal' waters
must be explored. In the USSR, a tenfold increase in the use of these
sources is planned, although a high price will have to be paid. In 1988,
for example, the cost-price of one kilowatt-hour of the Crimean solar
power station-5 was 26 roubles, while the average cost-price of electric
power is 1.2 copecks for one kilowatt-hour (1 rouble = 100 copecks). My
questions are these: who can pay a thousand roubles a month for
electricity, and what is going to happen to our country in a period of 5-10
years if, by that time, we are short of 120 million kilowatts? The USSR
will no longer be among the developed countries. At present, about 3
kilowatt-hours of electric power are required per each rouble of the
national income.

Commonsense suggests that nuclear power stations cannot be
dispensed with; but, at the same time, human beings must be assured of
the complete reliability and safety of these power stations. Scientists and
experts today are greatly concerned about the level of nuclear ignorance
which exists among the general public. Even a five-year old child knows
that it can hold an electric battery in its hand but it cannot stick its
fingers into a socket. How far does the knowledge of radiation go?
Some people are appalled by the knowledge that the radiation
background of granite is two or three times higher than the average and,
at the same time, they take in their hands a source of caesium plucked
out of the device. Experts know the, so to say, smell of radiation. It may
sound threatening to speak of Roentgens per hour, instead of Roentgens
per year, but I am convinced that radiophobia is the consequence mainly
of ignorance.

People throughout the world were and are concerned about the
Chernobyl tragedy, and I must admit that in the first days after the
disaster we made a number of mistakes. For example, we should have

invited specialists to the USSR immediately after the event. We had enough people and enough machinery but the radioactive dust was spread by lorries all over the neighbourhood, and that covered an area of thousands of square kilometres. In the town of Prypat, which is the town of nuclear specialists, very few people knew exactly what should be done in the case of a nuclear event. This is nothing less than ignorance and criminal negligence.

Ecology is of course the most urgent problem today. We all know that the mineral supplies of the earth are not as infinite as people has assumed them to be for a long time. Many forests are perishing; some species of fauna and flora are disappearing; mineral resources are dwindling; fresh water is a matter of general concern. Incidentally, before the last century, Europeans used untreated underground and surface water; only in 1829 in Chelsea, London, was the river water first passed through multi-media sand filters, such as those we use today, with the purpose of improving its quality.

Today, specialists are experimenting with new and better treatment methods, but, unfortunately, the intensive contamination of rivers, lakes and other water bodies by industrial wastes reduce all these efforts to zero.

I am not a specialist in this field, but the members of the USSR's delegation are experts on the problems of potable water: Academician Boris Laskorin is a well-known Soviet scientist and Nikolay Tzarik is chief engineer of the Kiev Water and Sewage Treatment Administration.

In my capacities as President of the International Federation of Engineering Societies and Chairman of the USSR Union of Scientific and Engineering Critics, it is a special honour to mention the fact that British scientists and engineers make a considerable contribution to the work of this International Federation, and are held in high regard by their colleagues in the Soviet Union.

1. Water supply and disposal in the City of Kiev following the accident at Chernobyl nuclear power plant

N. TZARIK, Kiev Water and Waste-Water Treatment
Administration, USSR

Treatment Administration

Kiev is the capital of the Ukrainian Soviet Socialist Republic, and is the USSR's third largest city, with a population of 2.7 million people.

The city water supply is dependent on three sources: two surface ones, i.e. the rivers Dniepr and Desna, and one underground one. The average total water consumption of the city amounts to 1.5×10^6 m^3/day, including 800×10^3 m^3/day from the Desna water supply plant, 400×10^3 m^3/day from the Dniepr water supply plant, and 300×10^3 m^3/day from subsurface aquifers pumped through artesian wells.

Industrial enterprises account for 20% of the city's water consumption. To meet the requirements of the potable water standards effective in this country, the water drawn from surface sources is conditioned at the treatment facilities of the Dniepr and Desna water supply systems, in compliance with the following treatment line: water intake, pumping plant, mixers, reaction chambers, horizontal settling basins, rapid trickling filters, ozone plants, clean water reservoirs, and repumping installation. Chlorine silicic acid, sulphuric aluminium, and ozone are used as chemicals.

The subsurface water needs no treatment since all of its indices conform with the standards. The groundwater is mined from the two aquifers located at a depth of 200-300 m, which belong to the Jurassic and the Senomanian.

Before being discharged to the Dniepr, the city municipal and industrial waste waters are subjected to mechanical and biological treatment. In summer, approximately 30% of the treated waste waters is extracted for irrigation of agricultural lands. Waste water sludge is treated in methane tanks, dehydrated in the sludge fields and used as a fertilizer. Methane is burned by the boiler plants for generating heat which is utilized by the biological treatment installation for meeting its own requirements.

The Chernobyl Power Plant accident posed a threat to the normal operation of the Kiev water supply system. In the circumstances, it became necessary to adopt the most urgent measures aimed at ensuring the non-stop delivery of potable water to the city under conditions of the potential radioactive contamination of water supply sources.

The Ministry of Public Health of the USSR had established the ad hoc norms for the permissible concentration of radioactive substances in foodstuffs. These norms were specified in conformity with the requirements of the Radiation Safety Standards (NRB-76) stipulating that there should be no excess of the following irradiation doses: thyroid gland - 30 rem; other organs and tissues - 10 rem. The permissible concentration of radionuclides in potable water as a function of the period of its consumption has been determined within the following limits: one month - 7×10^{-8} Ci/l; three months - 2×10^{-8} Ci/l; one year - 6×10^{-9} Ci/l.

Subsequently, the permissible concentrations of radionuclides in potable water were made tougher: initially, they were brought to 1×10^{-8} Ci/l according to total beta-activity, and then to 5×10^{-10} Ci/l for the sum total of ^{137}Cs and ^{134}Cs. The last norm is still effective today.

In compliance with the Radiation Safety Standards NRB-76, in the USSR, the permissible concentrations of radionuclides in potable water for the category B population (including persons who are likely to be exposed to the action of radioactive substances on account of residential conditions) amount to ^{137}Cs - 6.5×10^{-8} Ci/l, and to ^{134}Cs - 8.6×10^{-9} Ci/l.

Before the accident at the Chernobyl Nuclear Power Plant (NPP), the total beta-activity of water in water sources was 1×10^{-11} to 1×10^{-12} Ci/l.

Throughout the period from the day of the accident to the present, the concentration of radionuclides in potable water supplied to the city has not exceeded the permissible limits. The highest degree of water contamination was observed in May 1986, and was equal to 1×10^{-8} to 1×10^{-9} Ci/l according to total beta-activity. At present, the caesium total activity is 10^{-11} Ci/l.

Since the first day of the accident at the Chernobyl NPP, continuous round-the-clock monitoring of the radioactivity of water source water has taken place, including the control of water quality at various water treatment stages, the variation of radioactivity of different filter loading materials, and the radioactivity of waste waters, sludge and silt.

Our greatest concern was the threat of nuclear contamination of the Kiev reservoir. The upper reaches of this reservoir communicate with the Pripyat river on whose bank the Chernobyl NPP is located. The intake facilities of the Dniepr water treatment system are situated in the lower water of the Kiev reservoir at a distance of 120 km downstream of the NPP. The State Committee of the UkrSSR for Hydrometeorology and Environmental Control has made a comprehensive assessment of the pattern of contamination of the Pripyat river in the vicinity of the Chernobyl NPP, and of the potential threat of contamination by radionuclides of the Dniepr river basin, resulting from direct fall-out of radionuclides from the atmosphere and radionuclide transport by spring floods. Special hydro-engineering measures were taken to prevent the contamination of water resources of the Dniepr river, including the hydro-engineering projects at the NPP and at the Kiev reservoir, which buffers the inflow of waters of the Pripyat and Dniepr, as well as the dispersal of rain clouds at the approaches to the 30 km zone.

The analyses demonstrated that no excess of the permissible radionuclide concentration in water is to be expected, even in cases of flood and high water with a 1% flow probability.

However, despite the promising forecasts, several versions of the city's water supply in the event of higher permissible radionuclide concentrations were developed and implemented.

Version 1

Since the Kiev reservoir is the most vulnerable water supply source, it was decided that the water intake from the Dniepr should not continue for centralized water delivery purposes, and that Desna river waters should be fed to the treatment facilities of the Dniepr waterworks. To this end, in the span of just one month and a half, the following waterworks structures, which allowed the transfer of Desna waters to the intake of the Dniepr waterworks (some 350 000 m^3/day), were designed, built and put into operation

- new intake facilities with fish protection on the Desna river
- a floating pumping station with a capacity of 400 000 m^3/day
- power facility
- two pressure conduits (dia. = 1400 mm and dia. = 900 mm) with tunnel passages through the Dniepr river.

From 21 June 1986, the intake of water from the Dniepr river was discontinued, and the water supply of Kiev was effected from the Desna river and the underground sources. As a result, no disruption of water supply to the city occurred.

Version 2

Should the maximum permissible concentration of radionuclides be exceeded in not only the Dniepr river but also in the Desna river, the city water supply can be provided exclusively at the expense of subsurface sources, in which case the volume of the delivered water shall be reduced by 50%. Where the pumping stations of the artesian water supply system fail to create the appropriate hydraulic conditions, water dispensing points will be operating.

In keeping with the recommendations of the UkrSSR Academy of Sciences, the necessary corrections to treatment processes at the faucet water treatment plants have been made.

Such media as the Transcarpathian zeolite (10 000 m^3) and activated carbon (2000 m^3), grades A-3 and F-300, were used for filtering purposes. Filter media size fractions were 0.6-3.0 mm. The activated carbon F-300 (500 t) was imported from Belgium. The filter operation efficiency was studied with allowance for various combinations of filtering media.

The activated carbons, and particularly those of grade AG-3, are the best, compared with other filter media, at removing ^{131}I, ^{106}Ru from water, while the zeolites are good at removing ^{137}Cs, ^{90}Sr, ^{134}Cs, ^{106}Ru. During the first months of usage, their activity reached 1×10^{-8} Ci/kg, while the water radioactivity was reduced by 0.3 to 1 order of magnitude. Subsequently, the radioactivity of filter media decreased owing to the decay of short half-life isotopes. With the decrease of the water radioactivity, according to the general beta-activity, to 10^{-11}-10^{-12} Ci/l, the efficiency of zeolite and carbon filters is no higher than is the case with standard filtering media.

The filters with the quartz sand medium decreased the water radioactivity by trapping the suspended substances. On completion of each filtering cycle, the activity of filtering media was recovered and reduced to initial values.

In the event of significant deterioration of water quality, the technology of using powdered sorbents, such as activated carbon, bentonite and clinoptilolite, had been prepared. This process was not put into practice, however, although the laboratory research had demonstrated its fairly high efficiency. The radiological control was effected using the following radiation meters

SEG-C-06   -   gamma-spectrometry of the isotopes of caesium, strontium, ruthenium, etc.

RKB-4-1em   -   total beta-activity as determined by the express method

KRK-1   -   alpha-beta-activity of solid substances in water and in the air

SRP-68-01   -   gamma-activity

DP-5, DP-5B -   gamma-beta-activity of the general background in water, soil, and the air.

Since the sensitivity threshold of some instruments in measuring the alpha-beta-activity is 10^{-9}-10^{-10} Ci/l, while the radioactive contamination of water is lower by several orders of magnitude, the examined samples were prepared by evaporation of 3-50 litres of water.

The reduction of the radioactivity of water depends, to a great extent, on decreasing its turbidity at the expense of higher efficiency of reactants used during the coagulation.

At the Dniepr waterworks, basic aluminium sulphate instead of aluminium sulphate was used for coagulation of water. The former reactant was produced by the Pologov Chemical Plant 'Coagulant' at the request of the UkrSSR Academy of Sciences' Institute of Colloid Chemistry and Water Chemistry. The basic parameters of the synthetic coagulant are as follows: Al_2O_3 content: 16.0-16.8%; alkalinity: 1.6-2.0%; sediment insoluble in water: 1.6-2.5%. The basic modulus of the coagulant/molar ratio SO_3:Al_2O_3/ amounted to 2.7.

The water preparation process at the treatment facilities of the Dniepr waterworks was implemented in compliance with the following procedure: the coagulant, dissolved in the storage tank, was fed to the intermediate tank, where its density was brought up to 1.08-1.09 g/m^3; then it entered the mixer, to which the pre-chlorinated water was added (chlorine dosage was 3 mg/l).

At the last treatment stage, if required, the flocculant, the sol of activated silicic acid, was added. Following the mixer processing, the reactant-processed water was supplied to the reaction chamber. Water clarification occurred at the horizontal settling basins. After passing through the high-rate trickling filters, the purified water entered the pure water reservoirs. The settling time was 3.5-4 h, the filtration rate was 5.5-6.0 m/h, while the duration of the filtering cycle amounted to 24 h. The results obtained indicate the rising of the coagulant capacity of the basic aluminium sulphate against the standard aluminium sulphate. The average daily doses of aluminium sulphate alone and in combination with the sol of activated silicic acid were 46.4 and 49.8 mg/l respectively. The similar figures for the basic aluminium sulphate constituted 31.9 and 31.3 mg/l. The coagulant dose saving in this case amounted to 30% and 37% respectively.

The turbidity of water decreased between settling basins by an average of 10%; the colour was virtually the same; while the residual aluminium content decreased by 38%. When using the sol of activated silicic acid (5% with the solution of aluminium sulphate and 3% with the solution of basic aluminium sulphate), the differences between the above indices become even more pronounced: turbidity is reduced twofold.

The basic aluminium sulphate was developed by the UkrSSR Academy of Sciences AV Dumansky Institute of Colloid Chemistry and Water Chemistry (42 prosp. Vernadsky, GSP, Kiev-142, 252680, Teletype 'AKVA').

The costs of the performed construction and erection work, and the work related to city water supply and disposal processes, amounted to some 30 million roubles.

Definite changes in the quantitative and qualitative composition of the Desna river fauna have been observed since the Desna river became the principal water supply source for Kiev following the cessation of water intake from the Dniepr.

In May 1986, a five to tenfold decrease, compared with the previous years, of the number of Crustacea, including the Copepoda, Conchostraca and Cladocera was recorded. Representatives of the Amphipoda order had almost completely vanished. By mid-June 1986, the qualitative species composition of zoo-organisms had recovered, except for Amphipoda and Colurella which did not reappear until 1989. The hydrobiological changes of natural water did not affect the water-conditioning technology nor the quality of potable water.

With the increase in the radioactivity of potable water, an increase in the radioactivity of sewage waters, sludge and silts also occurs.

In May 1986, the average radioactivity of waste waters entering the treatment facilities was 8×10^{-9} Ci/l, while that of the treated waters equalled 3×101^{-9} Ci/l. In June 1986, these figures amounted to 3×10^{-10} and 2×10^{-10} Ci/l respectively. Subsequently, the waste-water radioactivity was in constant decline, constituting as much as 3×10^{-11} Ci/l at the present time.

The state of activated sludge at the treatment facilities featured a number of peculiarities. Around 20 May 1986, a great quantity of dead Colurella, accompanied by a noticeable increase of Arcella and Centropyxis, were observed; some cysts were also observed. At the end of May, free-swimming organisms prevailed. There were many

11

filamentous organisms; large-shape amoebae were observed in mass quantities; certain zooids increased in size, and were sometimes deformed; there was an increase in the number of food vacuoles and fluorescent inclusions, and of the representatives of ciliary infusoria, hitherto only seldom encountered. The sludge tended to float.

In June 1986, the situation showed no dramatic change. A 'plethora' of active amoebae with increased body size could be seen, while Gastrotricha could be observed more often than usual. By the end of the month, the large amoebae had suddenly disappeared, while the abundant growth of Zooglea ramigera became evident. The free-swimming organisms (Colpidium, Zionotus, Aspidisca) were dominant, while fixed organisms were few.

In July-September 1986, the activated sludge condition was back to normal. As its qualitative composition improved, a sufficient number of fixed organisms were observed along with the free-swimming organisms. In October-November, the deformed infusoria, again with fluorescent inclusions, and an increased number of nuclei and food vacuoles, could be observed. The number of amoebae has also increased, but they are of a smaller body size, and there is an abundant growth of Zooglea ramigera. Subsequently, and throughout 1987, 1988 and 1989, no drastic changes in the activated sludge were manifest.

As for the standard sanitary-and-hygiene indices, the waste water treatment quality complied fully with the requirements of the surface-water protection rules and it did not differ from the quality indices of the past years. With the BOD_{20} (biological oxgyene demand) of the incoming waste waters equal to 250 mg/l, the sewage BOD_{20} is 20 mg/l.

The radioactivity of sludge and silt, formed as a result of waste-water treatment in May 1986, was 10^{-8} Ci/l according to the total radioactivity (beta-activity) at a humidity of 97%.

The decision was made with regard to the implementation of special sludge accumulators with a water-impermeable base for the storage of sludge and silt, which was subsequently put into effect. At the present time, the radioactivity of sludge and silt is 2×10^{-9} Ci/l.

Conclusions

In order to improve the stability of the operation of urban water supply systems in the face of radioactive contamination of water sources, it is necessary

- to have several water supply sources with, preferably, an underground source among them, sealed by impermeable formations
- to operate flexible water conditioning flow charts which allow the use of various filtering media, chemicals and sorbents under the varying radiological situation conditions
- to ensure the continuous round-the-clock radiological, hydrobiological, chemical and bacteriological monitoring of water quality by equipping the laboratory with adequate instrumentation and computer systems.

2. Safeguards against the escape of radionuclides into the environment from nuclear power installations

J. L. GRAY, BSc, FEng, FIMechE, South of Scotland Electricity Board, UK

SYNOPSIS   Small amounts of radioactivity may be released to the environment in routine operation and larger amounts in accidents either at a power station or at nuclear fuel processing works or during transport of irradiated fuel between the two. The object in design and operation of the plant is to minimise the frequency and severity of such risks. The regulatory framework and the technical practices adopted throughout the life of the plant are described, with emphasis on the principle that radioactive discharges should be as low as reasonably practicable.

INTRODUCTION

1.   The primary condition for licensing a nuclear power installation is that it should be shown to be safe both to the station staff and to the public. It has always been argued that British safety principles adequately control the possibility of an unacceptable release of radioactivity into the environment. However, public confidence was shaken by the Chernobyl accident and the principles now have to be shown to be able to withstand more critical questioning than they previously did. It now has to be demonstrated that the whole concept of the reactors licensed in this country precludes an accident on the scale of Chernobyl. Much of the public concern, at least as expressed by spokesmen of anti-nuclear pressure groups, stems from the assumption that any significant accident involves a massive release of radioactivity from the station and that even odds of a million-to-one against such an accident are unacceptable. In fact the intention of the industry and of the licensing authorities is that even at this level of confidence the maximum accidental releases that could occur would be relatively small. In the vast majority of potential accidents activity would be largely contained within the reactor pressure circuit. Further accidents or failures would be necessary to affect the human population. Even serious accidents to the reactor do not necessarily cause it to fall over a cliff-edge into total catastrophe. The point is dramatically made by comparison of the Chernobyl and Three-Mile Island accidents. In each case the release of

radioactivity from the nuclear fuel was about the same. The release to the environment was about ten million times greater in one case than in the other, thanks to the difference in reactor design.

2. Similar scrutiny has to be applied to a variety of works and installations auxiliary to the nuclear power station itself. These include the refinement and enrichment of uranium, fabrication of the fuel elements, transport and reprocessing of the spent fuel and disposal of radioactive waste materials. The major potential hazards arise only when the fuel has been irradiated in the reactor core. The neutron bombardment there generates large sources of radioactive substances emitting alpha, beta and gamma radiation with half-lives ranging from fractions of a second to hundreds of thousands of years. It is these substances that have to be contained, whether they are in the reactor, in storage, in transport or undergoing chemical treatment to recover useful fissile materials.

3. Some ninety-five percent of the radio-nuclides in the irradiated fuel emerge as a small volume of high-level waste. The remainder is in a much larger volume of low-level and intermediate-level waste. All of these waste streams have to be disposed of ultimately in a way that excludes any unacceptable risk of their entering the human eco-system, particularly by long-term contamination of the water courses.

4. The chemical and power-generating ends of the industry have set up management systems aimed at preventing the kind of episode to which this conference is giving its attention. A "nuclear event" could conceivably begin with a reactor accident, a fuel transport accident or a pollution accident now or in the very long term. It is necessary to look at the whole range of possibilities in order to put the risks into perspective.

REACTOR SAFETY
5. When designing a nuclear power station an overriding consideration is to ensure that the risks are acceptable. Consideration has to be given to the possible releases of radioactivity from the reactor in both normal and fault conditions and the effects of these releases on the population. Risks to health and safety are obviously not unique to the nuclear power industry. They have to be considered in the design and siting of almost all industrial plant. In any such enterprise there is a balance of benefits such as prosperity and employment on the one hand and debits such as accidental releases to the environment that can have some effect on the health of the population on the other.

6.   The specific risks associated with nuclear power fall
into two broad categories, those resulting from the very
small amounts of radioactivity released in day-to-day
operation and the much more unlikely but potentially bigger
releases that might result from major faults in the plant.
The day-to-day releases are of most significance to the
power station staff but some very small doses could be
received by people living very close by.   Such amounts are
very small indeed by comparison with the doses incurred from
background radiation.   In the U.K. less then
0.1 per cent of the total radiation people receive
originates in the power industry.

7.   In the United Kingdom the responsibility for giving
consent to the construction of a nuclear power station and
to approve its start-up and operation is given to the
Nuclear Installations Inspectorate (NII) of the Health and
Safety Executive under various Acts of Parliament.   The
responsibility for demonstrating the safety of the station
to the NII is, however, with the licencee which, in
practice, means the electricity undertakings and British
Nuclear Fuels.   This responsibility on the licencee is
absolute and cannot be absolved even when NII itself or any
other official agency has given its consent.   The NII have a
wide measure of discretion in granting a licence.   They
specify conditions with which the licencee must comply.
These demand specific consents or approvals for activities
over the whole range of construction, operation,
maintenance, modifications, the control of nuclear materials
and preparation for nuclear emergencies all on the basis of
detailed submissions from the licencee and whatever
inspections and interventions the NII see fit.   This
flexible approach allows the NII more scope for upgrading
the standards of existing plant or plant in the course of
construction than is the case for example in the United
States where the practice is to prescribe specific detailed
requirements.

8.   The licensing of a power station is carried out in a
number of stages and the applicant can only continue from
stage to stage when the NII are fully satisfied with
performance so far.   Consents and approvals are required
before construction begins, at certain intermediate stages
during construction, before loading fuel and before raising
power.   At the start of construction the site licence is a
fairly short document but by the time the station is ready
to raise power it has become extensive and details all the
key legal requirements and conditions, e.g. it requires the
production of safety reports which describe the owner's
entire safety case for the station.   The final,
comprehensive, report is required to be submitted and
approved before fuel is loaded into the reactor.

9. The licensing process continues throughout the station's life. The NII appoint their own inspectors to each power station. They monitor its operation and if not satisfied they can order the station to be shut down at any time. However, the operators have their own nuclear safety departments which work closely with the NII. They are independent of the production function. They advise on safety standards and maintain surveillance of all aspects of operation to give added assurance that the standards are being met. This is one of the means of ensuring that the operators discharge their own responsibility for the safety of the plant. In addition, they are required to set up a Nuclear Safety Committee consisting of senior members of their Engineering and Operations Divisions and independent members recognised as knowledgeable in nuclear safety and technology. This Committee has a number of responsibilities specified under the site licence but amongst the most important are the control and approval of important modifications to the plant or its operating rules and any experimental work to be carried out on it. The NII would not itself approve a proposal for modification until the Safety Committee had approved it and recorded the case for that approval. The significance of these provisions will not be lost on anybody who has looked at the reports of the Chernobyl accident.

10. The licence to raise power once given is not for life. One of the licence conditions is that nuclear reactors must be shut down at regular intervals, currently every two years, for inspection, examination and testing and can only be restarted if a fresh consent is given by the Inspectorate.

11. It is instructive to look more closely at the nature of the safety reports, taking the new Scottish AGR station at Torness and its sister station in England, Heysham II, as examples. The nuclear plants at the two stations are substantially identical and the two generating Boards have independently assessed all aspects of the design. The demonstration that the design meets its safety and design code requirements is recorded in a range of documents. The head document is the station safety report, a massive work in 62 volumes, but this is supported by some hundreds of additional reports substantiating the design in detail. Each document originated within the design organisation, NNC Ltd., and was subject to their own internal independent review as required by their internal quality assurance procedures. The quality assurance procedures of the generating Boards, NNC and the individual contractors are themselves subject to a hierarchical approval process headed by NII. The documents submitted by NNC were assessed by the Design and Construction Divisions of the generating Boards

and independently by the nuclear safety departments. The
staff carrying out the several independent stages of
assessment are technically qualified and experienced in
their own field. This procedure has in fact picked up
problems, albeit not of a fundamental nature, that led to
changes of design and operating rules. Similarly, the
commissioning procedure when plant is tested to demonstrate
satisfactory performance has revealed the need for
modifications. All such modifications are fed back into the
assessment system for approval.

12. It has to be emphasised that the production of safety
reports is not seen as sufficient in itself to ensure
safety. Rather they are the visible output of the
procedures used in the design process to monitor, control
and document the development of all aspects of the design
work that have any safety significance. The safety report
provides the final discipline in which the adequacy of the
design as it finally evolves is tested.

13. The aim of ensuring that the risks associated with
nuclear power generation are acceptable means that it is
necessary to have stringent risk targets for the designer to
work to from the earliest conceptual stages of a project.
It is not enough to instruct the designers to make the risks
extremely small. What is required is a means of
interpreting the requirements for each facet of the design
against a defined standard. In practice, the safety
standards have been detailed in two key documents. These
are publicly available and were extensively discussed at the
Sizewell 'B' Public Inquiry.

14. The first is the NII's "Safety Assessment Principles for
Nuclear Power Reactors" (ref.1). This is essentially a
guide to the NII's own inspectors as to the principles they
should consider when assessing the safety of a design. Its
format is a statement of principles rather than specific
requirements, thus expressing the fundamental principle that
the licencee of the plant is fully responsible for its safe
design and NII's concern is with ends rather than means.

15. An example of the second document is the "AGR Design
Safety Guidelines". This was developed by the CEGB in
consultation with the SSEB and is specific to this type of
reactor. There is a corresponding document for the PWR type
being built at Sizewell.(ref.2) It is aimed at the
designers so that they have guidance as to the safety
requirements to be embodied in the plant from the earliest
stage. It is consistent with the NII's safety assessment
principles but its format reflects its different purpose.
It consists of 16 main sections detailing the safety
requirements for all the relevant aspects of station

design. It specifies limits for radioactivity dose rates in day-to-day operation and accidents. It gives specific requirements for the reliability of safety related plant and systems and it specifies the hazard conditions that the station must withstand, such as earthquakes, floods and fires.

16. Over-riding all specific limits and conditions is the requirement on the licencee to ensure that releases should be as low as reasonably practicable (the ALARP principle). There are many examples within current designs where the application of the ALARP principle has assured that releases in normal operation and in fault conditions are much lower than allowed by the Design Safety Guidelines. Indeed in almost all reactor accidents identified and analysed in Station Safety Reports, predicted off-site releases are either zero or much lower than the permitted limits. In many instances this is due to the relatively benign reaction of the AGR to faults, but it is assisted by the conservative design of the engineered safety systems.

17. The concentration of radioactive materials in any reactor core is potentially hazardous and fully justifies this level of scrutiny. Nonetheless the investment in safety assessment is unmatched by that of any other energy or process industry in the world despite the potential for major hazards that many of them present.

POLLUTION CONTROLS
18. An employer has a legal duty to protect employees and the public against ionising radiations arising from their work with radioactive substances. The Ionising Radiations Regulations 1985 lay down the rules and the NII monitors their application at nuclear power station sites. The Regulations require an employer to ensure that the exposure of people does not exceed specified limits and in addition impose the same ALARP principle as is applied to reactor design. The ALARP requirement is dominant in practice; exposures are normally well below the specified limits.

19. In addition, the Radioactive Substances Act, 1960 requires that radioactive wastes may only be disposed of or dispersed in the environment after an authorisation, detailing the quantities of activity and method of disposal or dispersal, has been given to the operator. Authorisations are issued by H.M. Industrial Pollution Inspectorate for Scotland and by corresponding officials in other countries. They call upon the operator to ensure that the radiation exposures caused by the discharges are as low as reasonably practicable (the ALARP principle again).

20. Every nuclear installation will emit some radioactivity throughout its life. In the types of power station we have in Scotland most of this will come from routine leakage of the slightly radioactive coolant gas. Most of the leakage is vented to the atmosphere through filters which substantially remove any radioactive particles. Some of the radioactive isotopes are gaseous and are not filtered out. Smaller quantities in liquid form are discharged with the condenser cooling water to the sea.

21. Specialist Health Physics staff control and measure radiation exposures at nuclear power stations. They are responsible to the Station Manager but independent of the production and engineering departments. They include Radiation Protection Advisers whose appointments have to be notified in advance to the Health and Safety Executive.

22. The level of exposure of workers and others is controlled so that the risk of harm is very low. The limits imposed by the Health and Safety Executive are based on the 1977 recommendations of the International Commission on Radiological Protection (ref.3) and the National Radiological Protection Board and as currently applied in this country are as follows:

Exposure of individual workers   -   50 mSv/year
Exposure of most affected   -   5 mSv/year
  member of public   (1 mSv/year averaged
                                            over 70 year life)

23. The governing limit is in practice the 1 mSv/year lifetime average which is half the average exposure of 2 mSv/year from natural sources.

24. The recommended limits are based on observations of effects at very much greater doses and dose rates as suffered for example by the Japanese victims of atomic bombs and patients subjected to certain medical treatments. These effects have been extrapolated downwards so that any dose or dose rate is assumed to impose a proportional risk of injury. It is known that the most recent review of the survival data of the atomic bomb victims will show an increase in risk of about a factor of three. As a result of this review the ICRP may well recommend a lowering of the above limits. They would still be well above those occuring in practice.

25. There is little or no evidence that injury does follow such low doses but this assumption is on the safe side and has been generally accepted as a proper basis for safety regulations.

26. On this assumption, experience at AGR power stations shows that the additional risk of contracting a fatal cancer by exposed workers is between 1 in 10,000 and 1 in 100,000 per year. The corresponding risk to the most exposed member of the public is of the order of 1 in 1,000,000 per year. Moreover, the measures taken in the design of modern power stations ensure that the summated risk of injury from all potential faults is many times lower than the risk arising from normal operation.

27. The major routine source of radioactive discharge is not the power stations but the chemical works which reprocess the nuclear fuel after it is discharged from the reactor. Two main types of nuclear fuel are produced in the United Kingdom, namely natural uranium metal fuel for magnox gas-cooled reactors and enriched uranium oxide fuel, in which the concentration of the fissile isotope uranium-235 is increased, for other thermal reactors such as the Advanced Gas-Cooled Reactor(AGR) and the Pressurised Water Reactor (PWR).

28. No significant problem arises during production since the fuel has not yet been irradiated. The radioactive discharge is mainly from the chemical works which reprocess the fuel to recover uranium and plutonium after it is discharged from the reactor.

29. Spent oxide fuel is stored in water at BNFL's Sellafield Works pending start-up of the Thermal Oxide Reprocessing Plant (THORP), scheduled for the end of 1992. AGR fuel can be stored under water for a long, but not indefinite, time before the stainless steel cans which contain it begin to corrode. The zirconium alloy cans of PWR fuel are even more corrosion resistant.

30. Magnox fuel can only be stored under water for a short time before the magnesium oxide cladding corrodes and releases radioactivity and it must therefore be reprocessed to an earlier timescale.

31. The reduction in the rate of growth of nuclear power and the discovery of new deposits of uranium have reduced the incentive for prompt reprocessing of oxide fuels. Preparations for long-term dry storage are therefore being made.

32. Of the radioactive wastes arising from reprocessing only low-level liquid wastes are dispersed, the remainder being either stored on the Sellafield site or disposed of by burial at the Drigg disposal site for low-level solid waste.

33. The main sources of low-level active liquid wastes are water purge from irradiated fuel storage and low-level effluents from reprocessing operations. They are chemically treated to reduce their activity to acceptable levels before being discharged to sea.

34. Over recent years the limits on allowable discharges of liquid effluent to sea have been reduced greatly (ref.4). Since the mid-1970s the following major treatment plants have been constructed: the Fuel Handling Plant, the Site Ion Exchange Plant (SIXEP) and the Salt Evaporator. These plants are in operation and have dramatically reduced discharges by a factor of forty or so on levels previously achieved.

35. Further reductions will be achieved by construction of an Enhanced Actinide Removal Plant (EARP) and plant for removal of solvents. The intent for 1992 is to achieve an upper alpha discharge limit of about 0.7 TBq (20 Ci) per year and an upper beta discharge limit of about 300TBq (8,000 Ci) per year and to maintain this until magnox reprocessing ceases, when these targets are expected to fall by a further factor of four.

36. It is expected that the dose received by members of the critical group of the public (i.e. the persons most affected) from low-level active discharges at Sellafield will fall below 10 percent of the ICRP subsidiary dose limit of 5 mSv a year by the early 1990s as recommended by the Radioactive Waste Management Advisory Committee and should continue to fall until about the year 2005. The highest critical group dose in 1985 was estimated to be less than 1 mSv and doses to typical members of the public were very much lower at about 0.02 mSv.

RADIOACTIVE WASTE DISPOSAL
37. Two aspects of waste disposal might affect the public water supply, namely transport of irradiated fuel from the power station to the reprocessing works and disposal of waste in the longer term.

38. There is no great controversy amongst informed people about the safety of transporting low-level waste or even intermediate-level waste despite the public agitation about it. The sensitive area is the transport of irradiated fuel. This was the subject of a special public inquiry for our new station at Torness and got a lot of attention at the Sizewell 'B' Inquiry. The method is to load specially designed massive steel containers or flasks of irradiated fuel on to trains at a local siding for removal to Sellafield by rail. The flasks weigh more than 50 tonnes. They are designed, constructed and used in compliance with

the regulations of the International Atomic Energy
Authority (ref.5). The Department of Transport is the
authority for approving the arrangements for safe conveyance
of fuel in these flasks. They have to be satisfied that the
flasks have been properly designed and tested and that the
management system under which flasks are filled, transported
and maintained is satisfactory before they issue an Approval
Certificate which allows the flask to be put into service.

39. The flask design has been validated by a combination of
model tests and theoretical calculation. The soundness of
the magnox design has been verified by dropping a full-sized
loaded flask 9 metres on to a rigid concrete base as
required by the IAEA specification and it was the subject of
a spectacular demonstration train crash. The locomotive in
that crash was wrecked but the flask was virtually
undamaged. The IAEA Regulations also prescribe the
resistance of the flask to fire and other hazards. With
such a specification and design and development process
behind it the method of transporting irradiated fuel is so
safe "as to be of no concern" to quote the phrase ultimately
agreed by opponents at the Sizewell 'B' Inquiry. (ref.6)
Flasks have, in fact, been transported many hundreds of
times over many years without significant incident. It is
difficult to conceive a genuine emergency involving a fuel
flask but nonetheless a well rehearsed emergency plan exists
just as it does for the power station itself.

40. The methods of disposal of radioactive waste have
merited a series of conferences to themselves and the
details are not very much to the point for our present
purpose. We can restrict ourselves to looking at some
fundamental concepts.

41. The practical proposal for waste disposal is not to bury
the radioactive substances in a haphazard fashion.
Isolation from potentially potable water supplies is a
fundamental objective of the repository. The main features
may be summarised as follows:

(a) packaging the wastes in steel or concrete containers
    capable of excluding groundwater until the radioactivity
    of soluble elements has decayed to a low level;

(b) selection of a repository site at which groundwater flow
    is extremely slow on account of the local geology and
    hydraulic gradient;

(c) disposal of the waste packages at great depth to
    minimise risk from inadvertent intrusion and to ensure a
    long transit time for groundwater to move from the
    repository to the biosphere (typically greater than

100,000 years);

(d) grouting of the packages with cement backfill, which
    establishes alkaline reducing chemical conditions under
    which the long lived radio-nuclides are very insoluble
    in water.

42. The combination of these features gives confidence that
even groundwater in contact with the waste packages will not
become highly contaminated and all but a few radio-nuclides
of extremely low specific activity will decay away during
the long journey to the surface. The potential annual dose
to a member of the critical group (i.e. the small section of
the public most at risk from the repository) under these
conditions is less than 0.1 mSv. This is a very small dose
indeed, being much less than the geographical variation in
dose from natural rock formations in the U.K. The ALARP
principle also applies to the authorisation of waste
disposal.

43. Preparations are being made for this deep disposal
technique to be implemented as soon as public confidence
allows; in the meantime much of the waste material that
might be buried is being stored safely at the power station
sites and at Sellafield.

DECOMMISSIONING
44. The earlier nuclear power plants are nearing the end of
their useful lives and will have to be closed down and
safely disposed of. The method of handling the job when the
time comes will be decided on both cost and environmental
health considerations. The first stage of decommissioning
will consist of taking out the remaining fuel for
reprocessing or disposal. It is governed by essentially the
same rules and constraints as applied during the operating
phase.

45. Part of the second stage is identical for fossil fuel
fired and nuclear stations and consists of dismantling all
the plant and buildings that have not been irradiated or
contaminated. In addition, components outwith the
biological shield which are classed as radioactive at low-
level or intermediate-level will be removed for disposal.

46. The methods and costs of these stages are very
conventional and predictable. The third stage, to make the
site available for other uses, needs a different approach.

47. It would be extravagant to dismantle the reactor within
its concrete pressure vessel or biological shield
immediately and the workers would be exposed to radiation
unnecessarily. The demolition of the Windscale prototype

INTRODUCTION

AGR is demonstrating that it is technically feasible but it
does depend on expensive robotic equipment. It makes more
sense to defer demolition of the core for say 100 years
until the radioactivity has substantially decayed. This is
a major consideration for it will be possible for workers
using normal precautionary techniques to enter the
biological shield and dismantle the core by "hands-on"
methods by that time. Costs incurred in 100 years' time,
discounted back to the station's commercial lifetime, have a
very small effect indeed on current electricity costs.

48. The relevant question for present purposes is the
potential hazard to surface drain water due to having the
radioactive core (excluding the fuel) in place for a century
or more. The building that would remain for the 100 years
is a small fraction of the original. It is a simple matter
to seal it within the original biological shield structure
and provide adequate weather proofing.

49. Quantitative assessments have shown that the risk to
water supplies is negligible even assuming social decay and
gross neglect.

INTERNATIONAL EVENTS
50. The discussion so far has concentrated on the methods
adopted in this country to prevent contamination of the
environment by either routine pollution or accident. It
must nevertheless be acknowledged that some major risks are
not necessarily subject to those controls. The great
majority of radioactivity incidents reported throughout the
world from the 1940s up to date were not attributable to
nuclear power installations at all but these are outwith the
scope of this paper. The major concern in the present
context is that there is only the beginning of a uniform
international nuclear safety culture, whereas the Chernobyl
accident has had a profound impact far beyond the country
where it happened. However, the International Atomic Energy
Agency did examine the implications of that incident and
took a number of important initiatives.

51. It drew up its "Basic Safety Principles for Nuclear
Power Plants" (ref.7), corresponding in essentials to the
British regulatory documents discussed above. All member
nations are committed to the observance of these principles
in the design, construction and operation of new power
stations.

52. For existing stations, the IAEA set up a system of
sample inspection by international Operational Safety Review
Teams (OSART). Power stations in Korea, Yugoslavia, Brazil,
France, Mexico, Finland, Hungary, Sweden, Netherlands,
Germany, Italy, Canada, USA, Spain, Uruguay and USSR have

been assessed by this process so far. The first assessment of a British station, Oldbury on the Severn, is about to take place. The purpose of these inspections is not only to reveal any shortcomings in the stations examined but to report good points and bad to the managements of utilities throughout the world and build a broad consciousness of what needs to be done and what can be done.

53. A further initiative stemmed from the need for a continued exchange of information amongst the operators of nuclear plant. The World Association of Nuclear Operators was set up in 1988 with members in twenty-nine countries and offices in Paris, Moscow, Tokyo and Atlanta Georgia. Its purpose is to collect and disseminate information particularly about operating experience and practices so that all operators can learn from one another.

REFERENCES

1. HEALTH AND SAFETY EXECUTIVE: Nuclear Safety: Safety Assessment Principles for Nuclear Power Reactors, London, 1983.

2. CEGB: Design Safety Criteria for CEGB Nuclear Power Stations, London, 1982.

3. NRPB: Recommendations of the International Commission on Radiological Protection. Statement by the NRPB on their Acceptability in the UK, London, 1978.

4. R.J. BERRY and D.J. COULSTON. How Good is BNFL's Health and Safety?, Atom, April 1978.

5. IAEA: Regulations for the Safe Transport of Radioactive Materials, Vienna, 1985.

6. SIZEWELL 'B' PUBLIC INQUIRY: Report by Sir Frank Layfield, Vol.3, London, HMSO, 1986.

7. IAEA: Basic Safety Principles for Nuclear Power Plants, Vienna, 1989.

3. How UK nuclear power stations are designed to be safe

D. R. SMITH, OBE, MA, FEng, NNC Limited, Knutsford, UK

SYNOPSIS. The accident at Chernobyl and the scale of the consequences were due to shortcomings in the design and operation of the reactor. In the UK the extremely high standards applied to the design and operation of nuclear power stations are intended to minimise the likelihood of faults. Suitable protective equipment is provided to ensure that any faults which may occur, do not lead to serious consequences. The paper illustrates the UK standards and provisions by reference to the latest Advanced Gas Cooled Reactors at Heysham 2 and Torness and the Pressurised Water Reactor under construction at Sizewell.

INTRODUCTION

1. The accident at Chernobyl occurred on a reactor design which, in both concept and detail, has features which impaired ultimate plant safety. This reactor would not be licensable in the UK because it does not meet the Safety Criteria of either the NII or the CEGB. A fundamental principle of UK Safety Criteria is defence in depth, in which potential human or equipment failures are compensated by several layers of protection including successive barriers preventing the release of radioactive material to the environment.

2. The main features of the Chernobyl reactor and the events, including operator error, which led to the accident illustrate the shortcomings that can be contrasted with the U.K. approach.

3. The CEGB Design Safety Criteria and the more detailed Design Safety Guidelines include numerical targets which restrict the frequency of faults which could lead to an uncontrolled release of radioactivity. These targets influence the redundancy and diversity of the automatic protection equipment. In addition the design must ensure that hazards, especially fires, cannot invalidate these safety functions. For some parts of the design, eg. structures, it is impracticable to provide redundancy and

adequate assurance is obtained through the design codes and standards.

4. The U.K. philosophy is that by virtue of the automatic protection equipment the operator is not called upon to take any action within about half an hour of a fault occurring. However, the design must ensure that the plant is not vulnerable to operator errors.

5. In the following sections, these safety aspects are illustrated by reference to the Heysham/Torness AGR and the Sizewell 'B' PWR.

CHERNOBYL ACCIDENT

6. The accident at Chernobyl occurred during a test at low power on reactor No 4. The Soviet acronym RBMK stands for high power boiling reactor. The design is unique in that it is a pressure tube reactor in which the light water coolant is boiled as it passes up through the vertical fuel channels but it has a graphite moderator through which the channel tubes pass.

7. The design concept was examined in 1975 by NNC and was judged then to be unlicensable in the UK. The shortcomings which were identified are listed below.

(i)   No in-core emergency spray system
(ii)   No containment building
(iii)   Core structure not seismically robust
(iv)   Core structure vulnerable to pressure tube rupture
(v)   The reactor had a positive void coefficient
(vi)   The shutdown margin was inadequate
(vii)   The power distribution was unstable
(viii) There was no diverse shutdown system
(ix)   The graphite moderator had too high a temperature

8. Apart from (i), (iii) and (vi) the remainder all contributed to the severity of the accident. The most serious shortcoming was associated with (v), the positive void coefficient. A positive void coefficient means that, when the reactor power increases and more steam is produced in the fuel channels, the steam voids increase the reactivity which in turn tends to increase the power. At power this is compensated by an increase in fuel temperature through the so-called negative doppler coefficient of reactivity and a positive void may not, in itself, be an unacceptable feature. However, the RBMK characteristics are such that, at low power, this effect is outweighted by the void effect and the reactor has a positive power coefficient, i.e. any increase in power will give rise to a further increase and so on, unless terminated by control rod insertion. Because of this characteristic, the rules forbade operation below 20% power.

9. In preparation for the test, when power was being reduced, the operator inadvertently took the reactor below the 20% level. Due to the unstable nature of the reactor response, and so that the test would be able to continue uninterrupted, he incorrectly switched off a number of the protection trips. Also, in attempting to maintain the reactor power, albeit at a rather low value, he withdrew the control rods beyond the normal permitted travel. The test was intended to study the rundown of the main circulating pumps while they remained connected to one of the main turbo-alternators when the latter was isolated from the steam supply and disconnected from the grid. When this action was initiated, the positive power coefficient caused the reactor power to increase. Because of the control rods being too far withdrawn, they were ineffective when the operator initiated their insertion.

10. The resulting power excursion and explosion was due to the many factors discussed above which can be grouped under the headings:

Design inadequacy   – un-safe characteristics
                    – inadequate protection equipment

Implementation   – test badly planned and conducted
                    – operator disregard for rules

11. It should be noted that, since the accident, the Soviets have carried out modifications to improve some of the design shortcomings and have tightened up their operating practices.

DEFENCE-IN-DEPTH

12. The defence-in-depth principle which has governed the evolution of reactor safety in the UK as well as the majority of countries with nuclear power programmes has two related aspects. The first is the provision of successive physical barriers between the fission products and the environment. These are:

(i)   the fuel matrix
(ii)   the fuel cladding
(iii)   the primary coolant boundary
(iv)   a containment building

13. The latter may not be a complete pressure tight containment, depending on reactor type and alternative provisions, for venting and filtering discharges.

14. The second aspect is that the frequency of faults which could threaten these barriers must be minimised. This is achieved by:

(v)   conservative design
(vi)   control during normal operation
(vii)   protective systems

15. These design related topics are part of a total safety culture which embraces manufacture, construction, commissioning, operation and the quality assurance of all of these activities. Item (v) includes the basic characteristics of the reactor, item (vi) includes operator actions and procedures. The frequency targets are outlined in the next section.

SAFETY CRITERIA AND GUIDELINES
16. The overall probabilistic design safety criteria applying in the UK require that the total frequency of all accidents that could lead to an uncontrolled release of radioactivity should be no greater than about 10^{-6}/reactor-year.

17. The criteria also limit the frequency of an uncontrolled release from any single accident to 10^{-7}/year in order to avoid individual faults causing a major contribution to the overall risk. Higher frequency faults are acceptable if limited releases arise.

18. The practical interpretation of these guidelines in terms of the design development has been to provide effective protective features and systems to ensure that the reactor pressure vessel, internal structures, and fuel are maintained within safe limits for all fault sequences more frequent than 10^{-7}/year. Thus, a design basis is determined within which the total envelope of initiating faults and fault sequences is considered. The aim is to show that even for the most limiting sequences, the possibility of any accidental release of a significant quantity of radioactivity can be discounted. The frequency of those sequences falling outside the design basis is calculated and shown to be acceptably low.

19. Good design, with the objective of reducing the probability of faults occurring, and the provision of reliable protective systems form the basis of the design approach. Reliability is achieved through the adoption of appropriate design standards and the use of redundancy. Following the more frequent faults (ie. faults where frequency is greater than approximately 10^{-3} per year) for which very high reliabilities of protection are needed, it is considered that redundancy alone within a single system is not sufficient. The safety guidelines require that diverse means of protection are provided as a defence against common mode failure (CMF). The probability of a CMF affecting plant items of one type must not be assumed to be less than 10^{-5} failures per demand.

20. The guidelines require specific attention to be given to the potential consequences of internal hazards, i.e. those arising from failures within the power station, and external hazards, i.e. those which are a feature of the site in terms of both natural and man-made phenomena. These guidelines are responsible, in particular, for the layout, segregation and qualification of plant and systems as necessary for each of the possible hazards, which can themselves be considered as potential common cause failures.

21. Safety considerations other than the probabilistic targets also influence the redundancy of plant items provided in the design. In particular, the deterministic 'single failure' criterion requires that, following a fault (or hazard) any necessary safety function can be performed despite the loss of equipment as a consequence of the fault (or hazard), the unavailability of equipment owing to maintenance and the failure of any single item of equipment.

PROTECTION EQUIPMENT
22. Although good design can reduce the frequency of significant faults occurring directly, or prevent minor disturbances developing into more serious faults, there is nevertheless a need to protect the reactor against such occurrences by systems which perform several key functions.

(i)   Fault detection and reactor trip initiation
(ii)   Reactor shutdown by insertion of neutron absorber
(iii)   Decay heat removal

23. The protective systems which provide these functions are described in turn.

Fault detection and reactor trip systems
24. Automatic fault detection is provided by sensing a number of physical parameters and plant conditions which are carefully chosen as prime indicators of fault conditions. On the AGR the parameters measured include:

    fuel channel gas outlet temperatures
    circulator gas outlet temperatures
    neutron flux level
    neutron flux period
    gas circulator supply voltages
    gas circulator speeds
    gas circulator inlet guide vane positions

25. For each parameter at least four (and usually more) separate measurements are made and majority voting used to initiate a trip if any 2 or more out of 4 channels exceed specified limits.

26. At least two such independent parameters are provided

to initiate a trip for each initiating fault although for
most faults additional parameters may be effective.   All
parameters are connected into a LADDIC or magnetic logic
guardline system which directly initiates reactor shutdown.
In total 18 parameters are monitored by the main guardline
(MGL) system.

27.   The MGL is designed as far as possible to be
fail-safe and can readily and regularly be tested.
Theoretically, its reliability is sufficient alone to
satisfy the frequency requirements discussed in para 18.
However, as a further defence against CMF an entirely
separate and diverse guardline system (DGL) using relays is
also provided.

28.   The DGL system uses outputs from 4 trip parameters
independently to initiate reactor shutdown.   The parameters
chosen are those which are effective for higher frequency
initiating faults and therefore those for which the
assumption of a limit to the probability of failure for the
main guardline system because of CMF would lead to higher
than acceptable fault sequence frequencies.

29.   On the PWR the number and type of monitored
parameters differ, but the same principle of redundancy of
measurement applies to each parameter and two diverse
protection systems are provided;   the primary protection
system(PPS) with 24 monitored parameters is based on
microprocessors;   the secondary protection system(SPS) with
about half that number of parameters is based on solid state
logic elements.

Reactor shutdown systems
30.   On the AGR the trip signals from either the main or
diverse guardlines interrupt the holding supplies for the
contacts of redundant sets of relays in four separate
groups.   Each group of relays controls an electrical supply
to the electromagnetic clutches of about twenty control rods
of the primary shutdown (PSD) system.   Interruption of the
clutch supply to any group causes each associated rod to
fall under gravity into the reactor core.   The redundancy
and diversity of design of relays and the number of control
rods (89) provided is such that the theoretical reliability
is extremely high.   The control rods are virtually fully
inserted within about 5.5 seconds of the trip signal.

31.   However, in order to give the necessary diversity as
a defence against CMF an independent secondary shutdown
(SSD) system is also provided which uses nitrogen gas at a
high pressure, injected directly into the reactor via
pipework which penetrates the bottom of the reactor pressure
vessel.   The operation of this system is completely diverse
from the primary shutdown system and it is initiated

automatically should be primary system rods fail to insert
within a predetermined time interval. In this unlikely
event nitrogen would enter the core within 8 seconds of the
initial trip signal.

32. The primary shutdown on the PWR is through the
insertion of control assemblies within several seconds in
response to a trip signal from either the primary or
secondary protection systems. If there is a failure of 3 or
more of these control assemblies to insert, the secondary
shutdown system will operate to inject boron into the
primary coolant passing through the reactor.

33. In both reactor types there is provision for the
operator to initiate a tertiary shutdown system in the
longer term. On the AGR boron glass beads are injected, on
the PWR either the normal chemical control or emergency
charging system can be used to increase the boron content of
the primary coolant.

Emergency cooling
34. The requirements for post-trip cooling differ
depending on whether or not the fault is associated with a
breach of the primary circuit. These post-trip actions are
initiated automatically by the protection systems on
detection of a fault.

Intact primary circuit
35. Because faults in this category are relatively
frequent it is necessary to provide diversity in the heat
removal systems. The four main boilers of the AGR can
receive feedwater by the main feed pumps continuing to
supply feedwater from the deareator through 10% feed lines
or by 4 emergency boiler feed pumps drawing water from
emergency feed tanks. In the unlikely event of all gas
circulators failing to operate, natural circulation in the
primary circuit can provide adequate heat removal to the
feedwater circulating through the main boilers.

36. In addition to the main heat transfer surface, each
boiler contains a decay heat bank which can be fed by 4
pumps with water from a dump condenser which is completely
separate from the main and emergency feed systems and which
rejects the heat to the atmosphere.

37. Adequate post trip cooling is provided by a single
main boiler with either of its associated gas circulators
or a single decay heat boiler with either of its gas
circulators or one main boiler receiving feed and natural
circulation.

38. On the PWR, post trip feed is taken from the main
feedpumps (4 running and 2 on standby). If this fails, two

33

diverse sets of auxiliary feedwater pumps (4 in total)
supply water to the steam generators via separate nozzles on
each steam generator. Two pumps are motor driven and the
other two are driven by steam turbines.

39. A route is provided for rejection of heat, after
reactor trip, to the atmosphere. This route operates in the
event of failure of the normal heat rejection route to the
sea.

Breached primary circuit

40. For the less frequent faults associated with loss of
primary coolant through a breach in the pressure circuit it
is not necessary to provide diversity. On the AGR the
required flow of primary coolant is maintained by the speed
of the main gas circulators being raised from the normal
post trip level of 15% to full speed as the pressure falls.
Heat is removed in the main boilers but for less severe
faults, the decay heat boilers are adequate and, in all
faults, they can be used after a few hours.

41. The most severe faults require four circulators and
associated main boilers to operate but in many, two
circulators with one main boiler are adequate if CO_2
injection is used to maintain the primary circuit pressure
above 2 bar.

42. The systems provided for the PWR differ because of
the two-phase nature of the primary coolant. For the most
severe faults, injection of primary coolant is from four
accumulators and at lower pressure, from low-head safety
injection pumps. Due to the low frequency of these faults
the accumulators are rated at 50% and two 100% pumps are
aligned for this duty. However these pumps can be augmented
by the two containment spray pumps and vice versa.

43. For smaller breaches, four 100% high-head safety
injection pumps are provided.

Electrical supplies

44. Many of the post trip functions are dependent on
electrical supplies for successful operation. These are
normally available from the turbo-generator or grid but,
should these be unavailable, alternative supplies are
provided. On the AGR, four diesels are available for the
gas circulator and decay heat boiler supplies. A second
set of four diesels supply power for the emergency feed
system. Although the diesels are basically similar, some
components e.g. those related to starting are different to
ensure that diversity is maintained. This is in addition to
the diversity provided by normally making grid supplies
available to all essential plant post-trip.

45. The PWR has 4 main diesels which supply power to the electrically driven protection equipment following loss of off-site power. In the event of failure of both normal off-site and emergency diesel power sources, steam driven equipment is provided to meet required safety functions such as feed to the steam generators and charging flow for protection of the reactor coolant pump seals. This equipment does not itself require electrical power, but electrical supplies for monitoring and control must be maintained. To meet this requirement, batteries are provided along with 2 battery charging diesels which are of diverse manufacture from the 4 main diesels.

HAZARDS

46. Protection against hazards is a requirement of the safety guidelines and their possibility and consequences are specifically taken into account in the design approach. Internal hazards are those whose source is attributable to failures within the power station while external hazards are those whose source is outside of the station and include both natural and man-made phenomena. These are discussed in turn.

Internal hazards

47. The design approach followed is to recognise hazards by their consequences and systematically examine the plant and systems within the power station to identify potential causes. Internal hazards considered include fire, flooding, dropped loads, hot gas or steam release, pipe whip, missiles from failure of rotating machinery or pressurised systems (eg. gas storage tanks) and release of toxic substances.

48. Defences adopted in the protection against internal hazards depend on the nature and potential consequences but may include:

(i)   Avoidance or minimisation of hazard potential, eg. use of non-combustible materials.

(ii)   Equipment provided for the detection and suppression of potential fires in order to limit their severity and the extent of damage caused.

(iii)   Layout, eg. remote location and careful orientation of high pressure storage tanks in respect of vital plant or systems.

(iv)   Separation, eg. provision of sufficient space between diverse systems or redundant parts of one system such that the consequences of a hazard are limited.

(v)   Segregation, eg. provision of rated fire barriers between groups of components to limit the extent of a hazard.

49. The recognition and treatment of hazards has a fundamental effect on the overall arrangement of systems through the principal separation and segregation provisions. This is carried through to the detailed segregation of electrical power and control cables which is arranged to satisfy principles which limit the impairment of redundancy within systems in the event of a hazard at any location on the station.

50. Application of these principles to the AGR ensure that a release of hot gas eg. through a sidewall penetration failure can only affect the equipment of one quadrant, ie. one boiler and its associated gas circulators. A fire in one essential services building can also only affect the supplies to the plant associated with one quadrant. A major failure of main feed and condensate eg. catastrophic deaerator failure can only affect the emergency feed system which is located in the same area; the decay heat boiler system is located elsewhere.

51. On the PWR the four-fold redundancy is maintained through segregation for all equipment required to establish or maintain a hot or intermediate shutdown. For equipment required to establish or maintain cold shutdown it is assumed that repair or restoration of unavailable equipment will be possible and that two-way segregation is sufficient.

External hazards
52. The design approach is initially a site survey to quantify the frequency and severity of potential external hazards. Clearly, the subsequent treatment of external hazards is site-specific. A comprehensive range of possible hazards is studied and the possibility of adverse effects on the power station is examined. In addition to site location and defences, those requiring specific design solutions for plant and systems to satisfy the safety guidelines are considered further. For Heysham II and Torness these are earthquake and high wind for which suitable qualification of plant and systems to withstand the consequences of these hazards is necessary.

53. Although layout and separation or segregation of plant and systems may be important in terms of limiting the consequences of failures induced by the specific hazards, these are not the prime defence adopted. The approach followed is to specify for the site an appropriate intensity for each hazard and then to qualify sufficient plant to withstand the effects of the hazard, including possible consequential effects of the failure of non-qualified plant, to ensure safe reactor shutdown and decay heat removal with adequate reliability.

54. For the earthquake, a safe shutdown earthquake (SSE) of 0.25g is specified for a return frequency of 1 in 10,000 years. The pressure vessel and associated systems, primary shutdown system, gas circulators (and auxiliaries), decay heat boiler feed system, and essential on-site electrical supplies are seismically qualified against this standard. The intention is to ensure that the probability of failure to shutdown or remove decay heat should not exceed about 10^{-3}.

55. A similar approach is adopted for a high wind although the qualified decay heat removal system in this case is the emergency boiler feed system.

56. Although the SSE specification for the Sizewell 'B' site is the same as for the AGR, in order to replicate the design at other sites with higher seismicity, the qualification tests for equipment will be at a higher level.

COMPONENT INTEGRITY

57. For a number of structures, where failure would place doubt on the ability to shut down without significant core damage, it is not possible to provide redundancy; on the AGR examples are the gas baffle, core restraint or the diagrid supporting the core; on the PWR the pressure vessel, main coolant pump fly-wheels, sections of the main steam lines.

58. The CEGB Design Safety Guidelines allow a fault to be discounted if one of the following can be demonstrated:

(i)   adequate forewarning and preventive action can be guaranteed.
(ii)   the occurrence of the fault can be discounted by engineering judgement based on appropriate preventive measures.
(iii)   the probability of the fault can be shown to be less than 10^{-7} per reactor year.

59. Usually approach (i) or (ii) is adopted and is illustrated from Sizewell 'B'.

60. Some of these measures make a positive and direct contribution to the achievement of integrity, whilst others contribute to an understanding of the behaviour of the component and enable a satisfactory demonstration of safety to be put forward.

Achievement of integrity

61. The required integrity is achieved through conservative design and careful construction by an established manufacturer, in accordance with an established code of practice supplemented by a detailed design specification. Rigorous quality control, inspection and testing procedures are applied. The plant is operated in a

carefully controlled manner, and is subject to in-service inspection and monitoring for evidence of degradation.

62. These measures form an integral part of the safety case put forward for Sizewell 'B' and are based on experience accumulated both on the reference SNUPPS plants and elsewhere, and include a number of improvements relative to past practice, which can be illustrated by reference to the reactor pressure vessel (RPV):

(a)   use of ring forgings to eliminate axial welds.
(b)   use of SA508 Class 3 as the basic material specifications with additional controls on various alloying elements to improve weldability, and to minimise degradation of properties due to irradiation and ageing.
(c)   the application of rigorous controls on welding procedures, and on welder qualifications.
(d)   comprehensive volumetric examination, by ultrasonics, more stringent than those required by the codes, or carried out previously on PWR pressure vessels.

Demonstration of integrity

63. The demonstration of integrity consists of a demonstration that the size of defects which are of safety concern are large in relation to those which are expected to be present, taking into account the measures adopted to avoid the incidence of defects, the comprehensive range of inspections applied during manufacture and the programme of ISI.

64. The demonstration therefore relies upon detailed thermal, stress and fracture analysis for all the important regions of the component, and for all plant states, to derive critical or limiting defect sizes. This analysis is substantially more rigorous and more comprehensive than that called for in any existing design code.

65. The limiting (or "critical") defect sizes must then be compared with the size of defect which can be reliably detected by the inspection processes, and a suitable margin between them shown to exist. This margin is defined in terms of the validation factor (VF) where:

$$VF = \frac{\text{limiting defect size}}{\text{validation size} + \Delta a}$$

66. Where Δa is the predicted fatigue crack growth during the full operating life of a defect equal to the validation size at the start-of-life. For most situations a target value of 2 has been adopted for the validation factor.

67. The validation size for a particular component has been established from extensive validation trials which provide confirmation that the ultrasonic inspections achieve a specified detection capability. For the reactor vessel the validation size is 25mm generally, and is 15mm in specific near-surface regions.

OPERATOR

68. Experience shows that most severe accidents have a human factor associated with them. Considerable importance is therefore placed on this aspect in the various stages of design, manufacture, construction and commissioning. Once the plant is operational the emphasis is on the correct maintenance and operation of the plant. In an emergency it is the operator at the control desk who has to make decisions and take appropriate action. Mandatory operating rules and procedures are provided and suitable training is given so that the operator is familiar with the characteristics of the plant and the significance of the procedures and rules. Nevertheless, the designers must recognise that operators can make mistakes and make provision to minimise the effect through suitable choice of plant characteristics and the systems provided.

Operating limits

69. The safety analysis on which the protective systems are based makes certain assumptions about the operating conditions of the plant. Operation outside these boundaries can invalidate the safety case, eg. at Chernobyl control rods were withdrawn beyond the operating limit and power was taken below the allowed value. In the UK automatic controls are used to maintain the plant within the specified limits of operation. Comprehensive alarm and display systems are used to alert the operator of significant changes. Interlocks are used to prevent unacceptable plant conditions from arising through incorrect action or equipment faults.

Plant availability

70. The reliability of the protective functions is dependent on the availability of sufficient equipment. The redundancy provided allows for a certain amount of equipment being unavailable due, eg. to maintenance during operation. The maintenance procedures and control room displays must ensure that the operator is aware of outages of safety related equipment. Clear and unambiguous requirements are specified in the operating rules for the minimum plant which must be available. If the plant does not meet these requirements the operator must reduce power or shut-down as required.

Operator actions post-fault

71. The recovery actions which the operator is required to take after a fault are specified in the operating instructions. The plant is designed to ensure that the operator has sufficient time to carry out required actions, and the necessary information to determine both the need for such actions and the effect on safety of any actions carried out.

72. Sufficient time is provided by ensuring that any response required in the first half hour is initiated automatically by the protective systems. This reduces the incentive for the operator to intervene precipitously in the early stages of a fault. This approach is supplemented by design provisions which restrict the ability of the operator to intervene in an unsafe manner. In particular, the operator's ability to inhibit automatic safety systems, either by blocking the actuation signal (as at Chernobyl) or by switching off the systems (as at Three Mile Island), is restricted by design.

73. Necessary information is provided in dedicated displays with associated alarms. The displays provide information only on the few plant parameters and systems that are important to safety. Therefore the operator is immediately aware of the effect on safety of his actions, without having to sift through all the other information provided for plant operation.

CONCLUSIONS

74. It can be seen that, in the UK, the CEGB Design Safety Criteria and Design Safety Guidelines have a major influence on the protective equipment provided for the safe shutdown of and post-trip cooling of a reactor following a fault. The examples from the Heysham II/Torness AGR and the Sizewell 'B' PWR illustrate the application of these standards.

75. A further reassurance on the adequacy of the safety provisions is that any reactor design is vetted independently by the NII against their own Safety Assessment Principles.

76. The importance of the operator in relation to severe accidents has been dramatically highlighted in several instances in recent years and, in the U.K., the selection and training of operators together with suitable protective systems are aimed at minimising the likelihood of significant operator errors.

Discussion

Academician B.N. Laskorin, *USSR Academy of Sciences Chairman of Environmental Protection Committee of the USSR Union of Scientific and Engineering Societies*
The protection of the vital qualities of natural water is the main issue underlying the survival of humanity.

Data on the Chernobyl tragedy have been widely discussed at many conferences and symposia held by the International Atomic Energy Agency and other agencies under the aegis of the United Nations. Also during the three years following the Chernobyl accident, we have been in close co-operation and have had confidential consultations with scientists from Great Britain, Japan, the USA, France and Sweden. The aim of the present conference is to consider methods of preventing radioactive pollution of natural waters in the event of a nuclear accident. The critical remarks, heard frequently, concerning the Chernobyl reactor are quite just. The protection of the vital qualities of natural waters is of extreme importance today if the global problems threatening all life on earth are to be solved.

Detailed information on the Kiev water supply after the Chernobyl accident is presented in Paper 1. There is no doubt that there was a huge fallout of radioactive products, measured in millions of curies, in the basin of the Pripyat river and the Kiev water storage reservoir. However, even in the crucial days following the accident, when the total radioactivity in the Pripyat river and the Kiev water storage increased one-hundredfold, the population was supplied with potable water of good quality even under the usual water treatment scheme. The level of radioactive products was within the adopted standards and did not exceed the maximal permissible concentration. (The total beta-activity was 10^{-11}-10^{-12} Ci/l before the accident and 10^{-8}-10^{-9} Ci/l after it.) However, radioactive products accumulated in the bottom sediments, and there was a threat of an increase in radiation activity as a result of storm water run-off and radioactive sludges lifting in stormy weather. That is why measures guaranteeing safe potable water supply were provided. All these are dealt with in Paper 1.

The groundwaters in the whole territory of radioactive contamination have not been subjected to any noticeable pollution and, as such, they have preserved their characteristics of 10^{-11}-10^{-12} Ci/l which they had before the event. Therefore, the groundwaters proved to be a safe potable water source, but here I must underline that the use of open wells is absolutely inadmissible because they accumulate impurities and they are very hard to clean. However, we must bear in mind that there are many natural water bodies, both fresh surface water sources, such as rivers and lakes, and underground sources, to say nothing of seas and oceans, which contain considerable quantities of natural radioactive elements such as uranium and radium. The concentrations of these elements very often exceed the permissible values established for anthropogenic activity. Geologists in the USSR and other countries very often use data on high uranium and radium content in natural waters, which often reaches 0.05-0.01 mg/l, as a criterion of uranium deposits, but it cannot be the only criterion.

The tragic experience of the Chernobyl accident, as well as all international practices of the nuclear industry and the use of radioactive materials in various fields of national economy, suggests that underground waters are the most reliable source of drinking water, as they are also in cases of non-radioactive pollution.

The use of underground waters in industry and public services should be prohibited: they must be preserved as a source of drinking water supply. Measures must be taken to prevent the pollution of underground waters from surface run-off. Underground waters must be regarded as the gold fund of pure drinking water. Closed water-recycling systems, as well as resource-saving techniques, are among preventive measures against radioactive and other pollution of natural waters, including inorganic, organic and biological pollution. All these measures result in reducing per capita water use. Detailed analyses of water use in all fields of industry, agriculture and public services suggest that there is a huge potential for reducing the per capita water use in the national economy. At present, advanced technologies of wastewater treatment provide 94-95% removal of organic matter and heavy metals, but they do not provide for the removal of biogenic elements and light metals. To meet the requirements on maximal permissible concentration, treated wastewater has to be diluted dozens of times; that is, we rely on water body self-purification in the long run.

At present, most rivers and water bodies, especially in Europe and the USA, are nothing else but diluted wastewater. Here, radioactive elements are not removed but redistributed among water organisms and the bottom sediments. In this process, toxic products accumulate, and this results in progressive deterioration of natural water quality. For 20 years, the USSR has been carrying out a programme of shifting some industries to closed water systems, with zero discharge into open water bodies. For the first time, closed water recycling schemes with zero discharge have been used in the uranium industry, at concentrating mills, and in metallurgical, chemical and other industries. In all cases a considerable reduction of per capita water use was achieved, as well as an ecological and techno-economic effect. Capital investments in the introduction of water recycling systems are repaid within 1 1/2-2 years.

Strict differentiation of wastewater must be observed in developing closed water-recycling schemes. Local treatment methods are widely used. These include highly effective flocculents and adsorption, extraction and membrane processes. For selective extraction of colour, rare metals and radioactive elements from wastewater, highly effective adsorbers have been developed. Scientists from all countries must combine their efforts and develop a scientific and technical programme to solve the global problem of protecting the vital qualities of natural waters.

Ms M.D. Hill, *National Radiological Protection Board, UK*
Further to Paper 1, it would be interesting to know what the basis is for the radiological standards used in the USSR for drinking water following the Chernobyl accident?

Dr D.C.W. Sanderson, *Scottish Universities Research & Reactor Centre*
I agree entirely with Mr Gray that it is helpful to hear of the many considerations being taken to ensure that modern British reactors are safe.Nevertheless, it can be suggested that the early Magnox design does not meet the full criteria of defence in depth, owing to the low margin of thermal safety in fuel cladding, and the penetration of biological and containment shields by primary CO_2 ducts. Could Mr Gray offer an opinion as to whether these plants would be licensed today in the UK if they were subjected to the full planning process?

Mr Gray, *Paper 2*
Of course progress has been made in the past thirty years in raising safety standards and developing designs to meet them. It would be disappointing if it were not so. It follows that a plant designed thirty years ago would not meet current licensing requirements of new construction, if only because its potential release of radioactivity would not be as low as reasonably practicable. Nevertheless, it has to be said that it would be very safe indeed in comparison with almost any other industrial structure. The long-term safety review carried out recently on our original Magnox plant at Hunterston has shown that it could be licensed for another extended period of operation, with only small modifications.

4. Radiological standards to be applied to drinking water in the event of an accidental release of radionuclides

M. D. HILL, MA, MSc, National Radiological Protection Board, UK

SYNOPSIS. Several sets of radiological standards have been established for application to drinking water in the event of an accident. Some of these sets were formulated prior to the Chernobyl accident, others after it. The debate about the appropriateness of these standards continues and while there seems to be a consensus on basic principles there is still a need to review and rationalise numerical values.

INTRODUCTION.
1. The radiological standards to be applied to drinking water in the event of an accidental release of radionuclides into the environment are of two basic types: intervention levels (also known as emergency reference levels, ERLs), and derived intervention levels (also known as derived emergency reference levels, DERLs). Intervention levels (ILs) are usually framed in terms of radiation doses to individual members of the public, while derived intervention levels (DILs) are expressed as concentrations of radionuclides or groups of radionuclides in drinking water. This paper describes the radiological protection principles involved in setting ILs and DILs and outlines the current advice of international organisations, and of the National Radiological Protection Board (NRPB) in the UK, on the levels to be used. It then goes on to indicate how this advice may change in the future. Although the paper deals specifically with drinking water, the principles described are applicable to other public exposure aspects of the use of water resources.

BASIC PRINCIPLES IN ESTABLISHING INTERVENTION LEVELS
2. The International Commission on Radiological Protection (ICRP) has recommended the following basic principles for planning actions to protect the public in the event of an accident (ref. 1):
   (a) serious non-stochastic effects* should be avoided by the introduction of countermeasures to limit individual dose to levels below the thresholds for these effects;
   (b) the risk from stochastic effects* should be limited by introducing countermeasures which achieve a positive net benefit to the individuals involved;

(c) the overall incidence of stochastic effects should be limited, as far as reasonably practicable, by reducing the collective dose.

3. As far as actions related to water resources are concerned, it is principles (b) and (c) which are most important because it is virtually impossible to identify an accident situation where doses to the public via water related pathways would be high enough to cause non-stochastic effects, and ILs set on the basis of principles (b) and (c) will automatically ensure that principle (a) is satisfied.

4. In order to use principle (c) in establishing ILs and DILs it is necessary to carry out "optimisation" exercises in which the costs of decreases in the health detriment in the affected population are balanced against the costs of the countermeasures. Costs in this instance are interpreted to mean not only financial costs but also less quantifiable factors such as psychological impacts and social disruption. Hence the balancing always involves an element of judgement and is not a simple numerical procedure.

5. The constraint on the optimisations is that principle (b) must still be satisfied ie, that the introduction of the countermeasure must be "justified" in the sense that it entails a positive net benefit to the people involved. This justification again involves elements of judgement because there will be aspects of the benefits of taking actions, as well as their costs, which are not readily quantifiable and which need to be taken into account.

6. Theoretically, the processes of justification and optimisation could be carried out at the time of an accident and ILs selected which are appropriate to the actual situation. Such a procedure is not, however, sensible in the case of actions which will only be effective if they are taken during the release of radionuclides or shortly after it has ceased, and even for actions which would not need to be taken until well after the accident there are advantages in establishing ILs for contingency planning purposes. For this reason, ICRP (ref. 1), the International Atomic Energy Agency (IAEA, ref. 2) the World Health Organisation (WHO, ref. 3) and, in the UK, the NRPB (refs. 4 and 5) have adopted an approach involving a two-tier system of dose levels. The lower levels are those at which consideration of the introduction of the countermeasure should begin, and below which action would not be warranted.

---

*Non-stochastic health effects are those for which the severity of the effect varies with the radiation dose, and so in general there is a threshold dose below which no effect occurs. Stochastic health effects are those for which the probability of an effect occurring, rather than its severity, is regarded as a function of dose, without threshold. The main stochastic effect of radiation is fatal cancer.

If predicted doses exceed the lower level, implementation of the countermeasure is desirable, but not essential. The upper levels are those at which it is expected that the countermeasure would be introduced, whatever the circumstances. When preparing emergency plans, the relevant authorities are advised to set site specific ILs which are between the upper and lower levels, and/or to set DILs which correspond to doses between the two levels. Table 1 shows the upper and lower dose levels recommended by ICRP, IAEA, WHO and NRPB for imposing restrictions on the distribution and consumption of food and water.

Table 1. Dose levels for restrictions on food and water

	Dose equivalent (mSv)	
	Lower level	Upper level
Whole body	5	50
Individual organs preferentially irradiated	50	500

ROLE OF DOSE LIMITS FOR THE PUBLIC IN ACCIDENT SITUATIONS

7. The dose limits recommended by ICRP (refs. 6 and 7) for members of the public do not apply to accident situations because these limits were established for the sum of the doses from a specified combination of sources of radiation exposure and this combination does not include radionuclides released into the environment as a result of accidents. The reason for this exclusion is that a distinction is made in radiological protection between existing exposure situations where any control involves intervention or remedial measures, and future exposure situations where the source can be subject to control during the design stages and in planning operations. The former category of exposure situations are considered on a case basis, with emphasis being placed on the extent of the complexity, cost and inconvenience of control measures, while the latter category are judged firstly on the basis of risks routinely accepted by the majority of population (the dose limits being set to correspond to the maximum acceptable risk), and then on the basis of whether it is worthwhile to reduce doses and risks by changes in design and operation.

8. Unfortunately, despite their original intentions, when it came to selecting upper and lower dose levels for accident situations ICRP made reference to dose limits and, in the case of restrictions on food and water, chose lower dose levels which are numerically equal to the dose limits for members of the public which were recommended at the time (ref. 1). This has caused confusion ever since and has led to a mistaken presumption by many people that, as dose limits change, dose levels for use in accident situations should change in a corresponding way.

9. Another important point to bear in mind in considering the distinction between dose limits for routine exposure situations and ILs for accident situations is that the former apply to doses which will actually be received while the latter are in terms of dose averted.* This distinction arises from the difference in the ways that dose limits and ILs are formulated and are intended to be used. As indicated above, dose limits are set to correspond to the maximum risk that would be acceptable in routine situations and represent the lower boundary of a "forbidden region"; they are used primarily at the planning and design stage. ILs, on the other hand, are set by balancing the costs of taking a countermeasure against the costs of the health detriment that that countermeasure would avert; they are for use both in emergency planning and in the case of an actual accident, but are not intended to be employed for obtaining criteria against which nuclear installations should be designed or operations at installations planned.

DERIVED INTERVENTION LEVELS – CURRENT ADVICE

10. DILs are a practical expression of ILs and are in terms of quantities that may be directly compared with measurements which would be made in the environment following an accidental release. In general, the process of obtaining DILs from ILs involves making assumptions about the characteristics and habits of individuals (eg, how old they are, how much food they consume and how much water they drink), and using mathematical models to calculate rates of radionuclide transfer through the environment and subsequent doses to people, as a function of time. In making assumptions about the characteristics and habits of individuals it is important to ensure that those chosen are reasonably representative of the habits and characteristics of the group of individuals whose projected dose is to be compared to the IL. Hence if the IL is in terms of the dose to an average person, then average habits are assumed, while if the IL is in terms of the dose to those likely to incur the highest radiation risks as a result of an accident, then habits appropriate to this group are assumed.

11. As far as drinking water is concerned, it is relatively straightforward to select overall consumption rates which are appropriate for obtaining general DILs, and to agree on the structure of and parameters for models for calculating doses per unit intake of radionuclides in water. Difficulties arise, however, in choosing models to predict rates of radionuclide transfer through the environment because there are such large differences between characteristics of water supply systems (eg. in the dilution which occurs, in water treatment plants and their effectiveness for removal of radionuclides, and in

---

*In many practical situations the dose averted by taking a countermeasure will be approximately equal to the projected dose in the absence of that countermeasure. Thus the term "projected dose" is often used in place of averted dose.

the time taken for transfer from deposition to consumption).
The approaches used so far in establishing general DILs for
drinking water have circumvented all these difficulties (and
others such as whether water is boiled prior to consumption) by
simply not attempting to model the transfer of radionuclides
from the time and place of deposition to the point of
consumption. While it would in theory be possible to undertake
such modelling on a site specific basis, obtain DILs for many
different sites and select general DILs from these, this
exercise does not yet seem to have been attempted either
internationally or by particular countries.

12. The first set of DILs to be established in the UK were
those calculated by NRPB (ref. 5); these were published in
March 1986, immediately prior to the Chernobyl accident, and
formed the basis for the NRPB advice not to drink rainwater
continuously for a week following the arrival of the Chernobyl
cloud over the UK. The NRPB DILs are in terms of the initial
concentrations of radionuclides, as measured in water at the
tap, which, when the water is consumed at a particular rate,
result in the ILs being exceeded at various times of exposure.
The DILs are calculated from the following formula:

$$DIL = \frac{IL.\lambda R}{I_w.D_{ing} (1 - e^{-\lambda_R T})} \qquad (1)$$

where DIL is the initial concentration of the radionuclide in
water (Bq l^{-1});
IL is the intervention level of dose (Sv, see Table 1);
I_w is the annual intake of drinking water (l y^{-1});
D_{ing} is the dose per unit intake of the radionuclide by
ingestion (Sv Bq^{-1}); and
T is the assumed period over which water consumption
continues.

Table 2 shows examples of the NRPB values for various
exposure times for isotopes of strontium, caesium, ruthenium
and iodine. The exposure times may be interpreted as times at
which substitutions of fresh water supplies are made, so the
DILs can be used to indicate the time at which action is
needed.

13. Also in 1986, but after the Chernobyl accident, the IAEA
published guidance on DILs (ref. 8). Those for drinking water
are expressed in terms of the peak concentrations of
radionuclides, and are calculated assuming that the
individual's annual intake of drinking water is contaminated
initially at the same level and that the only loss mechanism is
radioactive decay (ie, using the same formula as NRPB (ref. 5)
but taking an exposure time of one year). Examples of the IAEA
values are given in Table 3.

Table 2. Examples of NRPB DILs for drinking water

Radionuclide	DIL $(Bq\ l^{-1})$ for exposure time T (days)			
	T = 2	T = 7	T = 14	T = 100
^{90}Sr	$2.8\ 10^4$	$8.1\ 10^3$	$4.1\ 10^3$	$5.7\ 10^2$
^{106}Ru	$7.3\ 10^4$	$2.1\ 10^4$	$1.0\ 10^4$	$1.6\ 10^3$
^{131}I	$1.1\ 10^4$	$3.7\ 10^3$	$2.4\ 10^3$	$1.7\ 10^3$
^{134}Cs	$4.3\ 10^4$	$1.2\ 10^4$	$6.2\ 10^3$	$9.1\ 10^2$
^{137}Cs	$5.1\ 10^4$	$1.5\ 10^4$	$7.3\ 10^3$	$1.0\ 10^3$

Notes

a. The DILs given are based on the lower ILs in Table 1.
b. The drinking water intake rates assumed are 0.7 1 d^{-1}, 0.95 1 d^{-1} and 1.65 1 d^{-1} for infants (1 year old), children (10 years old) and adults, respectively. In all cases the DIL for the infant is most restrictive.
c. See ref. 5 for discussion of the procedure to be followed if more than one radionuclide is present in drinking water.

Table 3. Examples of IAEA DILs for drinking water

Radionuclide	DIL $(Bq\ l^{-1})$
^{90}Sr	$1.5\ 10^2$
^{106}Ru	$7\ \ \ 10^2$
^{131}I	$1.5\ 10^3$
^{134}Cs	$6\ \ \ 10^2$
^{137}Cs	$7\ \ \ 10^2$

Notes

a. The DILs given are based on the lower ILs in Table 1.
b. The drinking water intake rates assumed are as given in the notes to Table 2.
c. See ref. 8 for discussion of the procedure to be followed if more than one radionuclide is present in drinking water.

14. In a report published in 1988 (ref. 9), a group of experts convened by WHO used an approach which is even simpler than those adopted by the NRPB and the IAEA to obtain guideline DIL values for application after widespread radioactive contamination resulting from a major radiation accident. In this approach it is implicitly assumed that radionuclide concentrations in food and drinking water remain constant for a year. The DILs for drinking water are then calculated from:

$$DIL = \frac{IL}{Iw.D_{ing}} \qquad (2)$$

where DIL is the concentration of the radionuclide in water at
         the point of consumption (Bq l^{-1});
         IL is the intervention level of dose (Sv y^{-1}); and
         I_w and D_{ing} are as in equation (1).

Furthermore, instead of calculating DILs for each radionuclide, the WHO group simply divided radionuclides into two classes: those with "high" D_{ing} values (10^{-6} Sv Bq^{-1}) and those with "low" D_{ing} values (10^{-8} Sv Bq^{-1}), and they considered only the lower ILs given in Table 1. This led to two main guideline values for DILs for drinking water: 7 Bq l^{-1} for the "high" D_{ing} radionuclides (eg plutonium–239 and other actinides) and 700 Bq l^{-1} for the "low" D_{ing} radionuclides (eg iodine–131, caesium–137).

15. To conclude this section on current DILs it is necessary to mention developments within the Commission of the European Communities (CEC). In 1987 the Council of the European Communities adopted a regulation (ref. 10) which sets out the procedure to be followed by CEC for determining maximum permitted levels of radionuclides in foodstuffs and animal feeding stuffs placed on the market following a nuclear accident. The regulation contains values of maximum levels of radionuclides in dairy produce and other foodstuffs. Corresponding levels for liquid foodstuffs are currently being discussed and the regulation states that these values "should be applied to drinking water supplies at the discretion of competent authorities in Member States". Presumably the levels for liquid foodstuffs will be in the same form as those for dairy produce and other foodstuffs in that radionuclides are grouped into four classes: isotopes of strontium (notably strontium–90), isotopes of iodine (notably iodine–131), alpha–emitting isotopes of plutonium and transplutonium elements (notably plutonium–239 and americium–241), and all other radionuclides of radioactive half–life greater than 10 days (notably caesium–134 and caesium–137, but excluding tritium and carbon–14). It also seems likely that the values incorporated in a regulation will be established through a combination of technical discussions and consideration of other factors such as the degree of public concern, the implications for EC trade and the relationship to levels in use elsewhere in the world, because this was the case for the dairy produce and

other foodstuffs levels in the existing regulation (ref. 11). Hence these liquid foodstuff levels will not be derived directly from an intervention level of dose and cannot strictly be described as DILs in the sense that this term has so far been used in this paper.

POSSIBLE CHANGES IN STANDARDS

16.   The debate about the radiological protection standards to be applied in the event of a nuclear accident which began after Chernobyl is continuing nationally and internationally (see, for example, refs. 12–14). The discussions concern both the basic principles used in establishing ILs and DILs and the numerical values recommended by various organisations, and take into account recent revisions in the estimates of the health risks associated with exposure to ionising radiation (refs. 15–17). At the time of writing it is not clear what the detailed outcome of these discussions will be but it is possible to indicate the general direction in which thinking is moving.

17.   There seems to be a consensus that the principles recommended by ICRP for planning protective actions (see para 2) are sound but they need expansion and clarification. ICRP is expected to provide some of this in the forthcoming revision of their basic recommendations, and there is related work in progress at the Nuclear Energy Agency (NEA) of OECD, and the IAEA. At present it is anticipated that this expansion and clarification will not, as far as countermeasures related to exposure via water resources is concerned, differ substantially from that provided in this paper.

18.   The numerical values of ILs (see Table 1) require re-examination in the light of changes in estimates of radiation risks and further information about the costs and benefits of taking countermeasures. Following such a re-examination NRPB staff have suggested (ref. 14) that it may be more appropriate to use ILs for food and water restrictions which are a factor of 5 lower than those shown in Table 1. While it is too early to say what the relevant international organisations, and particularly ICRP, will recommend in terms of numerical levels, it seems clear that their ILs will either be reduced or stay at their present values; there are no suggestions that ILs should be increased.

19.   Of perhaps greater concern to most of those attending this conference are the likely changes in DILs. As will be apparent from paras 10–15, there are already several sets of DILs available, and the forthcoming publication of the CEC values will add another one. All the sets differ because each has been obtained on a different basis. Regardless of any changes in ILs, there is clearly a need to rationalise the DILs situation.

20.   In carrying out this rationalisation it is necessary to reconcile a number of conflicting aims. On the one hand it is desirable to have clear, straightforward guidance which can be

easily understood by both experts and the public; on the other hand the diversity of the characteristics of drinking water supplies and the countermeasures which could be applied to them is such that strict application of radiological protection principles could lead to a plethora of derived levels. Similarly, while simplicity is presentationally attractive, over-simplification could remove the flexibility to take those actions which are most appropriate to the circumstances if an accident actually occurs.

21. A further important point to bear in mind in establishing DILs for drinking water is the likelihood that they will ever be used. ICRP has stated (ref. 1) that, while the preparation of emergency plans should be based on consideration of a wide range of potential accidents, including those having low probabilities of occurrence, the degree of detail in plans should decrease as the probability of the accident decreases. The same principle applies in deciding on the effort to be devoted to setting DILs and site specific action levels.

22. Given the above discussion, the best approach seems to me to be to focus on setting a simple set of DILs which apply to those drinking water countermeasures which are most likely to be needed and which need to be implemented shortly after an accidental release occurs. For countries such as the UK, this would probably mean placing emphasis on DILs for banning the direct consumption by humans of rainwater and water taken from small sources which are open to the atmosphere and on which radionuclides released to the atmosphere may therefore be deposited. It may be that the CEC reference levels for liquid foodstuffs will be adequate for this purpose. For drinking water countermeasures which are less likely to be needed and/or which do not need to be implemented quickly it would seem better to set up procedures for determining whether it is appropriate to take action after an accident actually occurs, rather than devoting a great deal of effort to establishing DILs and action levels in advance for a whole range of specific sites and accident situations. Such procedures would include arrangements for carrying out environmental monitoring and for input of monitoring results into a computerised database, plus the use of computer programs to evaluate the merits and de-merits of various countermeasures options. In order to write these programs mathematical models would need to be constructed which enable doses to be predicted from monitoring data, on a site specific basis, and information gathered on the feasible countermeasures, particularly their financial costs and the speed with which they could be implemented, again on a site specific basis. To do this for all of the drinking water sources in a country would be a very large task and it would therefore be necessary to begin with those sources which by virtue of their location are more likely to be affected in the event of an accident.

REFERENCES

1. ICRP. Protection of the public in the event of major radiation accidents: principles for planning. ICRP Publication 40, Ann. ICRP, vol. 14 no. 2, 1984.

2. IAEA. Principles for establishing intervention levels for the protection of the public in the event of a nuclear accident or radiological emergency. IAEA Safety Series no. 72, IAEA, Vienna, 1985.

3. WHO. Nuclear power: accidental releases – principles of public health actions. A report on a WHO meeting, Brussels, 23–27 November 1987. WHO Regional Publications, European Series no. 16, WHO, Geneva, 1984.

4. NRPB. Emergency reference levels: criteria for limiting doses to the public in the event of accidental exposure to radiation. Chilton, NRPB, ERL 2, London, HMSO, 1981.

5. LINSLEY G.S et al. Derived emergency reference levels for the introduction of countermeasures in the early to intermediate phases of emergencies involving the release of radioactive materials to atmosphere. NRPB–DL 10, London, HMSO, 1986.

6. ICRP. Recommendations of the International Commission on Radiological Protection. ICRP Publication 26, Ann. ICRP, vol. 1 no. 3, 1977.

7. ICRP. Statement from the 1985 Paris meeting of the ICRP. Ann. ICRP vol. 15 no. 3, 1985.

8. IAEA. Derived intervention levels for application in controlling radiation doses to the public in the event of a nuclear accident or radiological emergency. IAEA Safety Series no. 81, IAEA, Vienna, 1986.

9. WHO. Derived intervention levels for radionuclides in food, Guidelines for application after widespread radioactive contamination resulting from a major radiation accident. WHO, Geneva, 1988.

10. EURATOM. Council Regulation (Euratom) No. 3954/87 of 22 December 1987 laying down maximum permitted levels of radioactive contamination of foodstuffs and feedingstuffs following a nuclear accident or any other case of radiological emergency. Official Journal of the European Communities L371, 11–13, 1987.

11. GRAY P.S. and LUYCKX F. Control of radioactivity in foodstuffs in the European Economic Community. Chapter 31 of Radionuclides in the Foodchain, ILS1 Monograph, Springer–Verlag, 1988.

12. NEA. Nuclear accidents, intervention levels for protection of the public. NEA/OECD, Paris, 1989.

13. IAEA. Revised guidance on the principles for establishing intervention levels for the protection of the public in the event of a nuclear accident or radiological emergency. TECDOC-473, IAEA, Vienna, 1988.

14. HILL M.D. et al. Protection of the public and workers in the event of accidental releases of radioactive materials into the environment. J. Radiol. Prot. vol 8 no. 4, 197-207, 1988.

15. UNSCEAR. Sources, effects and risks of ionizing radiation. 1988 report of the United Nations Scientific Committee on the Effects of Atomic Radiation, with annexes. UN, New York, 1988.

16. CLARKE R.H. Statement of evidence to the Hinkley Point C Inquiry. NRPB-M160, NRPB, Chilton, 1988.

17. STATHER J. et al. Health effects models developed from the 1988 UNSCEAR report. NRPB-R226, London, HMSO, 1988.

5. Radiological protection aspects of European Community legislation

G. FRASER, MSc, Commission of the European Communities, Luxembourg

The paper describes the evolution of the European Community basic safety standards for radiological protection pre-Chernobyl and discusses the possible role of maximum permissible concentrations in drinking water. In this light, it then describes the way in which the basic safety standards have developed since the Chernobyl accident, particularly as regards dietary contamination, and concludes by suggesting that while the overall implications for drinking water are limited to bottled and canned waters following an accident, this is not only an understandable but also a preferable situation.

The EC Legislative Procedure

Article 30 of the Euratom Treaty (1) requires Community basic safety standards to be established for the protection of workers and the general public against the dangers of ionizing radiation. For this purpose the Commission must first consult a standing expert committee set up under the terms of Article 31 before submitting proposals, for opinion, to the Economic and Social Committee. Having considered the advice of both Committees, the Commission then communicates its proposals together with the respective committee reports to the Council of Ministers which must in turn consult the European Parliament - the "Assembly" as it is referred to in the Treaty. Finally it is the Council which, acting on a qualified majority, decides on and enacts the Community legislation.

For the basic safety standards, such legislation is usually in the form of a Directive, which, while binding on Member States, does not automatically enter into national law. Instead, the individual Member State governments are required to make appropriate legislative and other provisions to ensure compliance. Within a period stipulated by the Directive. New national legislation may well require widespread consultation between various government departments and with representatives of the parties affected, and must then be submitted to the Commission in draft form for comment prior to being enacted.

The same sequence must be followed for introducing any revisions to the basic safety standards and hence such revisions are not to be undertaken lightly.

Should the Commission believe that a Member State is failing to comply with the standards, it may invoke certain procedures and ultimately bring the offending Member State government before the European Court of Justice if the problem is not resolved. Such failures may be purely technical, for example if national legislation does not provide adequate means for enforcing compliance, even if in practice all relevant limits are being respected. In cases of urgency, however, the Commission may itself, under the terms of Article 38 of the Treaty, direct a Member State to take all necessary measures within a period stipulated by the Commission and, in the event of continued non-compliance, proceed directly to the Court of Justice, by-passing normal procedures.

The Basic Safety Standards and their Evolution before Chernobyl

The first EC directive establishing the basic safety standards was enacted in 1959 (2) and was revised by further directives in 1962 (3), 1966 (4), 1976 (5), 1980 (6) and 1984 (7); a separate directive on medical practices was established in 1984 (8). In general these directives have followed the recommendations of the International Commission on Radiological Protection (ICRP) but are of a more practical nature, setting out not only maximum permissible levels and fundamental principles but also procedural requirements to ensure compliance with these levels and principles; this latter aspect recognizes the need to harmonize the provisions made by Member States as indicated by Article 33 of the Treaty.

Revisions of the basic safety standards since 1959 have reflected not only scientific advances but also to a certain extent the political consequences of increased technical resources within individual Member States. In 1959 nuclear power was in its infancy and there was a considerable incentive to pool the limited expertize then available. As such resources have increased, so also have Member States tended to become more independent, thus leaving a reduced role for the Community. In 1983, therefore, the Commission was unable to obtain Council endorsement for a review of bilateral radiological emergency arrangements, aimed at encouraging improvement through cross-fertilization and, to the extent appropriate, harmonization within the Community. (The work was, nevertheless, undertaken by the Commission on its own authority and within the limitations encountered, leading to a report published in January 1986 (9).)

The first basic safety standards directive enacted in 1959 (2) was almost entirely concerned with the protection of workers although it did specify a maximum permissible exposure for the population as a whole of 50 mSv (5 rem) per person, accumulated up to the age of 30; it also gave maximum permissible concentrations in water corresponding to the exposure limits for classified workers for almost 100 individual radionuclides, any mixture of fission products and for any mixture of alpha emitters. Because of the way in which the population exposure limit is expressed, however, it was not clear how equivalent concentrations could be inferred for members of the general population, but outside of controlled areas (areas in which persons subject to occupational exposure might receive more than 15 mSv (1.5 rem) in a year) the maximum permissible concentrations for classified workers were to be reduced by a factor of ten. Member States were required to carry out the necessary surveillance, inspection and, in the event of an accident, intervention; as a precaution against possible accidents, plans for the action to be taken by the competent authorities were to be drawn up in advance, appropriate resources made available and the Commission informed of the arrangements made.

The amending 1962 directive (3) extended the list of maximum permissible concentrations for workers to over 200 nuclides and 5 generalized categories, with values revised in the light of the latest ICRP recommendations. Subsequently in 1966 (4), the factor of ten to be applied outside of controlled areas to maximum permissible concentrations in water (as further extended and revised in respect of transuranic nuclides) was specified as appertaining to people who, residing in the vicinity of a controlled area, might thereby receive a higher exposure than that laid down for the population as a whole. The limit for the latter remained numerically unchanged but was defined as the genetic exposure.

The 1976 (5) revision, unlike those of 1962 and 1966, provided a completely new text, and a number of the changes incorporated are relevant.

- The maximum permissible concentrations in water were replaced by annual limits for ingestion of the various nuclides, singly and in combination, for <u>members of the   public</u>. It was stated that the annual limits were related to maximum permissible concentrations by the volume of all liquid ingested annually by an adult, assumed to be <u>0.8 m^3</u>. While it was noted that for application to children these limits might require correction, this was to be done, where necessary, by the competent national authority.

  [handwritten marginalia: 7 o gals / hts per day.]

- Moreover, the ingestion limits reflected an annual exposure limit of 5 mSv (0.5 rem) per year to the whole body for individual members of the public (or corresponding exposure limits for bone or bone marrow where appropriate.

- With regard to emergency planning, Member States were specifically required to stipulate action levels, measures to be taken by the competent authorities and surveillance procedures with respect to population groups liable to receive a dose in excess of the relevant limits. However, it was no longer necessary to inform the Commission of the arrangements made.

Finally, in a further complete revision, the 1980 directive (6) adopted the concept of effective dose (a means of taking into account the significance of the disparate doses to individual organs which results in a single value directly related to the overall associated risk). The 1984 amendment (7) provided a revised list of annual limits of ingestion for adults corresponding to an effective dose limit of 5 mSv per year for members of the public; again it was noted that these limits may need to be corrected for application to children. The requirements for emergency planning remained unchanged.

A 1985 Communication from the Commission (9) further

explained that, in applying concentration limits derived by Member State competent authorities from the annual limits of ingestion, it is the annual average concentrations which are relevant and that ultimately it is the annual dose limits, taking into account all exposure pathways, both internal and external, which have to be respected.

When the Chernobyl accident occurred, therefore, there were no Community radioactive concentration limits for drinking water for either normal or accident situations. In the former case, the annual limits of ingestion allow such limits to be derived but, since the basic limits are in terms of total dose, this would imply assigning a portion of the dose limit to the water pathway and there is no accepted approach to such apportionment; indeed it can be argued that to do so would only reduce the flexibility of the system to no good purpose. It should also be noted that the annual limits of ingestion given in the legislation correspond to a dose limit of 5 mSv per year and not to a lifetime annual average restriction of 1 mSv per year. The latter concept was first introduced by the ICRP in 1977 (10) but a recommended limit of 5 mSv in any one year was retained; however, by 1985, ICRP regarded 1 mSv per year as the principal limit, although it would be permissible to use 5 mSv per year for some years, provided that a lifetime average of 1 mSv is not exceeded (11). (In practice, the maximum recorded annual doses even to members of critical groups do not exceed 1 mSv). Finally, it must also be noted that the annual limits for ingestion given in the basic safety standards were for adults; a number of scientific papers had been published which would have allowed calculations for other age groups (e.g. by NRPB (12)) but there was no international agreement on the values to be assigned to the necessary parameters.

For the specific case of accidents there was no Community legislation or even guidance on ingestion levels prior to Chernobyl. A 1982 Commission report had suggested radiological criteria for controlling doses in the event of an accident (13), using the two-tier approach originally proposed by the NRPB (14) and described in Paper 4 by M.D. Hill, but the values proposed did not extend to ingestion. However, subsequent ICRP recommendations in 1984 (15), also taken up by WHO (Europe) and IAEA (16, 17), adopted 5 mSv as the lower criterion for ingestion exposure within the two-tier system and this provided a common starting point for further discussion. To the extent that EC Member States might have already formally adopted the ICRP proposal or extended it to derived intervention levels for the ingestion pathway, they were not required to inform the Commission.

However, before trying to convert dose criteria to maximum permissible concentrations in foodstuffs or drinking water, it is useful to consider what purpose such derived values might be designed to serve, either in normal or accident conditions.

The Potential Significance of Maximum Permissible Concentrations in Drinking Water

The decisive criteria for the control of radiation exposure are, as already stated, limitations on dose over a period of time.

For normal conditions, the current EC limit for members of the public is 5 mSv per year and the introduction of a long-term average limit of 1 mSv per year may be anticipated. These values refer to total exposure to man-made sources (other than medical treatment) and hence only a part could be assigned to exposure resulting from materials ingested within, say, some fraction allocated to the nuclear industry. Finally, it should be noted that if an average maximum permissible concentration based on the dose imparted over one year's intake at that concentration were to be agreed, this concentration could still be exceeded for limited periods without breaching the annual dose limitation. Hence there would be a need to agree on some (higher) concentrations to be used as short-term limits.

Some Member States have pursued this possibility to varying degrees but there is no international concensus. In practice, the application of the Community basic safety standards already ensures that the doses currently received by members of the public are at most a fraction of 1 mSv; moreover, drinking water makes only a very minor contribution. Even if the concentrations in such water were ever to attain what might be considered as intrinsically unjustifiable levels, the basic safety standards already require all exposure to be maintained at levels as low as reasonably achievable within the prescribed limits and hence would allow corrective action to be enforced. Conversely, any attempt to establish uniform EC limits simply on the basis of levels which may be regarded as being as low as reasonably achievable would have to take account of the least favourable situations in the Community, with the result that the many other situations, where conditions would allow lower values to be applied, the limits thus established would have little meaning. In these circumstances it is doubtful that efforts to obtain Community agreement on maximum permissible concentrations in drinking water would serve any useful purpose even if successful; indeed, as shown above, the trend has been to move away from such methods of control.

For accident conditions, however, even exposure limits are undefined since all such limits could be meaningless in advance of knowing what limits could be enforced in the particular circumstances of the accident; thus drinking water could only be banned if practicable alternative supplies to the population affected were available. However, there is one field in which some kind of alternative would almost certainly be possible and that concerns international trade in food; moreover, if we wish to avoid unjustified impediments to trade, general agreement is required in advance of an accident as to what contamination levels in food (including all bottled or canned drinks and hence natural waters) might be acceptable. Such agreement did not exist in advance of Chernobyl and this resulted in considerable difficulties even if such drinks were not specifically affected in that case.

Post-Chernobyl Legislation
The Chernobyl accident occurred on 26 April 1986, and over the following week resulted in significant radioactive contamination of

much of the European Community. The Commission immediately sought to collect all relevant information from Member States under the terms of Articles 35 and 36 of the Euratom Treaty, but the channels previously developed for this purpose were not geared to emergency situations and proved largely ineffective. Meanwhile a wide range of intervention levels were being imposed in various parts of the Community, aimed largely at controlling the short-lived nuclide iodine-131 in salad crops and in milk. The diversity of the levels imposed had immediate trade repercussions and it was this which allowed the Commission to avail itself of an entirely separate body of Community legislation - the Common Market Treaty (18).

This Treaty is aimed primarily at assuring uniform trade practices but, exceptionally, allows individual Member States to impose import restrictions where public health is at risk. Since non-radioactive contamination of foodstuffs is not uncommon, emergency information channels and procedures for resolving differences between Member States were already well established. These mechanisms were invoked on 2 May and allowed a Commission Recommendation to be issued on 6 May providing uniform limits within the Community for iodine-131 in the produce affected (19); this was rapidly followed by a temporary ban on imports from certain non-Community countries (20, 21). Attention then turned to the more diversified, long-term hazard presented by the radioactive caesium component of Chernobyl deposition.

The Group of Experts established under Article 31 of the Euratom Treaty (1) was consulted on 23 May and recommended a limit of 1000 Bq/kg for radioactive caesium in foodstuffs. This was necessarily a preliminary opinion on account of the time-scale involved but was felt to be reasonably conservative; it was aimed at limiting the dose in the first year to 5 mSv, the lower criterion in the two-tier ICRP system (15). In the event, the Council of Ministers took additional political factors into account and, on 30 May, adopted limits of 370 Bq/kg for milk, milk products and infant foodstuffs, and 600 Bq/kg for all other produce (22). The legal basis was still the Common Market Treaty (18) and strictly speaking these limits applied only to imports into the Community, although in practice, with certain qualifications, they were applied also to trade within the Community. Initially valid until 30 September 1986, they have been renewed on several occasions, most recently (23) until 31 December 1989, and could well be further extended. However, they are specific to the post-Chernobyl contamination and it was recognized that the Euratom basic safety standards should be expanded to provide for any future major nuclear accident.

For this purpose, the Article 31 Group of Experts had to:

-        consider the various radionuclides which might be released by different types of nuclear accident (including liquid releases) and their toxicities as a function of age of the recipient;
-        quantify representative contributions of various foodstuff classes to the total diet, again a function of age;
-        assess the likely effective annual average levels of dietary

contamination which might result from the application of intervention levels.

In all, 19 nuclides and 5 classes of foodstuffs were examined but, to produce a more practical system, these were reduced to 3 nuclide and 3 foodstuff categories plus minor foodstuffs. The levels recommended by the experts corresponding to a dose not exceeding 5 mSv in the first year are given in Table 1. The Commission then had to draw up a proposal for Council and to consult the Economic and Social Committee; the Council in turn had to consult the European Parliament. The final outcome of all the debate and consultation involved is given in Table 2 which combines two Council Regulations (24, 25) which, unlike Directives, are of direct application in national law.

The differences between the two tables result from a combination of factors, not all of a scientific nature. Iodine and strontium have now been split into separate nuclide categories: "Babyfoods" form a new category and "Liquid foodstuffs" replaces "Drinking water"; provision has also been made for animal feedingstuffs but the values have yet to be agreed. Moreover, for dairy produce and other major foodstuffs the values adopted are reduced by a factor of four, relative to the experts' recommendations, in respect of long-lived beta-gamma emitters, in order to take account of values applied outside of the Community and to maintain public confidence. The resulting differences between milk (dairy produce) and liquid foodstuffs being small, the values for the former have been applied to both. It should be stressed that since the regulations apply to all foodstuffs which "may be placed on the market", liquid foodstuffs are taken to include bottle or canned water but not tap water.

The new values will be brought into force by a Commission Regulation only when there is evidence that they are likely to be reached or have been reached as a result of some future accident and hence do not replace the current post-Chernobyl limits. They are intended to avoid short-term conflict and, in the particular circumstances then prevailing, other values may be found to be more appropriate. For this reason the Commission Regulation will be valid for only a maximum of three months; within the first month the Commission shall submit to Council a proposal to adapt or confirm the initial values, and Council shall act within the three month period. Further to these requirements, a 1987 Council Decision (26) imposes arrangements for the rapid communication of the data necessary to a review of the conditions existing subsequent to a radiological emergency. This Decision complements and extends the corresponding 1986 IAEA Convention (27).

A final aspect of trade: the values described will control foodstuffs marketed in the Community and hence also imports from third countries. In addition, exports of foodstuffs unacceptable within the Community is forbidden (28). There is no general legislation on what third countries will choose to accept but the Codex Alimentarius Commission meeting in July 1989 has recommended values which, in

TABLE 1. Derived reference levels (1) initially recommended by the group of experts appointed under Article 31 of the Euratom Treaty as the basis for the control of foodstuffs following an accident (Bq/kg)

	Milk products (3)	Other major foodstuffs (4)	Drinking water
Isotopes of iodine and strontium (2) Notably I-131, Sr-90	500	3000	400
Alpha-emitting isotopes of plutonium and transplutonium elements (2) Notably Pu-239, Am-241	20	80	10
All other nuclides of half-life greater than 10 days (2), (5) Notably Cs-134, Cs-137	4000	5000	800

Notes to Table 1

1. These derived reference levels are intended for general application: they are based on the lower RL discussed in the text, namely a committed effective equivalent of 5 mSv in a year and a committed dose equivalent to the thyroid of 50 mSv in a year. Values based on the higher RL would be 10 times greater.

2. Within each group of nuclides, the values relate to the total activity of all the nuclides in the group. Each group can then be treated as completely independent of the other groups.

3. Milk products include fresh milk and reconstituted milk drinks or foods prepared from dried milk preparations. Cheese should be considered as one of the "other major foodstuffs".

4. For minor foodstuffs, e.g. those with an annual consumption of less than 10 kg, values of 10 times those for major foodstuffs will be appropriate. It is not to be expected that restrictions will be needed on items such as spices and condiments.

5. Carbon-14 and tritium are not included in this group because of their low contribution to the doses for any foreseeable accident.

TABLE 2. EC maximum permitted levels for foodstuffs in the event of a radiological emergency (Bq/kg)

Nuclide category	Foodstuffs (1)				
	Baby foods (2)	Dairy produce (3)	Other foodstuffs except minor foodstuffs (4)	Liquid foodstuffs (5)	
Isotopes of strontium Notably Sr-90	75	125	750	125	
Isotopes of iodine Notably I-131	150	500	200	500	
Alpha-emitting isotopes of plutonium and transplutonium elements Notably Pu-239, Am-241	1	20	80	20	
All other nuclides of half-life greater than 10 days. Notably Cs-134, Cs-137 (6)	400	1000	1250	1000	

Notes to Table 2

1. The level applicable to concentrated or dried products is calculated on the basis of the reconstituted product as ready for consumption. Member States may make recommendations concerning the diluting conditions in order to ensure that the maximum permitted levels laid down in this Regulation are observed.

2. Babyfoods are defined as those foodstuffs intended for the feeding of infants during the first four to six months of life, which meet, in themselves, the nutritional requirements of this category of person and are put up for retail sale in packages which are clearly identified and labelled "food preparation for infants".

3. Dairy produce is defined as those products falling within the following CN codes including, where appropriate, any adjustments which might be made to them later: 0401, 0402 (except 0402 29 11).

4. Minor foodstuffs and the corresponding levels to be applied to them will be defined in accordance with Article 7.

5. Liquid foodstuffs as defined in the heading 2009 and in chapter 22 of the combined nomenclature. Values are calculated taking into account consumption of tap-water, and the same values should be applied to drinking water supplies at the discretion of competent authorities in Member States.

6. Carbon-14, tritium and potassium-40 are not included in this group.

most cases, are closely comparable with those adopted by the European Community.

Conclusions

In essence, therefore, there are no Community-prescribed concentration limits for drinking water except in accident conditions. Even in the latter case such limits will be temporary and will apply only to water reaching the market in bottled or canned form; they have been instituted because of the need to provide an orderly basis for trade to continue in the period immediately following an accident.

To develop permanent limits for routine conditions would involve Community-wide agreement regarding a number of problems for which there is no uniquely indicated scientific solution. Moreover, the limits when agreed would probably serve little useful purpose. That this is recognized is illustrated by the move away from such limits insofar as they were provided, at least for workers, in early versions of the Community basic safety standards.

For accident conditions, such limits are even less appropriate outside of trade applications, since it is not possible to determine in advance, values which might prove practicable in terms of the need to provide alternative supplies. Moreover, contamination following an accident can display very short-term fluctuations which makes it even more difficult to establish global limits based on the integrated annual intake. In view of this it is difficult to see how Community-wide limits for drinking water in general could ever be established on a sound basis; moreover, the effect of so doing could be counter-productive.

References
1.   Treaty establishing the European Atomic Energy Community. Rome, 25.3.57
2.   Directives fixant les normes de base relatives a la protection sanitaire de la population et des travailleurs contre les dangers resultant des radiations ionisantes. JO (Journal Officiel) 21/59, 20.2.59
3.   Directive du Conseil du 5.3.62 portant revision des annexes 1 et 3 des directives fixant les normes de bases en matiere de protection sanitaire. JO 1633/62, 9.7.62
4.   Directive du Conseil 27.10.66 portant modifications des directives fixant les normes de base relative a la protection sanitaire de la population et des travailleurs contre les dangers resultant des radiations ionisants. JO 3693/66, 26.11.66
5.   Council Directive 76/579/Euratom of 1.6.76 laying down the revised basic safety standards for the health protection of the general public and workers against the dangers of ionizing radiation. OJ (Official Journal) L 187/1, 12.7.76
6.   Council Directive 80/836/Euratom of 15.7.80 amending the Directives laying down the basic safety standards for the health protection of the general public and workers against the dangers of ionizing radiation. OJ L 246/1, 17.9.80
7.   Council Directive 84/467/Euratom of 3.9.84 amending Directive

80/836/Euratom as regards the basic safety standards for the health protection of the general public and workers against the dangers of ionizing radiation. OJ L 265/4, 5.10.84

8. Council Directive 84/466/Euratom of 3.9.84 laying down basic measures for the radiation protection of persons undergoing medical examination or treatment. OJ L 265/2, 5.10.84

9. CEC: Aims and practices of transfrontier emergency planning within the EC countries in case of an accident in a nuclear installation - a guide for use in bilateral agreements based on a review of existing practice by a group of experts convened by the Commission of the European Communities. Document No 2138/86, CEC, Luxembourg 1/86

10. ICRP Publication 26, Recommendations of the International Commission on Radiological Protection, adopted 17.1.77. Annals of the ICRP V1/3, 1977

11. Statement from the 1985 Paris Meeting of the International Commission on Radiological protection, 3/85. Annals of the ICRP V15/3, 1985

12. NRPB: Metabolic and Dosimetric Models for Application to Members of the Public. NRPB-G53, 1984 (London, HMSO)

13. CEC: Radiological protection criteria for controlling doses to the public in the event of accidental releases of radioactive material - a guide on emergency reference levels of dose from the Group of Experts convened under Article 31 of the Euratom Treaty. Document No V/5290/82, CEC, Luxembourg, 7/82

14. NRPB: Emergency reference levels - criteria for limiting doses to the public in the event of accidental exposure to radiation. NRPB DL-10, 1981 (London, HMSO)

15. ICRP Publication 40: Protection of the public in the event of major radiation accidents - principles for planning. Annals of the ICRP V14/2, 1984

16. WHO: Nuclear power, accidental releases - principles of public health actions. WHO European Series No 16, Geneva, 1984

17. IAEA: Principles for establishing intervention levels for the protection of the public in the event of a nuclear accident or radiological emergency. IAEA Safety Series No 72, Vienna, 1985

18. Treaty establishing the European Economic Treaty. Rome 25.3.57

19. CEC: Recommendation 86/156/EEC of 6.5.86 addressed to Member States concerning the co-ordination of national measures taken in respect of agricultural produce as a result of radioactive fallout from the Soviet Union. OJ (Official Journal) L 118/28 of 7.5.86

20. CEC: Decision 86/157/EEC of 6.5.86 suspending the inclusion of certain countries on the list of third countries from which the Member States authorize imports of bovine animals, swine and fresh meat. OJ L 120/66 of 8.5.86

21. Council Regulation 1388/86/EEC of 12.5.86 on the suspension of the import of certain agricultural products originating in certain third countries. OJ L 127/1 of 13.5.86

22. Council Regulation 1707/86/EEC of 30.5.86 on the conditions

governing imports of agricultural products originating in third countries following the accident at the Chernobyl nuclear power station. OJ L 146/88 of 31.5.86

23. Council Regulation 3955/87/EEC of 22.12.87 on the conditions governing imports of agricultural products originating in third countries following the accident at the Chernobyl nuclear power station. OJ L 371/14 of 30.12.87

24. Council Regulation 3954/87/EURATOM of 22.12.87 laying down maximum permitted levels of radioactive contamination of food stuffs following a nuclear accident or any other case of radiological emergency. OJ L 371/11 of 30.12.87

25. Council Regulation 2218/89/EURATOM of 18.7.89 amending Regulation 3954/87 laying down maximum permitted levels of radioactive contamination of foodstuffs and of feedingstuffs following a nuclear accident or any other case of radiological emergency. OJ L 211/1 of 22.7.89

26. Council Decision 87/600/EURATOM of 14.12.87 on Community arrangements for the early exchange of information in the event of a radiological emergency. OJ L 371/76 of 30.12.8727. IAEA: Convention on early notification of a nuclear accident, Vienna, 26.9.86. IAEA Infcirc/335 of 18.11.86

28. Council Regulation 2219/89/EEC of 18/7/89 on the special conditions for exporting foodstuffs and feedingstuffs following a nuclear accident or any other case of radiological emergency. OJ L 211/4 of 27.7.89

Discussion

Dr D.G. Miller, *Water Research Centre*

Water suppliers in all member states of the European Community are used to having water quality controlled by the Directive on Water for Human Consumption. Radioactivity, however, is not included. Emergencies are covered under Article 10, and water can be supplied above the established maximum admissible concentrations, provided that there is no other alternative source available and there is no unacceptable risk to health.

Radioactivity is much more complex than other chemicals. In Paper 4, Ms Hill is helpful in explaining the difference between DILs (DERLs) and standards to protect the public. In this case, costs and inconvenience have to be balanced against dose provided. What still has to be agreed is the level of acceptable risk. Ms Hill has conceded that there is the possibility of confusion here, with different numbers in different documents. In Paper 5, Mr Fraser also deals with limits for emergencies, but drinking water has been left to member states. Does this mean that drinking water could be prohibited in bottles or cans but allowable above these limits in the tap? The public will find this difficult to accept. They like simple yes/no limits. It must be agreed that flexibility helps practice but it can undermine the confidence of the public.

Ms Hill suggests that modelling of systems might be considered, particularly for high-risk sources. This could be helpful, but a more important question is what can be done if limits are exceeded. Is substitution feasible? The effort justified would, in turn, depend on whether the limits were likely to be approached. This would depend on the limits ultimately set. With lower and upper DERLs, it is probably not worthwhile; but if, for example, the EC regulation numbers were divided by a factor of 5, the levels could conceivably be approached.

Dr G. Oskam, *Water Storage Corporation, Brabantse Biesbosch Ltd, The Netherlands*

The calculation of DILs according to equation (1) in Paper 4 is said to be based on scientific principles. Yet one principle in scientific standards setting is omitted. As there are other pathways of exposure, it is necessary to allocate only a proportion of the admitted dose to ingestion of drinking water. In deriving MAC values for many toxic substances in drinking water, the World Health Organization often allocates 10% of the intake to drinking water, and in case of carcinogenicity this percentage is even lowered to 1%. So what I miss in the formula is an allocation factor of say 0.1 (or even less) to accommodate the exposure to other pathways such as food. Without such correction, I would not call the approach scientifically sound. Of course, the calculated DILs will then be proportionally lower. What are the reasons for neglecting this factor in the setting of radiological standards?

My second comment refers to Ms Hill's remark that the IL of 5 mSv/a was not meant for application under accidental circumstances. Now that the National Radiological Protection Board has advised the UK government to adopt a dose of 0.5 mSv/a as a long-term average for members of the public, it seems to me that a tenfold increase - compared with what might be called normal - could be quite applicable in exceptional conditions.

Mr R.G. Castle, *North West Water*
The DILs calculated by the National Radiological Protection Board and published in March 1986 do not seem to take account of radiation doses from sources other than water, such as air and food contamination. I should like to ask Ms Hill if this is the case, and, if so, does she not consider that other sources of contamination should be taken into account when calculating DILs?

Mr N. Tzarik, *Kiev Water and Waste-Water Treatment Administration*
I understand from Paper 4 that in western Europe there are no standards for radionuclides in water. I should like to ask Ms Hill what is being done to produce such standards, and what is her evaluation of the standards currently in use in the USSR?

Ms Hill, *Paper 4*
Dr Miller is correct that there is the possibility of confusion between standards to protect the public in normal circumstances and DILs (DERLs) for accident situations, and different numbers in different documents. As I tried to point out in my paper, a compromise needs to be reached between simplicity of standards and the flexibility to take the action which is most appropriate for the circumstances, bearing in mind the costs and risks involved. I do not think that it is possible, or right in principle, to try to agree on one level of acceptable risk, and hence one set of standards for both normal and accident situations. Nevertheless, something simpler than the present sets of DILs is obviously needed.

I agree with him that it is very important to determine how likely it is that limits will be exceeded, and to ascertain what can be done if they are. Ideally, this information should be an input to setting the limits in the first place, not an afterthought.

In reply to Dr Oskam, the reason for ignoring other exposure pathways when setting DILs for drinking water is that the intervention levels of dose (ILs) from which any DILs are derived are set so that the risks averted by taking a countermeasure are greater than the costs, financial and otherwise, associated with taking the countermeasure. Both the risks and costs are specific to that countermeasure, and so is the intervention level of dose. It follows that it is wrong in principle to then make an allowance for other exposure pathways when the DIL is calculated from the intervention level of dose.

My comment about 5 mSv/a was that this was the recommended dose limit for members of the public in routine situations and that such limits do not apply in accident situations. It may be that the appropriate IL is 5 mSv/a but this would be numerical coincidence. The basis for establishing ILs is quite different from that for establishing routine limits, as is explained in my paper.

With regard to Mr Castle's question, the Dils calculated by the NRPB do not take account of doses from sources other than water, and should not do so, for the reasons outlined in my reply to Dr Oskam.

I am sorry if I gave Mr Tzarik the impression that there are no standards for radionuclides in water in western Europe. Every country has standards, but these are not necessarily incorporated in law, because legal systems vary from one country to another. In the UK, detailed standards tend to be issued by way of Government publications and through recommendations (for example, those of my own organization), but not to form part of the laws actually passed by Parliament, which are more general. Hence our ILs and DILs for drinking water are recommendations. Some other countries have a different approach and do incorporate detailed standards in laws. Mr Fraser explained the position on European Community regulations.

I have not looked in detail at the water standards currently in use in the USSR, but from Mr Tsarik's paper they do appear to be much more restrictive than our own DILs. It would be interesting to know what the basis is for the standards in the USSR.

Mr Fraser, *Paper 5*
In his remarks, Dr Miller noted that Article 10 of the EC Directive on Water for Human Consumption allows the established maximum admissible concentrations for the (non-radioactive) substances cited to be exceeded in emergency - provided that no alternative sources are available. This corresponds to the fact that this Directive is not primarily intended for emergency situations.

In the case of radioactive contaminants, the Directive to which I referred is aimed specifically at emergency conditions; concentrations in normal circumstances are far below what might be considered as appropriate limits on the grounds of the risk to health. In such situations, it is the ALARA principle - the principle that all exposure shall be as low as reasonably achievable - which serves to limit radioactive concentrations, and this principle has itself the force of law; this is also relevant to Mr Tzarik's comment.

Should an emergency arise, supplies of seriously contaminated bottled and canned water (and foodstuffs) should be relatively easy to replace from other less affected or unaffected sources. Tap water is in a different category: to enforce a ban on its use as drinking water would require all tap water to be cut off; but even if it remained available for other purposes, its replacement for drinking (and culinary practices) could be much more difficult and, to a degree, strongly dependent on the particular local circumstances. Therefore, to set generally applicable concentration limits for emergency conditions, would be inappropriate. Instead, governments of Member States will continue to be bound by the ALARA principle; in effect, the greater the risk the greater the justification for making whatever efforts are necessary to arrange alternative supplies. The absence of numerical limits does not give carte blanche.

Regarding the remarks by Dr Oskam and Mr Castle, insofar as the EC limits for foodstuffs are concerned, account was taken of the possible additivity of the different dietary components other than drinking water. This has been treated more independently for two reasons: firstly, accidental releases to atmosphere are likely to be of much less significance in respect of drinking water contamination relative to other foodstuffs; secondly, for liquid releases, not only is the contamination of the water likely to be of a transitory nature (few installations discharge into closed waterbodies) but also a relatively small range of other dietary components will be significantly affected. The effects of additivity, therefore, will be rather limited in both cases.

6. The UK national response plan for nuclear accidents overseas

M. W. JONES, PhD, Her Majesty's Inspectorate of Pollution,
Department of the Environment, London, UK

SYNOPSIS. This paper describes the National Response Plan
set up by the United Kingdom (UK) Government to deal with
the consequences of nuclear accidents overseas. The
Department of the Environment (DOE) through Her Majesty's
Inspectorate of Pollution (HMIP), has responsibility for
co-ordinating implementation of the Plan.

INTRODUCTION
1.   The UK has long established plans for dealing with the
consequences of nuclear accidents within its own shores.
However, following a careful review of the Chernobyl
incident, the Government decided that a new contingency
plan, the National Response Plan, was necessary for
dealing with nuclear accidents overseas.

2.   The Department of the Environment is responsible for
co-ordinating design and implementation of the National
Response Plan.   An important part of this Plan is the
establishment of a network of continuously operating
radiation monitors capable of detecting independently any
radioactivity arriving over the UK. This network is known
as RIMNET, short for Radioactive Incident Monitoring
Network.

3.   RIMNET is to be installed progressively in phases
(ref. 1). The Phase 1 RIMNET system has now been set in
place providing a means of detecting radiation arriving
over the UK and handling the response to it (ref. 2).
This paper gives details of this Phase 1 system, and
describes the way in which it will be used, together with
a description of proposals for Phase 2 development.

4.   Government departments, local authorities and the
UK nuclear industry have all participated in the planning
of the RIMNET programme through membership of a
national co-ordinating committee - The Radioactive
Incident Co-ordinating Committee (RIMCC). The Committee

will continue to guide the operation of the Phase 1 system, and to co-ordinate the development of later phases. It will also review exercises designed to test the Phase 1 system performance.

5. The Phase 1 RIMNET system is expected to operate for a period of 2-3 years while the more extensive and fully automated later phases are planned, installed and commissioned.

6. International agreements negotiated since Chernobyl should ensure that the United Kingdom (UK) Government is notified, through HMIP, of any nuclear accident overseas resulting in a significant release of radioactivity. Operation of RIMNET system will mean that, even if these notification arrangements fail, any unexpected increases in radiation levels over the UK, of the kind that could result from an overseas accident, can be detected immediately.

RIMNET PHASE 1
7. RIMNET provides a national system for detecting and measuring radiation levels in the air over the UK. It also provides modern information technology facilities for the national dissemination of information and advice concerning the incident.

8. The Phase 1 RIMNET system is based on gamma-ray dose rate monitoring equipment installed at 46 field stations throughout the United Kingdom in June 1988. The locations, which are all meteorological observatories, are shown in Figure 1. A picture of the RIMNET gamma-ray dose rate monitoring equipment is shown in Figure 2.

9. The radiation detector, monitor and line driver are housed in a weatherproof cubicle located within a meteorological field station enclosure. The detector and monitor assembly is connected by cable to the observers office and operates a hard copy printer.

10. Regular gamma-ray dose rate readings are taken by the meteorological observer, usually every hour. The readings are transmitted to the Bracknell headquarters of the Meteorological Office along with other meteorological data and then transmitted to the Central Database Facility (CDF), which is located at the Department of the Environment (DOE) in London, and to a back-up computer installed at a DOE office in Lancaster.

11.   Data from all RIMNET sites is analysed within the CDF. An alarm will automatically trigger in the event of any unexpected rise in gamma-ray dose rate readings satisfying one of three algorithms covering different eventualities.   The CDF computer and its associated communications equipment, were handed over to DOE by the installation contractor at the end of 1988 and commissioned early in 1989.

12.   In the event of an overseas nuclear accident being notified or detected, the provisions of the National Response Plan will be implemented to assess its effect on the UK.   The Secretary of State for the Environment will be the lead Government minister.   The Director of Her Majesty's Inspectorate of Pollution (HMIP), will be responsible for advising Ministers about any subsequent actions.

13.   If it is clear that there will be an effect on the UK, Parliament, relevant official bodies and the public will be informed, and appropriate alert messages will be issued.   National Response Plan   arrangements described in the following sections of this paper will be initiated.

NATIONAL RESPONSE PLAN ARRANGEMENTS
14.   The form of the National Response Plan arrangements is shown in Figure 3.

15.   The Government's response will be managed by a Technical Co-ordination Centre (TCC) staffed by officials from Government departments, the National Radiological Protection Board (NRPB) and the Meteorological Office. Staff in this Centre will have access to data stored on the CDF and will be responsible for liaising with the departments and agencies which they represent to obtain radiological assessments.   The TCC will provide a fully co-ordinated response.   In particular it will ensure that all information and advice bulletins issued by Government Departments and other statutory bodies are consistent.

16.   Additional Government monitoring programmes will commence.   These will cover water, food, livestock, crops, and people and goods coming into the country from affected areas overseas.   Provision of advice on the contamination of drinking water is another specific DOE responsibility, and pre-prepared plans for monitoring of supplies in the event of an incident have been drawn up.

FIGURE 1
PHASE 1 RIMNET MONITORING SITES AND BULLETIN REGIONS

FIGURE 2
RIMNET MONITORING EQUIPMENT

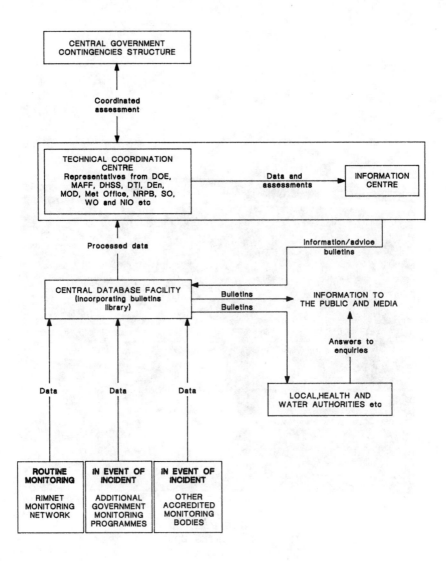

FIGURE 3
FORM OF NATIONAL RESPONSE PLAN SYSTEMS

17.   Other monitoring data supplied by accredited organisations will also be collated on the CDF to assist the TCC with its work.   Data links with other Government departments to enable the necessary information to be entered into the CDF and accessed remotely are being planned.

18.   On the basis of the information provided by the TCC, staff in the DOE Information Centre (IC) will prepare regular press releases. National and regional information will also be broadcast on viewdata and teletext systems (CEEFAX and PRESTEL) to ensure that the public are kept up to date.   Regional information will be based on the ten areas shown in Figure 1.

19.   Data held on the CDF and additional information and advice will be supplied daily to official bodies such as local and water authorities offering to help keep the public informed.   Telecom Gold electronic mail will be used for this purpose. This will help these organisations answer enquiries from the public on local radiation matters.   Local authorities may wish to act as the main focal point for local public enquiries.

20.   Where an individual Government department has direct statutory responsibility for a specific matter, that department may also supply its own media and public briefing provided the TCC is kept informed.

21.   The Phase 1 TCC and IC facilities are based in the DOE emergency operations room in London SW1.   The necessary information technology terminals (teletext, viewdata, electronic mail etc) and CDF access facilities have been provided.

ROLES OF ORGANISATIONS OUTSIDE THE DOE UNDER PHASE 1

Role of Other Government Departments
22. Government departments with relevant responsibilities will be represented in the TCC.   These may include the Department of the Environment (DOE), the Ministry of Agriculture, Fisheries and Food (MAFF), the Department of Health (DH), the Ministry of Defence (MOD) and the three territorial departments - the Scottish Office, Welsh Office and Northern Ireland Office.   The National Radiological Protection Board and the Meteorological Office will also be represented.

23.   Following an incident Government departments will continue to discharge their normal statutory responsibilities.   However the departmental representatives at the

TCC will ensure that decisions and actions are fully co-ordinated. These representatives will also provide the details and assessments necessary for the TCC and IC to prepare information and advice bulletins.

24. To discharge their wide range of responsibilities in Scotland, Wales and Northern Ireland, and to provide local information and advice, the three territorial departments will set up their own incident control centres in Edinburgh, Cardiff and Belfast. The work of these centres will be co-ordinated with the national response through their TCC representatives.

25. If departments commission supplementary monitoring programmes for their own purposes, the results, and assessments of them, will be available to the TCC.

Role of Local, Health and Water Authorities

26. In England, Scotland and Wales the local authorities may wish to act as the main focal point for local public enquiries in the event of any future overseas nuclear incident. A number of lead local authorities have been identified with the help of the local authority associations, and will be amongst the DOE contact points for the initial incident alert message. They may disseminate the initial alert information to other authorities. Similar arrangements are being planned with the water authorities. Health authorities will be informed by the appropriate Government departments.

27. In Northern Ireland, a Government department group, established to advise on peacetime radioactive emergencies, will act as the main focal point for public enquiries. In addition local authorities will be kept informed and will assist by dealing with enquiries at more localised levels.

28. Information officers in local, water and health authorities will have access to the regular information and advice bulletins issued via viewdata and teletext systems ie, CEEFAX and PRESTEL. Lead local authorities will also have access to the more detailed information distributed by electronic mail. This will assist the authorities in dealing with public enquiries at the local level.

29. Local, water and health authorities may collect radiological monitoring data of their own during an overseas incident. Where such data is available it will be used to obtain more detailed analysis of the distribution of radioactivity across the UK.

Role of the National Radiological Protection Board

30. In the event of an overseas nuclear incident the National Radiological Protection Board (NRPB) will advise Government departments on the interpretation of radiological monitoring data. The NRPB will be represented at the TCC, and have direct access to the CDF from their headquarters at Chilton, Oxfordshire. They will also supply monitoring data which they collect to the CDF.

Role of the Meteorological Office

31. The Meteorological Office will use a model to estimate and forecast radionuclide concentrations in air and surface deposition activity. The model will draw on meteorological and radiological data to predict the movement of the radioactive material released from the accident over Europe and the sea around the UK. The results will be sent to the Meteorological Office representative in the TCC to enable assessments to be made both on the likely movement of any plume of radioactive material across the UK, and on the pattern of deposition of radioactive material on the ground.

Role of the Nuclear Industries

32. In the event of any future overseas nuclear incident, the Central Electricity Generating Board (CEGB), British Nuclear Fuels plc (BNF), the United Kingdom Atomic Energy Authority (UKAEA) and the South of Scotland Electricity Board (SSEB) have expressed their willingness to collect supplementary monitoring data at their various sites to assist with the response to an incident. They would also assist with the analysis of samples from elsewhere.

ACCREDITATION OF SUPPLEMENTARY DATA SUPPLIERS

33. An accreditation system will establish a register of supplementary data suppliers able to provide specific monitoring results to the CDF. This will enable additional information on radionuclide concentrations in the environment to be obtained.

INTEGRATION WITH OTHER CONTINGENCY PLANS

34. The National Response Plan provides for a response to a nuclear accident abroad. Plans exist for dealing with nuclear accidents within the UK. These are the responsibility of the Department of Energy (DEn), the Industry Department for Scotland (IDS), the Ministry of Defence (MOD) or the Department of Transport as appropriate. Arrangements for accidents in the UK are

described in the booklet 'Emergency Plans for Civic Nuclear Installations' published by HMSO. Data from RIMNET will be available to the relevant Government department in the event of a UK nuclear accident.

PROPOSALS FOR LATER PHASES
35. Later phases of the RIMNET programme, will increase the number of monitoring stations to about 85. Additional monitoring facilities will be provided, at some sites. These will include automatic air sampling and deposition measurement. All monitoring stations will operate automatically and supply readings to the CDF.

36. The CDF will have improved analytical and display facilities to provide electronic assessment and the automatic preparation of draft view data pages and press releases.

SUMMARY
37. Within the National Response Plan, the Phase 1 RIMNET system provides a national means for monitoring the radiological effects of any nuclear incident overseas and for informing many organisations and the public of its implications. The systems will detect any overseas nuclear incidents effecting the UK, even if these incidents are not formally reported to the United Kingdom or there are delays in notification. Data from the RIMNET system will be available to the appropriate lead department in the event of a domestic nuclear incident.

REFERENCES
1. DEPARTMENT OF THE ENVIRONMENT. The National Response Plan and Radioactive Incident Monitoring Network (RIMNET). A Statement of Proposals, Her Majesty's Stationery Office, London 1988.

2. DEPARTMENT OF THE ENVIRONMENT. The National Response Plan and Radioactive Incident Monitoring Network (RIMNET). Phase 1. Her Majesty's Stationery Office, London 1988.

7. Monitoring water for radioactive releases in the United States

C.R. PORTER and J.A. BROADWAY, PhD, PE, Eastern Environmental Radiation Facility, US Environmental Protection Agency, Montgomery, and B. KAHN, PhD, Environmental Resources Center, Georgia Institute of Technology, Atlanta, USA

SYNOPSIS. The major radiological environmental monitoring programs for water in the United States are described. The applications of these programs for monitoring radioactive fallout, routine discharges from nuclear facilities, and releases due to accidents at such facilities are discussed, and some examples of measurements are presented. The programs monitor rainfall, surface water, and water supplies. Samples are usually collected and analyzed on a monthly or quarterly schedule, but the frequency is increased in response to emergencies.

INTRODUCTION
1. Several U.S. agencies undertake environmental radiological monitoring programs or require them of those whom they regulate in order to assure that radiation and radioactivity levels near nuclear facilities and in food and water supplies are at acceptable levels. Monitoring includes external radiation and radionuclides in air, airborne particles, dry and wet deposition, vegetation and food crops, soil and sediment, food animals and wildlife, milk, and surface water, groundwater, and drinking water. Calculational models based on these monitoring data and on special studies of environmental pathways and radionuclide dispersion are used to predict or estimate the radiation doses to populations and the most exposed persons. Described here are efforts devoted specifically to monitoring water for radionuclides from fallout, effluents at nuclear facilities, and the accidents at the TMI-II and Chernobyl nuclear power stations.
2. The U.S. Environmental Protection Agency (EPA) operates the national Environmental Radiation Ambient Monitoring System (ERAMS) (ref. 1). Its water-related aspects are described in Table 1. Data are published in the quarterly report Environmental Radiation Data. Rainfall collection provides an early indication of airborne radionuclide deposition. The surface water and water supply collection sites shown in Fig. 1 were

Table 1. ERAMS sample analyses and frequencies

Type	No. of Stations	Collection Frequency	Analysis	Analytical Frequency
precipitation	67	every event (composited monthly)	^{3}H; gross beta and gama spectrometry	every monthly composite
			^{239}U; ^{238}U; ^{235}U; ^{238}Pu; ^{239}Pu; ^{240}Pu	spring composite
finished water supplies for population centers or below nuclear facilities	78	quarterly (grab samples)	^{3}H	quarterly
			gross alpha and beta; gamma spectrometry; ^{89}Sr; ^{90}Sr	annual composite
			^{226}Ra; ^{234}U; ^{235}U; ^{238}U; ^{238}Pu; ^{239}Pu; ^{240}Pu	if gross alpha 0.07 Bq/L
			^{228}Ra	if ^{226}Ra is between .11 and .19 Bq/L
			^{131}I	one quarterly sample per year per station
surface water below nuclear facilities	58	quarterly (grab samples*)	^{3}H gamma spectrometry	quarterly spring sample

* Monthly composites of hourly samples are collected downstream of Oak Ridge National Laboratory and Savannah River Laboratory. All other stations submit single quarterly grab samples.

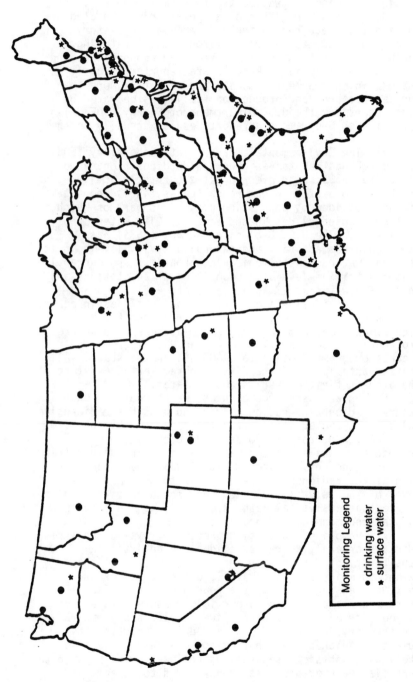

Fig. 1. Drinking water and surface water sampling stations

selected downstream from nuclear facilities to determine
possible releases of radioactivity from liquid effluents.

3. Each of the 126 nuclear power units, located at
65 sites, is required by the U.S. Nuclear Regulatory
Commission (NRC) to perform environmental monitoring,
including deposition, surface water and groundwater, and
nearby water supplies. Results are reported annually to
the NRC in environmental monitoring reports. More than 20
nuclear research and production facilities operated by
contractors for the U.S. Department of Energy (DOE) also
perform such programs and report results annually to the
DOE.

4. The Environmental Measurements Laboratory (EML)
of the DOE has maintained a worldwide deposition network
since the 1950s, with over 70 sites currently active. The
EML has also performed numerous studies, including intake
of radionuclides by population groups, as part of which it
measured radionuclides in the New York City water supply
(refs 2-3). The U.S. Geological Survey (USGS) has
measured gross activity and natural activity levels in its
national water quality monitoring programs, and currently
measures tritium levels in deposition at 14 stations and
in surface water at 12 locations (refs 4-6).

5. Individual states monitor radionuclides in public
water supplies on a 4-year cycle in response to EPA
regulations; perform confirmatory measurements downstream
from nuclear power stations under an NRC program; and
operate programs similar to ERAMS within the state. All
states participate in the first program, but the extent of
the other activities varies among states.

6. Under most circumstances, water contains only
naturally occurring radionuclides and possible radioactive
fallout. Elevated levels of natural radium-226 and -228,
radon-222, and uranium-238 and -234 occur in some
groundwater, while surface water may contain fallout (ref.
7). One function of water monitoring in the absence of
significant radionuclide releases is to determine the
level of the natural radiation background in water and to
assure that analytical methods can distinguish between
natural and manmade radionuclides.

7. Sampling, collection frequency, type of analysis,
identity of analyzed radionuclides and analytical
sensitivity differ greatly among programs, hence the
extent to which radioactivity is detected varies among
systems. As suggested by the fourth column in Table 1,
gross alpha and gross beta particle measurements are used
to look for elevated radionuclide levels, and gamma-ray
spectrometry is a convenient method for detecting the
numerous radionuclides that emit gamma rays. Specific
chemical or physical separations followed by alpha or beta
particle measurements must be performed to determine
radionuclides such as tritium, strontium-89 and -90,

uranium-228, and plutonium-239.

FALLOUT FROM TESTS OF NUCLEAR DEVICES IN THE ATMOSPHERE

8. Fallout radioactivity levels in water increased gradually from the early 1950s, peaked after the major United States and USSR tests of fusion devices in 1961-1962, and then decreased gradually as deposition and decay lessened the inventory of these radionuclides in the atmosphere. Tests by the Republic of China and France from 1967 to 1980 periodically inserted short-lived radionuclides and added to the long-lived ones in the atmosphere. Continued leaching and resolubilization of long-lived radionuclides earlier deposited in soil and on vegetation also contributes to the activity in water.

9. Typical time-sequence patterns of radioactivity levels in Fig. 2 show this peaking for the commonly measured long-lived fallout constituents, strontium-90 and cesium-137, in New York City water (refs 2-3). More recently, cesium-137 measurements during 1987 in the Savannah River upstream from the Savannah River Plant averaged 0.0002 Becquerel per liter (Bq/L). This level could be detected only by concentrating cesium from large volumes of water (ref. 8). Tritium in the Susquehanna River, shown in Fig. 3, originated mostly in atmospheric tests of fusion devices and only to a small extent at an upstream nuclear power station. It had considerably higher levels, and peaked later (refs 5-6). Recent levels, at approximately 3 Bq/L, could only be measured after electrolytic concentration. Since its inception in the mid-1970s, the ERAMS network has obtained similar results for tritium and strontium-90, but the more recent values are just below its detection limits. Gamma-ray-emitting radionuclides and plutonium in ERAMS samples have been below their respective detection limits of 0.3 and 0.001 Bq/L.

10. The usual approach to monitoring fallout is that an atmospheric nuclear test is announced, monitoring networks are alerted, and samples are collected and analyzed more frequently than in the routine program. The greater frequency assures prompt detection, reporting, and protective response if needed. Fallout from a recent test is usually detected first in airborne particles and rainfall, and characterized by short-lived fission products. An indication that tests have recently occurred is shown by elevated strontium-89 results as seen in Fig. 2 for the 1958 - 1963 period. The later decrease of 50-d strontium-89 levels below 28-y strontium-90 suggests that no further major tests were held.

DISCHARGES FROM ROUTINELY OPERATING NUCLEAR FACILITIES

11. Fission and activation products are discharged in liquid effluent at BWR and PWR stations in the United

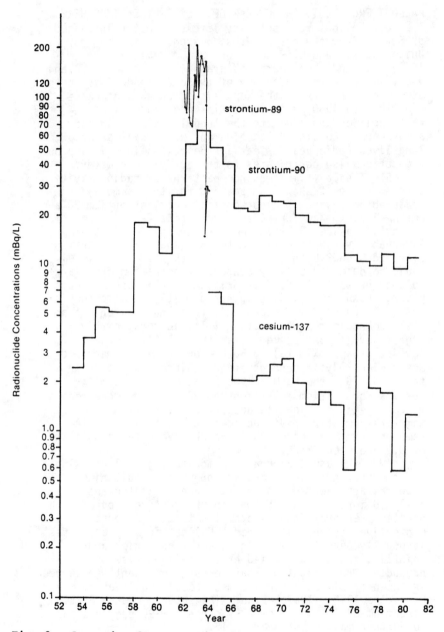

Fig. 2. Strontium-90, strontium-89, and cesium-137 concentrations in New York City tap water, 1954-81 (references 2,3)

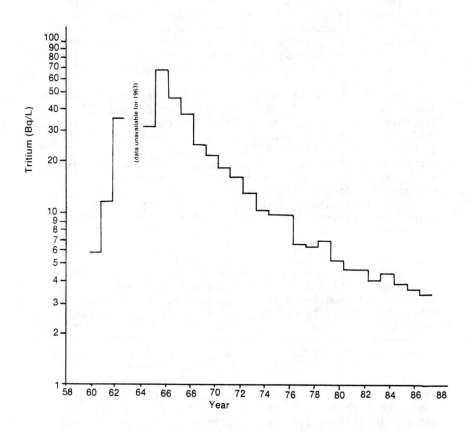

Fig. 3. Tritium concentration in the Susquehanna River, State of Pennsylvania, 1960-87 (references 5 and 6)

States at concentrations that, once diluted in receiving waters, are difficult to measure unless the radionuclides are concentrated from large volumes or determined with ultra-low-level methods (ref. 9). In ERAMS reports, tritium and gamma-ray-emitting radionuclides have typically been at or below detection levels downstream from monitored nuclear power stations. Some examples of positive findings immediately below the outfall are given in environmental reports by nuclear power stations. In a report for the Susquehanna Station, levels for tritium were about 8 Bq/L, and activation products that emit gamma rays such as chromium-51, manganese-54, cobalt-58, cobalt-60, and zinc-65 were at levels of about 0.08 Bq/L (ref. 10).

12. The ERAMS has consistently observed tritium at levels in the range of 100 Bq/L downstream from the DOE Savannah River Plant. The facility environmental report confirms this finding and also reports downstream levels of 0.001 Bq/L for cesium-137 and 0.02 Bq/L for strontium-90 (ref. 8). Only one other ERAMS sampler below a DOE facility has occasionally detected elevated radionuclide levels, also due to tritium.

13. Information on the extent of therapeutic use of short-lived radiopharmaceuticals such as iodine-131 and technetium-99m suggests that they will enter surface waters at low but occasionally detectable concentrations. Finding these radionuclides in sewage-plant sludges indicates some removal from sewage effluent. Iodine-131 at a concentration of approximately 0.04 Bq/L both upstream and downstream at the Susquehanna station was attributed to discharges at a hospital further upstream (ref. 10).

ACCIDENT AT THE THREE MILE ISLAND II NUCLEAR POWER STATION

14. Three ERAMS deposition samples from sites that were within 300 km of TMI II were collected for analysis 15 days after the accident on March 28, 1979. All contained combined wet and dry deposition. There was no detectable iodine-131 in any of the samples. Tritium and gross beta particle activity in these samples were comparable to levels at other sites and at these sites in previous months.

15. Within the first week after the accident, EPA placed additional deposition collectors at 14 locations within 5 km of the site at Middletown, PA. A control sampler was placed in the Susquehanna River 14 km upstream from the station, and an indicator sampler was placed 24 km downstream from the outfall. Samples were collected daily during May and June 1979 and weekly thereafter from the river and at every rainfall from the deposition collectors. They were analyzed for tritium and gamma-ray emitting radionuclides. This program has continued to the

present.

16.   No radionuclides were detected in the deposition
samples.   The surface water samples contained low levels
of tritium and iodine-131 both upstream and downstream due
to the sources approximately 150 km upstream identified in
ref. 10, but any contributions from TMI II were less than
instrument detection limits of 0.4 Bq/L for iodine-131 and
4 Bq/L for tritium (see Fig. 4).

ACCIDENT AT THE CHERNOBYL NUCLEAR POWER STATION

17.   Within 3 days of the accident at Unit 4 of the
USSR reactor station on April 26, 1986, the ERAMS was
activated for emergency response.   Arrival of radioactive
airborne particles was observed in the northwest United
States on May 5 and throughout the country in the
following week.   The major radionuclides in air were
ruthenium-103, iodine-131, tellerium-132, cesium-134, and
cesium-137; other fission products, such as ruthenium-106
and barium-140, were found at lower concentrations.

18.   These radionuclides in rain are shown in the
gamma-ray spectrum in Fig. 5.   The pattern of iodine-131
deposition in the United States for May, in Fig. 6, is
based on summing measurements of each rainfall sample at
the 67 sampling stations.   The maximum monthly deposition
was 680 Bq/m^2 in Idaho, and all deposition above 150
Bq/m^2 occurred in the northwest, except for an elevated
value in Vermont.   Little additional deposition occurred
in the months following May.   Deposition in the United
States was negligible compared to Europe.   A typical
pattern of iodine-131 in rainfall at Olympia, Washington,
following the Chernobyl accident is shown in Fig. 7.

19.   No radioactivity attributable to Chernobyl was
found in surface water or water supplies by ERAMS.   At the
detection limits of 0.04, 4, and 4 Bq/L for strontium-90,
iodine-131 and cesium-137, respectively, and an intake of
2 liters of water per day for 30 days, the respective
radiation doses are estimated to be less than 1×10^{-3}
(to bone), 1×10^{-2} (thyroid), and 5×10^{-4} (thymus)
millisievert (mSv) per person.   The average dose in the
United States due to this accident by milk and food
ingestion was estimated to be about 0.02 mSv to the most
exposed organ, the thyroid.   The highest organ dose was
0.5 mSv to infant thyroids in the state of Washington
(ref. 11).

DISCUSSION AND CONCLUSIONS

20.   The various environmental radiation monitoring
programs appear to form a sufficiently dense network for
adequate coverage in detecting and quantifying radioactive
releases into surface waters.   Although the monitoring
intervals are monthly or even longer, the ongoing programs
can be converted rapidly to more frequent sampling and

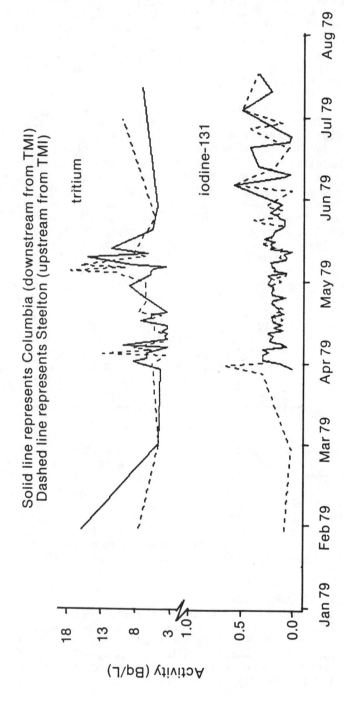

Fig. 4. Tritium and iodine-131 concentrations in the Susquehanna River, Pennsylvania, February to August 1979 (reference 10)

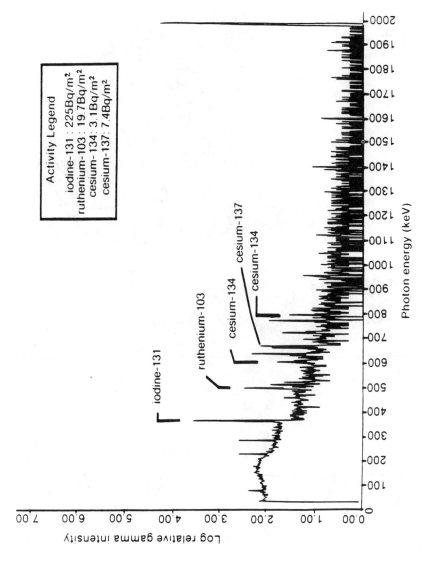

Fig. 5. Radioactivity in rainfall, Spokane, Washington, 12 May 1986

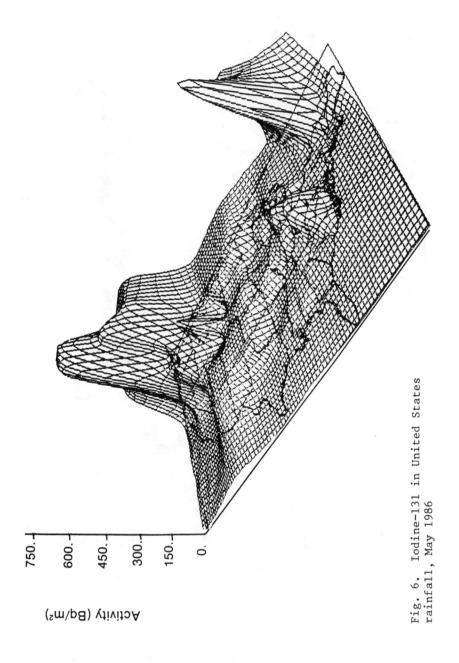

Activity (Bq/m²)

750.
600.
450.
300.
150.
0.

Fig. 6. Iodine-131 in United States rainfall, May 1986

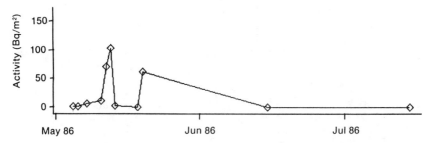

Fig. 7. Iodine-131 in precipitation, Olympia, Washington, May - July 1986

analysis. The existence of radiological laboratories devoted to environmental monitoring provides the capability for intensively monitoring an emergency, a cadre of professionals that can respond to and interpret the significance of elevated environmental radioactivity levels, and available reporting systems for informing officials and the public.

21. The monitoring data must be related to radiation doses to persons drinking or otherwise utilizing the water by calculational models as described in ref. 11. This can be done directly for water-supply monitors, but for measurements of plant effluents and surface waters requires consideration of factors such as dilution, uptake on sediments, and purification by water treatment. The monitoring data must also be used to infer radiation doses through alternate pathways, such as fish consumption and external exposure at the shore or while swimming, and may suggest special monitoring programs for such pathways.

22. An overview of these activities suggests obvious opportunities for improvement. The possibility of coordinating the various programs should be explored. If radioactive contamination of water by airborne deposition is considered a significant exposure pathway, sampling sites at a number of major supplies not downstream from nuclear facilities should be added to ERAMS. Analytical detection limits for the various radionuclides should be related to the radiation dose rates to determine whether the detection techniques must be made more sensitive or can be relaxed. Finally, installation of sequential or batch composite radionuclide monitoring devices at water supply distribution systems near nuclear facilities to enable prompt control might be worth the additional effort and cost.

REFERENCES

1. Porter, C.R., Broadway, J.A., and Kahn, B. Methodology for surveillance of the food chain as conducted by the United States. Radionuclides in the

food chain, M.W. Carter, ed., chap. 22.
Springer-Verlag, Berlin, 1988, pp. 302 - 322.

2. Hardy, E.P. Personal communication, U.S. DOE
   Environmental Measurements Laboratory, New York NY
   10014, 1989.

3. Hardy, E.P. Environmental Measurements Laboratory
   Environmental Report. U.S. DOE Report EML-405, pp.
   II-301-302, 1982.

4. Michel, R.L. Tritium deposition over the continental
   United States, 1953 - 1983. Atmospheric deposition,
   J.W. Delleur, ed. International Association of
   Hydrological Sciences Press, Oxfordshire OX108BB UK,
   1988, pp. 109 - 115.

5. Wyerman, T.A., Farnsworth, R.K., and Stewart, G.L.
   Tritium in streams in the U.S., 1961 - 1968. Radiol.
   Health Data Rept. vol. 11, 421-439, 1970.

6. Michel, R.L. Personal communication, U.S. Geological
   Survey, Reston VA 22092, 1989.

7. Kahn, B. Sources, occurrences, and health effects of
   radionuclides in water supplies. International
   symposium on water-related health issues. American
   Water Resources Association, Minneapolis MN 55435,
   1987, pp. 77 - 84.

8. Mikol, S.C., Burckhalter, L.T., Todd, J.L., and
   Martin, D.K. Savannah River Plant Environmental
   Report, Annual Report for 1987. U.S. DOE Report
   DPSPU-88-301, 1988.

9. Kahn, B. Composition and measurement of
   radionuclides in liquid effluent from nuclear power
   stations. Effluent and environmental radiation
   surveillance, J.J. Kelly, ed. American Society for
   Testing and Materials STP 698, 1988, pp. 63 - 74.

10. Teledyne Isotopes. Susquehanna Steam Electric
    Station Radiological Environmental Monitoring Program
    1986 Annual Report. U.S. NRC Dockets No. 50-387,
    -388, 1987.

11. Broadway, J.A., Smith, J.M., Norwood, D.L., and
    Porter, C.R. Estimates of radiation dose and health
    risks in the United States population following the
    Chernobyl nuclear plant accident. Health Phys. 1988,
    vol. 55, 533-539.

8. The use and potential of aerial radiometrics for monitoring environmental radioactivity

D.C.W. SANDERSON, BSc, MPhil, PhD, and M.S. BAXTER,
BSc, PhD, Scottish Universities Research and Reactor Centre,
East Kilbride, and E.M. SCOTT, BSc, PhD, Glasgow University, UK

SYNOPSIS

THE BASIS AND BACKGROUND TO THE USE OF AERIAL SURVEY
METHODS ARE OUTLINED BRIEFLY. RECENT AND ONGOING WORK BY
SURRC INDICATES THAT THIS METHOD HAS CONSIDERABLE POTENTIAL
FOR RAPID HIGH RESOLUTION FALLOUT MAPPING. IT IS ARGUED
THAT THIS INFORMATION COULD BE VITAL TO FORMING RELIABLE
DECISIONS ON COUNTERMEASURES IN THE EVENT OF A NUCLEAR
ACCIDENT WITH WATER RESOURCE CONSEQUENCES.

INTRODUCTION

1. Aerial radiometric survey provides an extremely rapid
and economical means of locating high deposition areas in
the event of an accident involving the release of
significant quantities of gamma ray emitting radionuclides.
This paper outlines the basis and background to the method,
recent experience of it in the UK, and indicates some of
the possible uses which it may have to water resource
evaluation and protection.

BACKGROUND

2. The gamma rays which accompany many nuclear transitions
can penetrate up to several hundred metres in air producing
radiation fields which can be mapped with sensitive
spectrometry equipment operated from aircraft. The
distribution of terrestrial radionuclides, whether natural
or anthropogenic, can be determined by constructing
appropriate low-altitude flight paths.

3. These principles have been applied to mineral
exploration and geological mapping for over 40 years. Gas
filled detectors used in the late 1940's for mapping total
radiation fields around uranium reserves (refs 1-3), were
quickly supplanted by more efficient solid scintillation
detectors (refs 4,5). Early British work included studies
of total radiation mapping in mineral exploration (refs
6,7), a simple line survey of West Cumbria in 1957
following the Windscale fire (refs 8,9) and an appraisal

of the use of helicopter mounted equipment in emergencies (ref 10). Although the thrust of technical and applications work has been directed primarily to geological exploration there have been a number of environmental applications over the years. These include work conducted in 1978 when the Cosmos 954 satellite deposited the contents of a nuclear reactor over the Great Slave Lake in northern Canada (ref 11,12) and the rapid national mapping undertaken in Sweden after the Chernobyl disaster (ref 13)

4. The capability to use aerial survey for emergency response was not developed in the UK at the time of the Chernobyl accident. With hindsight it is clear a far more convincing and earlier understanding of the fallout deposition pattern could have been obtained had this technique been used to guide ground based efforts. As it was even after three years, the picture of deposition produced by ground based methods was at best incomplete, and in instances quite misleading.

5. Awareness of the inherent difficulties of using conventional methods to map fallout on a national or regional scale prompted SURRC to examine the potential of aerial survey methods for mapping detailed local variations in anthropogenic nuclides. This was first undertaken in a short feasibility study conducted in SW Scotland, and has been followed up by a continuing programme of research and survey flights to extend and apply the technique.

THE METHOD
6. The basis of the method lies in the character of gamma ray emission and transport from terrestrially deposited radioactivity and an airborne gamma ray spectrometer. The gamma ray fluxes comprise a mixture of primary (unscattered) photons, whose energies are characteristic of individual nuclides, and secondary (scattered) radiation resulting from partial energy transfer interactions in the path from nuclide to detector. Distributed radioactivity in water or soil can generates a surface gamma ray flux from depths of 20-30cm (mineral rich soil or rocks) or 40-50cm (organic or waterlogged matrix), which propagates into the air. As height above ground is increased both the total gamma flux and the relative amount of primary information conveyed by unscattered radiation decrease, by attenuation and scattering in the air path. Typical half depths for primary radiation in dry air range from 72m (for 137-Cs at 662 keV) to 158 m (for 2.62 MeV photons from 208-Tl).

7. A gamma ray spectrometer raised above the ground therefore records a spectrum comprising photopeaks, escape peaks, and scattered radiation, which becomes weaker with

TABLE 1. PRINCIPLE NUCLIDES OF INTEREST FOR AERIAL RADIOMETRICS

Nuclide	Energy/keV	Half Life	Origin	Comment
241-Am	59.5	433a	Activation product	Special method needed
131-I	364	8.02d	Fission product	Sensitivity to be determined
134-Cs	796	2.06a	Activation product	Readily detected
137-Cs	662	30.2a	Fission product	Readily detected
40-K	1462	1.28×10^9a	Primordial nuclide	Readily detected
214-Bi	1764	19.9m	238-U daughter (radon daughter)	Readily detected
208-Tl	2615	3.05m	232-Th daughter	Readily detected

TABLE 2. FACTORS AFFECTING SENSITIVITY OF AERIAL MEASUREMENTS

1. Survey altitude

2. Aircraft speed

3. Integration time

4. Detector size

5. Detector energy resolution

6. Extent of spectral interferences (especially for low energies).

TABLE 3. AERIAL SURVEYS CONDUCTED BY SURRC

Location	Date	Area /ha	Line spacing	Detector volume	Comments
Whithorn & Mull of Galloway	Feb 1988	30000	1 mile	7 l	fixed wing
N & S Uist, Benbecula	March 1988	30000	1 mile	7 l	fixed wing
West Cumbria	August 1988	45000	500m	7 l	Bell Helicopter
Upper Clyde Valley	December 1988	8000	1 km	7 l	Aerospatiale Squirrel
Central Highlands	December 1988	5000	1 km	7 l	Aerospatiale Squirrel
Eaglesham Moor	January 1989	8000	1 km	7 l	Aerospatiale Squirrel
North Wales	July 1989	32000	500m	20 l	Aerospatiale Squirrel
SW England	September 1989	225000	1km/500m	24 l	Aerospatiale Squirrel

increasing height. Table 1 summarises some of the gamma rays and nuclides which may be of interest to aerial radiometric survey.

8. The other important feature of raising a detector above ground is that the detection geometry opens up so that the area on the ground being sampled increases very rapidly. Typical areas of investigation are such as to give 90% of the detected signal from a circle diameter 4-5 times the height above ground (ref 14). Sensitivity depends strongly on detector characteristics, integration time and flight envelope - factors summarised in table 2. The most effective use of aircraft in aerial survey is achieved by matching the integration time to the time taken to cross a circle of investigation at safe flying speeds, and choosing a detector volume and altitude which will give satisfactory sensitivity under these conditions. Considerations of this type lead to selection of large volume (16-48 litre) NaI detectors for rapid fixed wing survey at high resolution, and smaller arrays (4-16 litres) for use from light helicopters.

9. Survey procedures comprise constructing systematic flight paths and recording detector spectra in conjunction with navigational and altitude data during the course of the flight. Data analysis principally comprises collation and validation of results, extraction of integrated, and spectrally deconvoluted photopeak counts, correction for altitude variations and other minor influences, and calibration to the response from reference fields. Whereas for geological work it makes sense to standardise results to a hypothetically homogeneous radiation field, there is as yet no consensus as to the most appropriate basis for calibrating anthropogenic sources. Surveys conducted by SURRC have been ground calibrated to comparable vertical depth distributions for layered sources; however other approaches also have merits. The final step is production of maps by computer based image construction methods.

SURVEYS CONDUCTED BY SURRC
10. Table 3 summarises the surveys conducted by SURRC since February 1988, using equipment which has been steadily developing over its course. The initial feasibility studies (ref 14) conducted in 1988 proved extremely successful; 137-Cs both from Sellafield coastal deposits and from Chernobyl inland was readily detected and could be extracted with ease from the natural components.

11. Subsequent work in the Western Isles showed the very slight extent of Chernobyl fallout in isolated locations ; results which were of considerable interest to the

population who had received no notification of monitoring results even two years after the event.
The survey of livestock restriction areas in West Cumbria commissioned by MAFF in 1988 (ref 15) made use of a light helicopter for safe low speed flying in mountainous areas. Despite poor weather it was possible to obtain a map of unprecedented detail in 2 weeks. This was subject to a rigorous independent cross comparison with ground based results from samples collected blind by MAFF, which overall confirmed the calibration procedures adopted.

12. More recent projects have included small scale surveys in Scotland for various purposes - the overall impression derived from the results is that the recently added Chernobyl component is more widespread and at higher levels than commonly supposed. Peak levels of more than 40 kBq/m^2 have been observed in the central highlands. A recent transect across the southern uplands suggests that comparable levels to those in the Cumbrian livestock restriction zone occur here also. Current projects include a survey of parts of North Wales, conducted in July, and a large scale survey in SW England which starts immediately after this meeting. It has been possible to extend both detector specifications and methodology at each stage. Currently we are using a multicrystal array of 8% resolution NaI detectors with full spectral recording via dual port PC based pulse height analysers. A comprehensive suite of acquisition and analysis software has been developed in house for this task.

POTENTIAL WATER RESOURCE APPLICATIONS
13. Before suggesting some of the ways in which aerial survey could contribute to water resource evaluation and protection in a nuclear emergency it is apposite to consider those factors which influence the radiological outcome of such an event. Table 4 summarises some of the considerations. Although it is fair to argue that high transfer time supplies, and those for which large dilution factors apply may only prove a minor exposure pathway in hypothetical nuclear accidents, this is clearly not so for small private water sources with rapid collection and limited dilution. The presence for example of half a million becquerels per square metre of 131-I in the central highlands from Chernobyl could very easily have led to alarming activity levels in some isolated supplies.

14. It seems very unlikely that single nuclide contamination up to DERL levels could be tolerated - since few postulated scenarios are either single nuclide or result in a single exposure path. There will therefore be a need both to control and also; since that part of dose

TABLE 4. FACTORS INFLUENCING THE RADIOLOGICAL CONSEQUENCES OF WATER RESOURCE CONTAMINATION FOLLOWING A NUCLEAR INCIDENT

1. Initial deposition

      - locations, levels,
      - physical and chemical form
      - isotopic composition, half lives

2. Transfer characteristics from catchment to supply

      - transfer times
      - losses by radioactive decay

3. Dilution with uncontaminated water

4. Storage Times/ Transfer times to the consumption point

5. Effect of treatments in removing nuclides

      - reduction in water
      - hazards due to waste

6. Consumption patterns and quantities

7. Individual radiological behaviour of each nuclide

8. The extent to which other exposure paths have, or will operate

9. Effectiveness of countermeasures

      - substitution of alternative supplies
      - use of blocking agents

exposure due to water resources reduces the available margin for other exposure paths; to assess the contamination of water supplies on an extremely short time scale.

15. It is here that aerial survey might well have a role to play, along with its other potential applications under such circumstances. The obvious application would be to determine catchment area inventories for large water supplies as well as deposition levels over bodies of water. The sensitivity of established methods could readily detect 10 Bq l^{-1} on water (or some 1 kBq m^{-2} on ground) of many fission products including 137-Cs. Incorporation of provision for such emergency surveys into contingency plans could make a vital contribution to constructing effective countermeasures on the time scale in which they would be needed. It is rather hard to imagine how reliable countermeasures could be enacted without a detailed knowledge of deposition; and aerial survey appears to be the only possible method to obtain sufficient information in time for such countermeasures to be effective.

REFERENCES

1. STEAD F.W. Airborne radioactivity surveying speeds for uranium prospecting, 1950,Eng. Min. J., 74-77
2. PEIRSON D.H. and FRANKLIN E. Aerial prospecting for radioactive minerals,1951, Brit. J. Applied Physics, Vol 2
3. GODBY E.A. CONNOCK S.H.G. STEHLES J.F. COWPER G., & CARMICHAEL H. Aerial prospection for radioactive minerals, 1952, Atomic Energy of Canada report 13.
4. PRINGLE R.W. ROULSTON K.E. BROWNELL G.W. LUNBERG H.T.F. The scintillation counter in the search for oil, 1953, Mining Engineering , 1255-1261
5. PEIRSON D.H. and PICKUP J. A scintillation counter for radioactivity prospecting,1954, J. Brit. Inst. Radio Eng., vol 14, 25-32
6. WILLIAMS D. and BISBY H., The aerial survey of terrestrial radioactivity,1960, AERE report R-3469
7. WILLIAMS D. and CAMBRAY R.S. Environmental survey from the air, 1960, AERE report R-2954
8. WILLIAMS D. CAMBRAY R.S. and MASKELL S.C. An airborne radiometric survey of the windscale area October 19-22nd 1957, AERE report R-2890
9. CHAMBERLAIN A.C. GARNER R.J. and WILLIAMS D. Environmental monitoring after accidental deposition of radioactivity, 1961, Reactor Science and Technology,14,155-167
10. PEIRSON D.H. and CROOKS R.N., Survey of environmental radioactivity:A preliminary assessment of the use of helicopters in an emergency.1961. AERE report M-927
11. BRISTOW Q., The application of airborne gamma-ray spectrometry in the search for radioactive debris from the Russian satellite Cosmos 954, Current Research,Part B, Geol. Survey of Canada paper 1978-1B,151-162
12. GRASTY R.L., 1980, The search for Cosmos 954, in Search Theory and Applications, ed HEVLEV & STONE,1980, Plenum Publishing Corporation.
13. LINDEN A. and MELLANDER H., Airborne measurements in Sweden of the radioactive fallout after the nuclear accident in Chernobyl, USSR.,1986 Swedish Geological Company, TFRAP 8606
14. DUVAL J.S. COOK B. and ADAMS J.A.S., Circle of investigation of an airborne gamma-ray spectrometer, J. Geophys. Res, 76, 8466-8470
15. SANDERSON D.C.W. SCOTT E.M. BAXTER M.S. PRESTON T., A feasibility study of airborne radiometric survey for UK fallout, SURRC report March 1988
16. SANDERSON D.C.W. & SCOTT E.M., Aerial radiometric survey in West Cumbria in 1988, MAFF FOOD SCIENCE REPORT N611

9. Monitoring of radioactivity in man after a nuclear event — the example of the Chernobyl reactor accident and the Scottish population

B. W. EAST, BSc, PhD, MSRP, and I. ROBERTSON, BSc, CPhys, MIP, Scottish Universities Research and Reactor Centre, East Kilbride, UK

SYNOPSIS. Following the reactor accident at Chernobyl in April 1986, the uptakes of thyroidal radioiodine (^{131}I) and whole-body radiocaesium (^{134}Cs and ^{137}Cs) were measured in members of the Scottish population. Thyroidal radioiodine averaged 16Bq in the Glasgow area, while body radiocaesium peaked at an average maximum value of 800 Bq (total) eight months after the accident and declined with a half-life of 267 days (^{137}Cs) thereafter. One individual, relying on a mountain water supply, had higher levels of each radionuclide. Milk and meat consumption influenced uptake and there were clear indications that body radiocaesium was higher in areas of higher fallout deposition.

INTRODUCTION

1. The reactor accident at Chernobyl in the USSR on 26 April 1986, resulted in atmospheric releases of radioactivity and the subsequent deposition of radioactive fallout over Scotland in early May. Soon after the fallout deposition occurred, a programme of high sensitivity thyroid and whole-body monitoring was started to measure the uptake of radioactivity in members of the Scottish population[1]. Radioiodine; ^{131}I ($t_\frac{1}{2}$ = 8 days) and radiocaesium; ^{134}Cs ($t_\frac{1}{2}$ = 2.06 years) and ^{137}Cs ($t_\frac{1}{2}$ = 30.2 years) were easily measurable by means of their gamma ray emissions. The age, sex, geographical location and details of individuals' diet were all recorded so that the influence of these factors could be assessed. Only limited data were however obtained on concentrations of the radionuclides in drinking water in the Glasgow and Lanarkshire areas immediately after the fallout so that only very limited inferences could be drawn as to the influence of this source, on uptake.

2. The quantities of radioactivity which were involved proved to be small, increasing the internal radiation dose rates above those normally received from the background by correspondingly small degrees. They were however easily detectable with the high sensitivity equipment used and although the Chernobyl accident occurred some 3000km away from Scotland, the study is an example of how the resulting radioactive contamination reaching man can be assessed by direct measurement after such an event.

METHODS

Sampling the population
3.   Volunteers from throughout Scotland were requested and during the period from 6 May 1986 until 29 February 1988, 251 individuals, representing children and adults of both sexes from many parts of the country were examined..   They were assumed to be healthy and were selected geographically from the 56 administrative districts in the country. A localised group of individuals from the East Kilbride and Glasgow area associated with the SURRC laboratory, formed part of the sample.   They made the predominant contribution in the early stages of the study, particularly to the thyroidal ^{131}I measurements, until examinations of volunteers from further afield began in February 1987.   Selection in terms of a representative population group was according to age and sex, and from each district the aim was to examine variously: an infant or young child up to 12 years of age; male and female teenagers (13-17 years); male and female adults (18-65 years) and an elderly person of either sex (over 65 years).   Some individuals were included because of special location, dietary, or other factors relevant to the study eg. venison eaters and residence in areas of higher fallout deposition.

Monitoring of volunteers
4.   Volunteers attended the Health Physics and Nuclear Medicine Unit at SURRC and were measured in a high sensitivity shadow-shield whole-body monitor[2] to determine their thyroidal radioiodine and body radiocaesium content. The procedure was very simple, requiring only the removal of outer clothing and shoes and the wearing of a gown, disposable hat and plastic "overshoes" before entering the monitor. No prior showering was necessary. Height, weight and age were recorded at the time of measurement. Details of the monitor are given below.

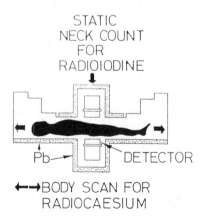

STATIC
NECK COUNT
FOR
RADIOIODINE

Pb DETECTOR

BODY SCAN FOR
RADIOCAESIUM

Fig. 1. Thyroid and whole-body monitoring

Thyroidal radioiodine

5.   Thyroidal ^{131}I was measured by positioning the neck beneath the upper detector of the body monitor and counting for 10 minutes.   The system was calibrated using polythene models of the neck containing a simulated thyroid gland filled with a known quantity of ^{131}I.   From the gamma-ray photopeak at 0.364MeV the radionuclide was identified and the net activity determined.   A diagram of the monitor is given in Fig.1 and a typical spectrum of the neck region is shown in Fig.2. Measurements were made on 11 volunteers from the Glasgow area, including 4 children under 10 years of age, and on an individual who relied on a mountain water supply. They were started 10 days after the Chernobyl accident, that is 4 days after the initial fallout over the UK on 2nd May.   Repeated measurements were possible in three cases to follow changes in thyroidal levels.

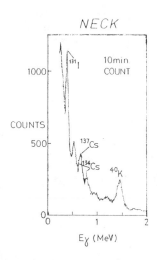

Fig. 2.   Spectrum of radioiodine, ^{131}I, in the thyroid

Body radiocaesium

6. Whole-body radiocaesium was measured in all volunteers and in 60% of cases, was repeated after 3 or 6 months, so that a picture of the magnitude of uptake, progressive increase, equilibrium and decrease of body radiocaesium with time was obtained.   The measurement was done by counting each volunteer supine on a motorised couch for approximately 20 minutes while scanning from head to foot between the two NaI(Tl) detectors, mounted above and below the body, as shown in Fig. 1.   Each detector was 29cm diameter x 10cm thick and shielded in the monitor system by 10cm thick lead to minimise the detector background and enable the small quantities of radioactivity in the body to be measured accurately. A whole-body gamma ray spectrum typical of a volunteer from the West of Scotland is

shown in Fig.3. The ^{134}Cs and ^{137}Cs activities from the Chernobyl fission products can be seen easily as also can the ^{40}K photopeak from the body potassium. The activities in Becquerels (Bq) of the radionuclides present were calculated by integration of the net photopeaks observed in the gamma-ray spectrum and the application of calibration factors previously obtained for the monitor with known quantities of radioactivity. For the various radionuclides the photopeak energies taken were: 134Cs - 0.796MeV. ^{137}Cs - 0.662MeV, ^{40}K - 1.46MeV.

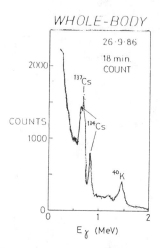

Fig. 3. Spectrum of radiocaesium in the body

7. Volunteers were informed verbally of their results at the time of measurement and the significance of the findings discussed. Written statements were not normally given to individuals and it was a condition of participation that this procedure was acceptable and that participants understood that their results would be coded as research data. The expenses of volunteers in attending were paid.

Dietary survey
8. Details of diet were obtained by asking volunteers to complete a questionnaire recalling their daily and weekly consumption of most types of food. From the returns, the consumption of the main categories such as milk and meat (including bacon) could be calculated and special dietary habits such as vegetarianism and venison eating identified. Principal categories were allocated as follows:
  (a) Omnivore
  (b) Vegetarian
  (c) No milk in the diet
  (d) Venison/game in the diet
  (e) Goat meat and products in the diet

(f) Diet not recorded

Cases where individuals took the precaution of not consuming fresh milk immediately following the accident were also recorded. The general accuracy of the dietary data was checked by comparison with findings contained in the Annual Report of the National Food Survey Committee 1986.[3]

Drinking water

9. A limited survey of drinking water from the town of East Kilbride near Glasgow, and from a nearby area of Lanarkshire was carried out. 500ml samples of tap water were monitored by high resolution gamma-ray spectrometry, using a Ge detector, to check for radioiodine and radiocaesium contamination.

RESULTS

Thyroidal radioiodine

10. Thyroidal radioiodine results, representing the activity present in the glands of individuals, are presented in Fig.4. Repeated measurements on an individual are linked by dotted lines and those on children are circled. The maximum value observed in the Glasgow area residents was around 30Bq and the overall average for the period, 16.4Bq. The volunteer using a mountain water supply, was clearly higher at 57.5Bq. Also in the one individual on whom a series of measurements was possible, radioiodine appeared to peak between 10 - 20 days.

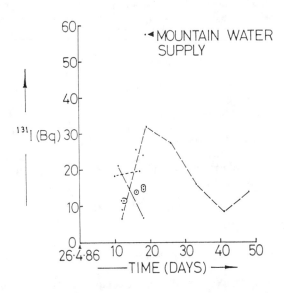

Fig. 4. Thyroidal ^{131}I in the Glasgow area after Chernobyl

Drinking water

11. Very small quantities of radioiodine and radiocaesium were transiently observed in the drinking water from East Kilbride and Lanarkshire during the month after Chernobyl. The average results were as follows:

Bq l^{-1}

	^{131}I	^{134}Cs	^{137}Cs	n (samples)
East Kilbride	2.2	1.3	2.6	6
Lanarkshire	1.6	1.5	ND	3

Whole-body radiocaesium

12. In all, 251 volunteers were measured. Repeat examinations at nominal intervals of 3 or 6 months were possible on 60% of individuals participating to determine their individual uptake and elimination patterns, enabling 487 observations to be reported in all. The population sample consisted of 46 children; 8 teenagers; 190 adults and 7 elderly persons. Volunteers from 45 of the 56 districts in the country were obtained covering all regions from Shetland in the north to the Borders in the south, and from the Western Isles to Aberdeen in the east. The pattern of ^{137}Cs uptake for all these areas is shown plotted semilogarithmically as a function of time after the accident in Fig.5. Radiocaesium content in the body is given in terms of Becquerels per gramme total body potassium (Bq $g^{-1}K$), a unit which simplifies comparisons between individuals of differing body habitus because potassium is related to body size. Repeat measurements on individuals are included in this plot but their connection is not identified. All the points lying above 10Bq $g^{-1}K$ can be attributed to at least one of the three special circumstances of; venison consumption; use of a mountain water supply; or goat meat consumption. After 200 days, 13 observations below 1Bq $g^{-1}K$ consisted of 3 children; 4 vegetarians an omnivore and a non-milk drinker. (Four of these individuals were measured twice and both points included).

DISCUSSION AND CONCLUSIONS
Radioiodine

13. ICRP data for an acute release, predict that the maximum for thyroidal ^{131}I occurs after 6-7 days[4]. In comparison with this, the observed maximum in the Glasgow area was somewhat

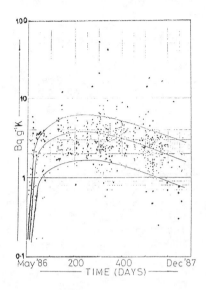

Fig. 5. Total body ^{137}Cs in the Scottish population after Chernobyl

later. Using the same prediction, the observed maximum for the group (30Bq) would imply an intake from an equivalent acute release of approximately 3×10^7Bq, had this occurred in the area. It is interesting to note that the total amount of ^{131}I which escaped from Chernobyl was estimated to be 3×10^{17}Bq, of which 1.5×10^{15}Bq was deposited on the UK[5].

14. The significant routes of intake for radioiodine are generally taken to be via inhalation and milk consumption. Radioiodine in the water supply could clearly contribute if at a high enough concentration, but at the very small amounts found in the local Glasgow area water supply this is not thought to have been a significant route. The comparatively higher activity seen in the volunteer with a mountain water supply however might indicate an intake from this source, although inhalation could also have contributed.

Radiocaesium
15. Following examination of the data by regression analysis, the overall mean was described by a composite line in which the data were represented in three phases:

  i.   an initial steep exponential rise from 5-35 days
  ii.   a less rapidly changing phase through the maximum from 36-400 days and

iii.   a decreasing exponential phase to infinity from 401 days.

The relationships obtained for these phases were respectively:

  i. $B = 0.04 \exp. (0.107t)$
 ii. $B = 1.15 + 2.06 \times 10^{-2}t - 3.96 \times 10^{-5}t^2$
iii. $B = 8.94\exp. (-2.6 \times 10^{-3} t)$

where B = body activity of ^{137}Cs in Bq $g^{-1}K$
      t = time in days after 1.5.1986

These relationships are shown in Fig.5 together with similar lines representing the upper and lower boundaries encompassing 80% of the population. It is concluded that levels of body radiocaesium in Scotland reached a maximum about 8 months after the accident ranging by a factor of 4 between the upper and lower boundaries. The mean maximum body ^{137}Cs level was 3.8Bq $g^{-1}K$ ($\approx$540Bq) with an upper boundary value of 6.2 and a lower boundary value of 1.6Bq $g^{-1}K$. The corresponding levels for ^{134}Cs were 1.7 ($\approx$240Bq), 2.8 and 0.7Bq $g^{-1}K$ respectively.

Factors influencing the uptake of radiocaesium

16. The data were analysed statistically with respect to the various influencing factors of interest; age, sex, diet and geographical location of residence, by the selection and grouping of appropriate observations. For the purposes of the present discussion, only ^{137}Cs is considered. ^{134}Cs would be expected to behave similarly in all respects, except that it has a shorter radioactive half and so would decrease in activity more rapidly.

17. Analysis showed that the sex of volunteers had no influence on radiocaesium uptake.

18. Comparisons between various age groups throughout 1987, showed that early in the year there was no significant difference in body radiocaesium. By the autumn however, the under-18-year-olds had significantly lower radiocaesium levels consistent with the fact that children have a more rapid turnover than adults and as the radiocaesium in the diet declined, their body content decreased more quickly.

19. The consumption of milk, and the ^{137}Cs levels measured in the first 5 months in nine selected volunteers from the Glasgow area were compared. Four of the group took no special dietary precautions, but the remaining 5 had stated that they had stopped consuming fresh milk immediately after the accident. It was found that initially, the two groups were distinguishable by their different rates of increase of radiocaesium. However, by September, all their body levels were converging so as to become indistinguishable, presumably because precautions had been stopped or reduced, and also because radiocaesium was being absorbed from other foods.

20. Although there were no statistically significant

differences in the ^{137}Cs levels found in omnivores and vegetarians, radiocaesium levels were consistently higher in the meat-eating volunteers.

21. Statistically, there were clear indications that body levels were higher in the West and South West and in the North and North East areas of the country where deposition of fallout was known to be higher. Although these increases were generally small it was evident that the intensity of fallout in a given area had a direct effect on the uptake of radiocaesium by inhabitants of that area.

Special cases with high body radiocaesium levels

22. In several volunteers, body radiocaesium was strikingly higher than the general spread of observed values (see Fig.5). The highest value of 52.7 Bq ^{137}Cs g^{-1}K (8110Bq) was observed in a male volunteer who ate goat-meat and associated products and who resided in the South West of the country. His corresponding ^{134}Cs level was 24.5 Bq g^{-1}K (3774Bq). An accompanying female volunteer eating a similar diet had 21.0Bq ^{137}Cs g^{-1}K and 9.7Bq ^{134}Cs g^{-1}K initially, falling to 16.9 and 5.8 respectively 9 months later. After her first measurement it was understood that she had not changed her diet and her observed rate of decrease *in vivo* corresponded to a half-life of 870 days.

Nine volunteers who ate venison were also measured. Six of these, stopped or reduced substantially their venison intake after their first measurement and 7 months later showed reduced levels which corresponded to a half-life for radiocaesium *in vivo* of approximately 195 days. Clearly this reduction was directly associated with the elimination of venison from their diet and it appeared that these volunteers would eventually attain levels within the normal spread.

One volunteer from the island of Arran (rainfall >20mm in places) also showed high values. She ate a normal diet but relied on a mountain water supply. Her initial level, 5.91 Bq ^{137}Cs g^{-1}K after 15 days was 10 times the population upper boundary at that time and rose to 12.4 Bq ^{137}Cs g^{-1}K 4 months later. A year later she had decreased to 3.88 Bq ^{137}Cs g^{-1}K, corresponding to the current population upper boundary. After passing through the maximum, her subsequent rate of decrease again corresponded to a half-life for radiocaesium in vivo of approximately 195 days and she rejoined the overall population spread after 17 months. No data were available for the radiocaesium concentration of her mountain water supply but it is likely that levels could have been elevated because of conservation in solution in the hilly acidic conditions, so contributing to her intake of radiocaesium.

Final conclusions

23. The overall picture which emerges from the study is that all members of the Scottish population took up radiocaesium to a greater or lesser extent as a result of the Chernobyl reactor accident. Fresh milk consumption appeared to be an influencing factor as exemplified by a group of individuals in the study who stopped its consumption in the months following the

accident and who showed correspondingly low body radiocaesium levels initially. Meat consumption was also important, and venison and goat meat eaters showed the highest body radiocaesium levels. However, these individuals formed only a small group and in the majority who consumed more commonly available meats no clear numerical relationship could be seen. Further to this, individuals who might have eaten contaminated ie. > 1000 Bq kg⁻¹ sheep meat could not be distinguished from the rest of the population in this study. It would appear that, in the circumstances of widespread contamination over the whole country, by the time radiocaesium finds its way into man, averaging factors such as food distribution, processing, metabolic variation and dietary variation tend to reduce differences, so that all individuals follow a similar broad pattern. Although the data on water supply characteristics were limited, the few observations which could be related to uptake, would fit in with a picture in which supplies from lowland or clay bearing areas would not be likely to make a significant contribution to intake because radiocaesium and radioiodine would be removed by absorption, whereas these radionuclides could be present in untreated or acidic run-off supplies where there is little absorption.

Radiation doses

24. Total mean dose equivalents for radiocaesium (^{134}Cs plus ^{137}Cs) were 31 μSv for the first year after Chernobyl, 20 μSv for the second year and 62 μSv for the overall dose commitment. In comparison with the dose due to natural background sources of radiation, the doses from radiocaesium received in the first and second years after Chernobyl represent increases of about 2% and 1% respectively. At these levels no observable clinical effects would be expected in the population.

Residual radioactivity

25. Up until February 1988, ^{137}Cs levels in the Scottish population appeared to be declining with an *in vivo* half-life of 267 days. This rate of decline must however be used with some caution to predict the longer-term ^{137}Cs pattern, as our previous knowledge of the behaviour of radiocaesium from the fallout from atmospheric bomb testing suggests that it will probably be more persistent than this and continued monitoring of population groups will be necessary to confirm the pattern. It should be noted that ^{134}Cs will decrease more rapidly than ^{137}Cs because of its shorter radioactive half-life of 2.06 years compared with 30.2 years for ^{137}Cs.

ACKNOWLEDGEMENTS

26. The support of the Department of the Environment for part of this work under contract No. PECD 7/9/386 is acknowledged.

REFERENCES
1. EAST B.W. and ROBERTSON I. Measurement of radioactivity from Chernobyl in population groups in Scotland. Department of the Environment Report No. DOE/RW/88.103, 1989.

2.   BODDY K., ELLIOTT A., ROBERTSON I., MAHAFFY M.E. and HOLLOWAY I. A high sensitivity dual-detector shadow-shield whole-body monitor with an 'invariant' response for total-body in vivo neutron activation analysis. Physics in Medicine and Biology, vol.20, 296-304, 1975.

3.   Annual Report of the National Food Survey Committee. In: Household Food Consumption and Expenditure H.M.S.O., 1986.

4.   Annals of the International Commission on Radiological Protection, Vol. 2, No. 3/4 (ICRP Publication 30, Part 1), Pergamon Press, Oxford, 1979.

5.   CLARK M.J. and SMITH F.B. Wet and dry deposition of Chernobyl releases. Nature, vol. 332, 245-249, 1988.

10.   Potential risks of using water resources as a basis for monitoring requirements after a nuclear accident

I. GANS, PhD, and H. RÜHLE, Institute of Water, Soil and Air Hygiene, Federal Health Office, FRG

SYNOPSIS
Radiation exposure of population by intake of radionuclides in drinking water is, generally, low compared to the exposure via other exposure pathways like intake in food or external irradiation. If, nonetheless, monitoring of drinking water in case of a regional or widespread conterrmination of the environment due to a nuclear accident is taken into consideration the differences in potential risks of different types of water recources should be taken in to account. While for unprotected water sources like creeks, rivers, reservoirs and lakes sampling and measurements might be necessary within a period of hours, days or a week after the onset of contamination, groundwater sources in most cases need only be monitored within periods of weeks, months or even years.

RADIATION EXPOSURE OF POPULATION BY RELEASES OF RADIOACTIVITY
Normal operation of nuclear installations
1.   When radioactive substances are released into the environment, either in gaseous or particulate form into air or in solute form into some water body, they will cause radiation exposure of man in some way or other. For normal operations of nuclear installations a number of steady-state models have been developed by which radiation exposure of population may be assessed (ref. 1-7). For these calculations the important exposure pathways have been identified in the environment.

2.   After discharge, airborne radioactivity is dispersed by atmospheric turbulence. The relevant exposure pathways are
-    external irradiation from the plume (beta- and gamma rays),
-    external irradiation from radionuclides deposited on the ground,
-    internal irradiation by inhaled radionuclides, and
-    internal irradiation by consumption of contaminated food.

3.   Radioactive liquid effluents are generally discharged into rivers, estuaries or the sea. The radionuclides are dispersed by water movement and sedimentation in the freshwater and in the marine environment. The principal exposure pathways are
-    external irradiation from sediments on the shore and on inundated areas,

-   internal irradiation by consumption of fish and other aquatic foodstuff,
-   internal irradiation by consumption of drinking water, and
-   internal irradiation by consumption of food contaminated due to irrigation.

The last two exposure pathways apply only to freshwater bodies.

4.   In addition to the pathways listed in paragraphs 2 and 3 a number of other ways are thinkable by which radionuclide releases may cause irradiation of man. The experience has shown that, by the selection of the pathways cited, their description by appropriate environmental models and the choice of suitable model parameters, it is possible to ensure that actual radiation doses are not substantially underestimated by the calculated doses.

5.   The consumption of drinking water taken from a river receiving liquid effluents is of minor importance for the radiation exposure as a whole. Calulations carried out with the model used in the Federal Republic of Germany for licensing procedures of nuclear installations (ref. 7) show that this exposure pathway may contribute about 10 % of the total dose (ref. 8). In this calculation, all processes that might decrease the radionuclide concentration, like bank infiltration and dilution by unaffected groundwater, are neglected.

6.   In normal circumstances the effects of airborne releases of radioactivity on those exposure pathways that are taken into consideration for the assessment of radiation doses by liquid releases like e.g., the consumption of drinking water, are small. The resulting doses may be neglected compared to the doses which are estimated for the normal pathways for airborne releases, like food consumption or external irradiation. This is due, mainly, to the fact, that after atmospheric dispersion and dry and wet deposition on vegetation and ground only a small fraction of the deposited activity reaches surface water or groundwater, where dilution with unaffected water additionally decreases radionuclide concentration.

Accident situations

7.   For the assessment of radiation exposure of population after a nuclear accident, time-dependent models are best suited (ref. 9-12). They cover airborne releases and the terrestrial environment. The time-dependency relates to the season of the year, particularly, during which due to the accident the radioactive contamination of the environment starts. The importance of this feature is clear when comparing consequences of a large scale contamination in winter and in early summer. While in the first case no agricultural products are affected, the last case may result in restrictions on the use of the crops of almost a whole year.

8.   The models used for assessing consequences of accidents beyond the design basis do, generally, not account for the impact of airborne releases on the aquatic environment. This is due to the fact that, in generic models, calculated radiation doses and risks by aquatic

pathways are low compared to those caused by atmospheric and terrestrial pathways. In models used for a realistic prediction of the consequences of certain accident scenarios, aquatic pathways could only be included on a site specific basis. Generic models used, particularly, to predict the impacts of accidental radioactive releases to the hydrosphere, also show that for land-based nuclear power stations aquatic exposure pathways are of minor importance (ref. 13).

9.   The doses resulting from normal routine releases of nuclear installations via the drinking water pathway are not only small compared to the total dose via all pathways, but also small in the sense that they are negligible compared to dose limits and compared to the natural radiation field. In the case of accidental releases the latter may no longer be true, especially if the transport of radioactivity from the directly affected area downstream to less contaminated areas, or the supply of drinking water over long distances are taken into account. In order to follow the principle of optimization in radiation protection it may be prudent in such cases to restrict the use of contaminated water supplies. Especially in these cases an assessment of the potential contamination risks of water resources is a necessary basis for monitoring requirements. Otherwise the monitoring programs for drinking water may interfere with monitoring programs for food which in most cases have highest priority in order to assess the actual radiation exposure. The experience we had after the Chernobyl accident in the Federal Republic of Germany showed the necessity for people dealing with public water supplies to be able to assess the potential risk of the different raw water resources.

CLASSIFICATION OF CONTAMINATIONS BY ACCIDENTS

10.   Radioactive contaminations of drinking water resources may result from a number of events. According to the area affected we may distinguish the following categories:
-    Local contaminations of soil and of groundwater by, e.g., transportation accidents involving radioactive material or uncontrolled releases of nuclear installations into soil and into groundwater.
-    Contamination of a river or other receiving water body by uncontrolled high liquid releases from a nuclear installation.
-    Regional or widespread contamination of the total environment, precipitation included, by high releases of radioactivity into air. (The source of the releases may be a nuclear facility or an explosion of an atomic weapon).

Depending on the causing event the severeness of the contamination will differ. A combination of the three categories is possible.

11.   Transportation accidents involving radioactive materials are only of local importance for contamination of water resources. Because of restrictive transportation regulations the limited quantity and the packaging of radioactive material provide for a very low contamination risk.

12.   Uncontrolled liquid releases from nuclear installations pose a problem to technical safety measures inside the installation. Releases of

this type are very unlikely and do not belong to the class of accidents within the design basis for nuclear power stations. An upper bound on the activity released is, in this case, the inventory of the primary coolant.

13.   The contamination of drinking water following severe reactor accidents or other nuclear events has been of some concern in Germany in the late sixties (ref. 14). In these cases direct deposition of radionuclides on the surface of, e.g., a river in the direct neighbourhood of the facility has been estimated in the order of 10^{13} Bq. In the years following it has to be expected that less than one percent of the activity per year deposited in the catchment area of the river is mobilized and transported in river water.

14.   The most severe reactor accident, combining a containment failure and a core-melt-down includes all three contamination categories mentioned in paragraph 10.

RISK ASSESSMENT FOR DRINKING WATER
Water resources at risk

15.   The degree of a potential contamination of drinking water depends on the source, the kind and amount of contamination, and, of course, on the type of water resource used for drinking water. Source, kind and amount of contamination have been briefly discussed in the last chapter. The type of water resource is important for the assessment of factors that might decrease the radionuclide concentration of the primarily contaminated water source. For while transfering the contamination from the primary source, e.g. precipitation, river water or ground water, to the raw water supply used for drinking water a number of processes take place which delay, reduce or even prevent the radioactive contamination.

16.   Accordingly, raw water sources may be ranked into the following three groups, starting with the water resource of the highest risk (ref. 14)
-   cisternes
-   unprotected water resources
        creeks and rivers
        reservoirs and lakes
-   protected water resources
        groundwater in karst and fissured rock areas
        artificially infiltrated groundwater
        natural groundwater in porous media.

This ranking is generally true in case precipitation is the primarily contaminated water source. In case only river water is transporting the contamination, the ranking would be
-   river water
-   artificially infiltrated groundwater
-   bank infiltrated groundwater
-   natural groundwater.

If groundwater itself is contaminated severely, a contaminated groundwater flow may give rise to a wide spread underground contamination and to a secondary contamination of river water.

Factors influencing contamination

17.   In order to evaluate the potential risk of contamination for drinking water the following factors are of special interest:

-    transport time of water between the primarily contaminated water body and the raw water source used for drinking water, e.g. residence time of rain and groundwater in the catchment area of a creek or river or of groundwater in a karst area,

-    raw water volume from noncontaminated sources which may contribute to the dilution of the contaminated water, e.g. the natural groundwater part of bank infiltrated groundwater

-    processes of sorption and desorption as well as precipitation which cause a retardation of radionuclide migration rates compared to water flow rates and a reduction of the contamination.

18.   In Table 1 a number of parameters are compiled which influence the contamination of raw water sources used for drinking water when by a regional or wide spread contamination rain water is the primary source of radioactivity.

19.   Only in special cases, cisternes are still used as drinking water supply. Depending on the volume of uncontaminated water present in case of a nuclear event, if dilution is high, it may be possible even to continue to use this water.

20.   If creeks and rivers are the raw water source, the characteristics of the catchment area like type of vegetation (and season of the year), type of soil and orography are of importane. They affect the mean residence time of the water and the sorption of radionuclides in the catchment area. Both factors diminish radionuclide concentrations: shortlived radionuclides like ^{131}I partly decay before reaching the surface water, longlived radionuclides like ^{90}Sr and ^{137}Cs are retarded in such a way that concentrations in the surface water stay on a minute level. For larger rivers the total flow rate, part of which may originate in less contaminated areas, may contribute an additional dilution. In contrast, urban areas, where most of rain water is precipitated on covered surfaces, may give rise to concentration peaks in the river which receives the run off.

21.   For lakes and drinking water reservoirs the characteristics of the catchment area are of similar importance as for creeks and rivers. Additionally, the particularities of these water bodies have to be taken into account. During summer time the thermal statification of the water body prevents mixing of freshly contaminated water with the bottom layers, from where, normally, drinking water is taken. Thus shortlived radionuclides decay before reaching drinking water. In the periods of water circulation late in the year, the large volume of noncontaminated water dilutes the radionuclide concentrations which originally existed at the surface or in the tributaries. The ratio of the total volume of the lake or the reservoir to the flow rate of water leaving gives an estimate of the mean residence time (ref. 14).

22.   For groundwater in karst areas and in fissured rock, the characteristics of the top soil in the catchment area are of special

Table 1   Parameters affecting radioactive contamination of drinking water when rain water is the primary contamination source

Raw water source	Parameters
Cisternes	- volume of uncontaminated water
Creeks and rivers	- characteristics of catchment area (vegetation, soil type, orography)
	- residence time of water in catchment area
	- flow rate
Lakes and reservoirs	- characteristics of catchment area (vegetation, soil type, orograpy)
	- stratification, circulation and water flow
	- volume of uncontaminated water
Groundwater in karst areas	- characteristics of top soil in catchment area
	- residence time of precipitation
	- volume of uncontaminated water
Infiltrated groundwater	- residence time of infiltrated water
	- dilution by natural groundwater
	- retention in aquifer
Groundwater in porous media	- flow rate in unsaturated soil
	- depth of aquifer below surface
	- soil characteristics

importance. A layer of humus is an efficient absorber of most radionuclides and may prevent an instantaneous contamination of the groundwater. Besides, similar to the situation for surface water bodies, the residence time of precipitation and the volume of uncontaminated water present at the onset of contamination have to be considered.

23. In case, river water is contaminated which is used for bank infiltration or for artificially infiltrating groundwater the residence time of the infiltrated water and the retention of radionuclides in the aquifer are the dominant factors reducing the danger of contamination. An additional dilution is due to natural groundwater.

24. Groundwater in porous media may be considered protected against contamination from rainfall. The flow rate in unsaturated soils in the order of a few meter per year and the retention of radionuclides in soil delay radionuclide migration in such a manner that only some longlived radionuclides like ^{90}Sr reach the water table after years. Only in special cases the protective soil layer may be penetrated, either naturally, e.g. by dead tree roots, which extend deeply into soil, or by human activities, e.g. by badly fitted bored wells.

Time scale for monitoring programs

25. In the last subchapter parameters affecting the contamination risk of different raw water sources were discussed. For monitoring purposes it is important to know what period of time after the onset of contamination, a rise in radioactivity might be expected in a raw water source. The two parameters affecting this time period are the residence time of water in soil or, the transport time between different water resources, and the retardation of radionuclides by sorption on soil particles. Table 2 shows best estimates for the former parameter. In Table 3 retardation factors are summarized for a few radionuclides typical for contamination conditions after nuclear events. For Tritium and ^{131}I retardation is negligible. Thus the transport times given in Table 2 determine the least time periods after which radioactivity should be monitored if necessary. In the most probable case, that rain is the primary source of contamination, this time span lies between a few hours and a year, depending on water resource and on the special conditions at the time of contamination. If river water is the primary (or secondary) source of contamination the infiltration into groundwater takes time in order of weeks to months. Because of the low flow velocities of groundwater the time period available for monitoring is in the order of years. Groundwater in karst and fissured rock areas may demand a faster reaction.

Levels of contamination

26. In order to evaluate the risk of radioactive contamination for different water resources it is worthwhile to recall the results of studies undertaken in the sixties, when the environment was contaminated by fallout of atomic weapons testing (ref. 14). During the maximum of fallout in 1963/64, for ^{90}Sr in surface water about 10 % of the

Table 2   Order of magnitude of transport times of water between different water resources (H = hours, D = days, W = weeks, Y = years)

Raw water source	Primary source of contamination		
	Rain	River water	Groundwater
creeks and rivers	H-D[1]	H-D[3]	Y
lakes and reservoirs	D-W-M[2]	-	Y
groundwater in karst areas	D-W[1]	-	W-M-Y
infiltrated groundwater	-	W-M	Y
groundwater in porous media	Y	-	Y

[1] depends on rain intensity
[2] depends on season and weather conditions
[3] depends on distance from contaminating source

Table 3   Retardation factors in saturated soils (sand) for typical radionuclides (order of magnitude)

Radionuclide	Radioactive halflife	Retardation factor
Tritium (^{3}H)	12 a	1
^{131}I	8 d	1
^{90}Sr	28 a	10
^{103}Ru	39 d	5
^{137}Cs	30 a	100

concentration in rain water were measured, similar concentrations in bank infiltrated water. In groundwater of karst areas ^{90}Sr concentrations were about as high as 1 % of the concentrations in rain water. Concentrations of ruthenium isotopes were similar, concentrations of ^{137}Cs lower than ^{90}Sr concentrations.

27. After the reactor accident of Chernobyl measurements for ^{131}I show similar relations between rain and surface water (ref. 15). The maximum concentrations in Southern Germany which was highly contaminated were about 350 Bq/l in the River Danube. In Northern Germany concentrations of ^{131}I ranged from 1 to 10 Bq/l in riverwater. Because of the short halflife of ^{131}I only bank infiltrated groundwater with infiltration time spans of a few days showed ^{131}I concentrations in the order of Bq/l. Neither drinking water from lakes and reservoirs nor groundwater in karst areas showed elevated radionuclide concentrations.

28. The concentration of radionuclides to be expected in a raw water source after contamination a primary water body may be estimated, generally, by the formula

$$C_{i,d} = c_{i,o} \cdot d \cdot e^{-\ln 2\ (R_i \cdot T_r)/T1/2,i} \cdot K$$

$C_{i,d}$	=	concentration of radionuclide i in raw water source used for drinking water (Bq/l)
$C_{i,o}$	=	concentration of radionuclide i in primarily contaminated water body (Bq/l)
d	=	factor of dilution by uncontaminated water
R_i	=	retardation factor for radionuclide i
T_r	=	mean residence time of water in catchment area or transport time between primarily contaminated water body and raw water source (s)
$T_{1/2,i}$	=	radioactive halflife of radionuclide i
K	=	correction due to any additional effects

If we consider the contamination of bank infiltrated water by ^{131}I, assuming a residence time of two weeks and a contribution of true groundwater of 50 %, the concentration in drinking water decreases to about 10 % of the original value in the river. If we compare this formula with the measurements after the reactor accident of Chernobyl in rivers the order of magnitude product of d and K may be estimated to be 0,01 to 0,1 for ^{131}I, and less for ^{137}Cs. For other types of water resources it is even less.

CONCLUSIONS

29.   After a reginal or widespread radioactive contamination of the environment following a nuclear event monitoring of drinking water may be appropriate even though radiation exposure by consumption of drinking water is of minor importance for the total irradiation. The monitoring programs should focus on water works using directly creek an river water and, with less intensity, on those, using surface water from lakes and reservoirs and groundwater from karst and fissured rock areas. Only under very unfortunate circumstances is there a need for monitoring other groundwater sources.

REFERENCES

1.   Fletcher, J.F.; Dotson, E.L. (compilers):
      HERMES - A Digital Computer Code for Estimating Regional Radiological Effects from the Nuclear Power Industry.
      USAEC Report HEDL-TME-71-168, Hanford Engineering Development Laboratory, Richland, Wa 71

2.   Disposal of Radioactive Wastes into Rivers, Lakes and Estuaries.
      IAEA, Safety Series No. 36, Vienna, 1971

3.   Soldat, J.K.; Robinson, N.M.; Baker, D.A.:
      Models and Computer Codes for Evaluating Environmental Radiation Doses.
      BNWL-1754, UC-11, February 1974

4.   Regulatory Guide 1.109
      Calculating of Annual Doses to Man from Routine Releases of Reactor Effluents for the Purpose of Evaluating Compliance With 10 CFR Part 50, Appendix I. U.S. Nuclear Regulatory Commission, Oktober 1977

5.   Bayer, A.:
      Die radiologische Belastung der Bevölkerung der Rhein-Maas-Region, Elemente für eine Abschätzung bis zum Jahr 2000.
      Bericht der Komm. der Europ. Gemeinschaften V/1647/77 (1978)

6.   Commission of the European Communities:
      Methodology for Evaluating the Radiological Consequences of Radioactive Effluents Released in Normal Operations. Joint Report by the National Radiological Protection Board, UK and the Commissariat a L'Energie Atomique, France. 1979

7.   Der Bundesminister des Innern:
      Allgemeine Berechnungsgrundlagen für die Strahlenexposition bei radioaktiven Ableitungen mit der Abluft oder in Oberflächengewässer (Richtlinie zu § 45 StrlSchV)
      GMBl 1979, Nr. 21, S. 371-435

Berichtigung
GMBl 1980, Nr. 30, S. 576-577
Berichtigung und Änderung
GMBl 1982, Nr. 33, S. 736-737
Berichtigung und Änderung
GMBl 1985, Nr. 19, S. 380-383

8. Gans, I.
Kontamination des Trinkwassers nach dem Tschernobyl-Unfall im
Vergleich mit anderen Lebensmitteln. ÖVGW-DVGW Symposium
"Radioaktivität und Trinkwasser", Salzburg, Oktober 1986, DVGW-
Schriftenreihe Wasser SW 2, Wien 1988, 23-41

9. Pleasant J.C., McDowell-Boyer L.M., Killough G.G RAGTIME: A
FORTRAN IV implementation of a time-dependent model for
radionuclides in agricultural systems
ORNL/NUREG/TM-371, Union Carbide Corp., Nuclear Division,
ORNL, USA 1980

10. Simmonds, J.R. The influence of the year on the transfer of
radionuclides to terrestrial foods following an accidental release to
atmosphere. Chilton, NRPB-M121 (1985).

11. Geiß, H., Paretzke, G.G., Münster, M. (Leiter der Vorhaben). Projekt
Sicherheitsstudien Entsorgung (PSE), Abschlußbericht Fachband 9,
Kennzeichen: KWA 3119/O, Berlin, Januar 1985

12. Whicker, F.W., Kirchner, T.B.
PATHWAY: a dynamic food-chain model to predict radionuclide
ingestion after fallout deposition
Health Physics, Vol. 52, No. 6, pp 717-737, 1987

13. Office of Nuclear Reactor Regulation, U.S. Nuclear Regulatory
Commission. Liquid Pathway Generic Study, Impacts of Accidental
Releases to the Hydrosphere from Floating and Land-Based Nuclear
Power Plants. NUREG-0440, February 1978, Washington D.C.

14. Arbeitsgruppe "Trinkwasser-Kontamination". Radioaktive Stoffe und
Trinkwasserversorgung bei nuklearen Katastrophen. Bericht der
Arbeitsgruppe, erstellt im Auftrag des Bundesministeriums des
Innern, Bonn, November 1971

15. Der Bundesminister für Umwelt, Naturschutz und Reaktorsicherheit,
Hrsg.: Impact of the Chernobyl Nuclear Plant Accident on the
Federal Republic of Germany, Comprehensive Report of the
Commission on Radiological Protection, Gastav Fischer Verlag,
Suttgart, New York 1988

Discussion

Dr F.S. Feates, *Her Majesty's Inspectorate of Pollution*
In the UK, we have a number of environmental monitoring programmes similar to those described in Paper 7. The National Radiological Protection Board and the UK Atomic Energy Agency (under contract to the Department of the Environment) undertake detailed national studies, as does the Ministry of Agriculture, Fisheries and Food -particularly for the marine environment and the nuclear operators. All publish summaries of their results, which can be obtained from the organizations concerned. The Department of Environment also publishes a comprehensive summary of all these monitoring results in an annual digest of environmental protection statistics.

Mr D.M.V. Aspinwall, *Engineers for Nuclear Disarmament*
With reference to Paper 6, I should like to ask what emergency back-up systems are available to ensure that the computer-based RIMNET is always operable (e.g. to cope with power failure)? Would these systems still work in the case of the worst imaginable nuclear 'event' (war implied but not stated)?

Mr G. Fraser, *Commission of the European Communities, Luxembourg*
The 1986 Vienna Convention was followed by a European Community system for urgent information in the event of a radiological emergency, intended to be compatible with and to enlarge the Vienna system (EC Council of Ministers 12/87). Any such system will rely not only on the comparability of the data in technical terms but also on uniformity of presentation allowing initial collation for analyses. On the latter aspect, the International Atomic Energy Agency and the World Health Organization have now published a manual providing the format and content of data to be communicated for the purposes of the Vienna Convention. To the extent that such data for the UK are collected within RIMNET, has the database been designed to take account of this?

Mr G.M. Roberts, *Yorkshire Water*
The discussion so far has centred on major events at power stations and other large nuclear installations. There are a very large number of smaller, but still terabecquerel concentrations of nuclear material

Nuclear contamination of water resources. Thomas Telford, London, 1990.   131

around the country. As individuals, we are much more likely to become involved in an incident involving one of these small sources, and although such incidents are unlikely to be of national significance, they can be the cause of considerable, and legitimate, local concern. Could anyone help me put such incidents into context, with particular reference to security and protection from accidental release and appropriate arrangements for public protection?

Ms M.D. Hill, *National Radiological Protection Board, UK*
Emergency plans exist for all those installations where an accident is likely to lend to a release of radioactive material of such a size that it may be necessary to take countermeasures to protect the public. Outside the nuclear industry there are very few installations where it is necessary to have off-site emergency plans because most accidents will have consequences only on site. Since the probability that countermeasures for water supplies will be needed is very low for accidents at UK nuclear installations, it follows that it is extremely small for UK non-nuclear industry premises.

Mr A. Blythe, *Woodspring District Council*
Over 340 local authorities now monitor for radioactivity. We at the sharp end of public suspicion of 'official' reassurances wonder how we can dispel such public anxiety to ensure that monitoring and official data are credible. Does local, independent monitoring help in that objective?

Mr R. Clayton, *Crowther Clayton Associates*
Dr Broadway (Paper 7) has stressed the importance of good communication with the public in the event of an accident, and the question has been asked why the public generally does not seem to believe the specialists and what should be done to improve their plausibility. A major reason for this distrust is because the expert technologist has been caught out too often being - in the words of Edmund Burke - 'economical with the truth'. Let me give just two examples in which specialists dealing with nuclear issues were shown by subsequent events to have been at best incompetent and at worst disseminators of untruths.

On 4 November 1976, the magazine New Scientist published an article by the exiled Russian dissident Zhores Medvedev in which he claimed that a dump of radioactive waste from nuclear reactors had exploded in 1957 near the town of Chelyabinsk in the Urals. This story was widely reported in the national press and the expert who was consulted by the press was Sir John Hill, the chairman of the UK Atomic Energy Authority. Sir John declared that Medvedev's story was rubbish, and in a letter to The Times on 23 December 1976, he wrote, inter alia, "I do not believe the burial of nuclear waste in Russia or anywhere else could have led to an accident remotely resembling that described in the New Scientist article ...... I feel I should make it absolutely clear that in my view the burial of nuclear waste could not lead to the type of accident described ....". At a press conference in Moscow on 19

December 1979, Professor Anatoly Aleksandrov, President of the Soviet Academy of Sciences, said "There has never been a nuclear accident in the Soviet Union".

However, since Glasnost, the Soviet Union has been much more prepared to talk openly about its technical problems, as has become clear at this conference. As recently as about six months ago, the Soviet Union finally admitted that there had, in fact, been just such an accident of the type claimed by Medvedev; in the summer of 1989, Medvedev himself was invited back to the Soviet Union to give evidence to a select committee investigating the disaster. The general public now sees that the technical expert was not only wrong but apparently culpably wrong, with the added suspicion that his denials possibly had a political basis, since both the British and American governments were burying nuclear waste and an accident such as that claimed by Medvedev could have been politically embarrassing.

Another example can be found in the Three Mile Island accident in March 1979. Shortly after the accident, when there was still a great deal of confusion, Jack Herbine, the Vice-President of Metropolitan Edison, the owners and operators of the Three Mile Island nuclear plant, said that there had been no recordings of any significant levels of radiation and none were expected outside the plant. The statement was untrue, and Herbine almost certainly knew it to be untrue when he made it. The level of reliability of the public statements made by the responsible technologists and the managers was so low that the Governor of the State of Pennsylvania, Dick Thornburgh, said "One has a tendency to grow very sceptical about whether every bit of information we receive is 100% accurate".

When the 'Truth' is unpalatable or politically inconvenient, the public's experience is that the 'Truth' is not told and, consequently, the public has become sceptical about all official claims, especially when told that there is nothing to worry about. As a consequence, the public tends to believe only the independent organizations such as Greenpeace or Friends of the Earth. The only way in which the technologist can be believed, it seems to me, is when that technologist is palpably independent - but for some people the technologist is, by virtue of being a technologist, 'on the other side' and therefore will almost inevitably be treated with scepticism.

E.G.W. Chambers, *Strathclyde Water*
Lack of public confidence has been mentioned. As long as there are inconsistent or unclear standards, public concern is likely to arise from both mischief makers and those with general concern.

With reference to Paper 7, could further comments be offered on current US thinking on action levels and intervention levels?

Dr S.J. Caughey, *Meteorological Office*
The modelling work being undertaken by the Meteorological Office should help direct aerial surveying of deposited radioactivity. The model output will provide deposition fields (both wet and dry). These

can be based on weather radar measurements of rainfall rates, thus providing excellent spatial and temporal resolution. The UK weather radar network will soon be extended to Scotland and coverage will then extend to the whole of the UK.

Dr M.W. Jones, *Her Majesty's Inspectorate of Pollution*
The Meteorological Office in liaison with Her Majesty's Inspectorate of Pollution, is developing models to predict the direction and rate of travel of radioactive clouds to enable estimates to be made of the deposition of radionuclides.

In the event of a nuclear accident, supplementary monitoring programmes will provide additional information which will enable the output from the models to be refined, which, in turn, may indicate additional areas where further monitoring would be appropriate.

Professor S. Bergström, *Swedish Meteorological and Hydrological Institute*
Experience from Sweden after Chernobyl showed that you have to be careful with airborne gamma-rays spectrometry on snow-covered ground. The rainfall penetrates the snowpack and the gamma rays are reduced by the water equivalent of the snow. This may lead to an underestimation of the deposition.

Mr J. Hill, *Sir Alexander Gibb and Partners*
Although we have heard that drinking water is likely to be only a relatively small source of radiation exposure, depending on circumstances we may still have to attempt to reduce contamination in supplies from surface water sources. From his knowledge of natural removal mechanisms, how efficient does Dr Gans (Paper 10) think water treatment processes would be in removing contamination, and can he suggest variations to the treatment process that would improve removal?

Mr R. Castle, *North West Water*
I wish to comment from the water industry on the point that most experts believe that water supplies are likely to remain relatively uncontaminated following a nuclear incident. While this is probably true, the general public does not, unfortunately, perceive this to be the case. Therefore, radioactivity monitoring of water supplies is essential to reassure the general public.

Dr Jones, *Paper 6*
Dr Feates refers to a number of publications summarizing the results of environmental monitoring programmes. In addition to these, the Department of the Environment will be publishing data from the first six months of operation of the RIMNET monitoring network. These will provide, on a monthly basis, the maximum and minimum gamma dose rate readings at each site, together with the calculated average dose rate and the standard deviation.

Mr Aspinwall asks about emergency back-up systems for RIMNET. At the heart of the RIMNET system are two computers, one in London and one in Lancaster. Both are updated at the same time so that the information on one is always a duplicate of the other. Thus if one computer fails the other computer is immediately available to carry out the RIMNET functions. In the event of a power failure there are back-up systems available in London. We are confident that RIMNET would work and be available in the case of the worst imaginable nuclear accident.

Mr Fraser asks to what extent the RIMNET database has been designed to take into account plans for the provision of data from the International Atomic Energy Agency and the World Health Organization. It is planned to transmit information from these organizations over the Global Telecommunications System (GTS). The United Kingdom is linked to the GTS via the Meteorological Office in Bracknell, and arrangements are being made to link RIMNET to this. It is of vital importance that international organizations agree on the extent and format of the data to be transmitted. International communication systems should be flexible in operation, otherwise the difficulty of securing agreement to future changes in these systems by other countries, and the cost of doing so, would create major difficulties.

Mr Roberts and Ms Hill refer to arrangements for public protection from incidents involving small radioactive sources. National arrangements exist for providing assistance to the police, and similar bodies, for handling incidents involving relatively small quantities of radioactivity: these are known as the National Arrangements for Incidents involving Radioactivity - the NAIR scheme. Briefly, they provide for advice and help to be given locally from the nearest organization with experience and equipment in handling radioactivity.

As a final comment, I should point out that one of the key aims of the National Response Plan (of which the RIMNET system is part) for handling the consequences of an overseas nuclear accident is to ensure that members of the public and concerned organizations are informed of the accident as soon as possible, and that consistent follow-up information is also made available quickly.

Dr Broadway, *Paper 7*

Mr Clayton discusses the problems presented when an expert technologist withholds complete information regarding a radiation incident. The examples he gives, as well as many others of which we are aware, demonstrates clearly the problems which result when an expert attempts to shield the public from the complete truth.

There is, however, another aspect of the problem of good communications which is of more general concern than the problem of misinformation. There is continued need to communicate the consequences of risky technology in a way that gives the public the most complete information to use in making decisions.

The Environmental Protection Agency in the United States has committed itself to improving the risk communication skill of its employees. Coursework, training sessions and case studies are used by employers to learn from past mistakes and to work towards more effective communications. Our agency would welcome the opportunity to share with other organizations any experiences or materials which have aided improved communication.

In reply to Mr Chambers, action levels for quantities of radioactivity as developed by different agencies within a given country or within several countries tend to be narrowly-tailored to the specific needs of the moment. Typically, little attention has been given to international uniformity or to ease of interpretation. As a result, most action levels tend to be overly complicated and related to concepts such as the effective committed dose equivalent instead of to concentrations which can be measured easily. There is an increasing consensus that agencies and different countries must work in close harmony to establish consistent and clear guidelines. Until that goal is reached, I am afraid that the difficulties mentioned by Mr Chambers will continue.

Dr Sanderson, *Paper 8*

Although welcoming the developments described by Dr Caughey and Dr Jones, I must sound a note of caution. One of the many salutary lessons of Chernobyl in Scotland was the complete failure of the published NRPB/MET office fallout maps, based on meteorological evidence, to identify the high levels of deposition in the Central Highlands - possibly the most heavily contaminated part of the UK. This seems to have been due primarily to a lack of field monitoring results rather than to poor rainfall data. Indeed the predicted map gave excellent results in West Cumbria and parts of South-West Scotland, where fallout levels were already known from ground sampling. It is vital that deposition predictions do not lead to similar gaps or delays in monitoring programmes in any future incident.

In reply to Professor Bergström, the shielding effect of snow, or heavy rainfall, has been known for 30 years; indeed aerial radiometrics has been used to predict meltwaters in the USSR, the USA and Canada over many years. The problem appears to be one of interpretation, but it may be worth pointing out that when fallout is covered by snow the direct radiation hazard is reduced, and that ground-based monitoring with portable instruments will under-respond in exactly the same manner as airborne observations.

Dr Gans, *Paper 10*

The discussion at this conference is very similar to the discussion we are having in the Federal Republic of Germany. There are two points of view when looking at the contamination of drinking water: one is that of the people engaged in radiation protection, the other is that of the water suppliers.

The former look at the consequences of a nuclear event as a whole. Generally, an analysis of the possibilities for exposure of population shows that among all the exposure pathways - inhalation, food consumption and external irradiation - the consumption of drinking water is of minor importance or even negligible. Therefore, from the viewpoint of radiation protection there is no need for setting forth concentration limits. Because of my occupational background, I belong to this group. On the other side, the water suppliers are used to drinking water standards - therefore, they also expect them in the case of radionuclides; furthermore, and I can understand this, they are confronted by a public which is used to standards or concentration limits and asks for verification that drinking water is safe.

The outcome of the discussion in Germany is that we have not introduced drinking water standards. Perhaps we will apply the EC standards when necessary. Our aim, however, is to inform the public water suppliers in such a way that they might assess the potential risk of contamination of the particular water source they are using, and estimate the need for monitoring drinking water. My paper is part of our effort in this area.

In reply to Mr Hill, during the period of fallout from nuclear weapons' testing, a great number of studies were performed in waterworks, using surface water to evaluate the decontaminating effects of conventional water treatment. A serious drawback of many of these investigations is that, owing to the state of measurement techniques in those days, the figures on removal efficiency etc., are based on gross beta measurements; as such, they are more or less useless for evaluating the decontamination effects for specific radionuclides like ^{131}I, ^{137}Cs ^{103}Ru. The few studies in which individual radionuclides were measured show a wide range of removal efficiencies, typically 10-90%. Therefore, I would hesitate to rely on the removal mechanisms of water treatment generally. It has to be borne in mind, however, that the removal of a radionuclide is identical with the removal of the corresponding chemical element. Therefore, in cases such as ^{131}I, ^{137}Cs and ^{90}Sr, the water supplier might get an idea of the order of magnitude of removal efficiencies by looking at the removal of I, Cs and Sr by the treatment processes.

11. The consequences of a nuclear event on water resources — the UK and other European countries

D. G. MILLER, PhD, MIChE, FIWEM, Water Research Centre (1989) plc, Medmenham Laboratory, UK

SYNOPSIS. Water suppliers in Europe did not give high priority to radioactivity in drinking water preparation prior to the Chernobyl accident. This incident demonstrated short comings in contingency plans and a lack of expertise in the water industry in this area. The major factors involved have now received attention and there is greater awareness of the importance of information exchange, scale of incident, nature of nuclides released and vulnerability of different sources. Although it is unlikely that such a major accident will occur in the future steps are being taken to cope with the consequences. Public assurance on the safety of drinking water is a major objective of the water industry.

BACKGROUND

1. For a long period prior to the Chernobyl accident radioactivity did not feature strongly in water supply planning except where groundwaters were used which contained naturally occurring radon. In these cases simple aeration treatment is normally sufficient to produce an acceptable drinking water.

2. During the period of above-ground weapons testing in the 50s and 60s some water supply utilities carried out spot measurements on raw and treated waters but safety was not a question frequently raised. This monitoring was largely discontinued prior to Chernobyl.

3. In 1985 the Association of European Water Suppliers (EUREAU) thought it important to draft a report on the potential hazards to water supplies from aqueous and atmospheric emissions resulting from the normal operation of nuclear facilities. This question has not featured prominently in the United Kingdom because all but one of the installations are located on the coast and the impact on water resources used for public supplies is minimal. This is not the case in other Member States where effluents discharge to major rivers which often flow across national boundaries. Because of the likely release of up to 30 fission and activation products, of which around ten or more will be longer-lived radionuclides, EUREAU saw the need to emphasise the importance of consultation at the planning stage, regulations on plant location, licensing of the discharges and

effective monitoring by the dischargers. With these conditions imposed EUREAU did not see a major threat to water supplies from normal operation of nuclear installations.

4. The Chernobyl accident interrupted the production of this report and caused much more attention to be paid to this form of threat. It is important to understand why the Chernobyl accident had such a major impact on thinking. Previous accidental releases from Windscale and Three Mile Island had not impacted on water supplies mainly due to the scale of the accidents. Table 1 shows the estimated total release of activity in the three cases (ref. 1,2). It can be seen that the total release and the principal radionuclides of concern were far greater in the case of Chernobyl where it was estimated that some 3.5% of the total core inventory was discharged.

5. It has also been calculated that the total release of activity from above-ground weapons testing over a number of years was some 4000 times that of the Chernobyl accident. The annual effective dose equivalent in the UK peaked at about 80 µSv per annum and has now declined to around 10 µSv/annum. Chernobyl on the other hand was estimated to produce an annual individual effective dose equivalent outside the Soviet Union in the first year of between 0.3 and 500 µSv, depending on the country. The average was 300 µSv but this declined rapidly after the first year. For the UK it is estimated that the effective dose equivalent was increased by 3% of the average dose from all sources in that year (ref. 3).

6. To understand fully the impact of the Chernobyl accident and its effect on water supplies it is also necessary to take into account the changing attitude of sections of the public concerning radioactivity and its potential effects on health. In most Member States there has been an increase in opposition to nuclear power generation and the campaigns have served to increase public awareness of the potential dangers of radiation. It has been more difficult therefore to obtain a balanced view of relative risk. This change has not been solely in relation to radioactivity but has also been part of an increasing concern over environmental hazards generally. Substances which have the potential to cause cancer have been particularly singled out and this has led to demands for measures to reduce risk to an absolute minimum. The dual approach in the United States, where water quality limits for potential carcinogens, including radioactivity, are set at zero as a long-term objective but with intermediate practically achievable limits, is typical of the trend in standard setting. In essence this is not very different from the principle of ALARA which is a basic philosophy of radiological protection. It is against this background that the water supplier must consider the question of wholesomeness of water including acceptable levels for radioactivity.

ACTIVITY BY WATER SUPPLIERS FOLLOWING CHERNOBYL

7. The Chernobyl accident demonstrated the lack of

preparedness in all Member States not least with water supply utilities. Lack of information exchange, inadequate knowledge of radioactivity by professional staff and shortage of analytical facilities were all demonstrated in the short-term following the incident. Subsequently national committees were established in a number of Member States to consider the requirements for coping with future events. The European Commission considered the problems of rapid exchange of information between Member States and with countries outside the Community. EUREAU drew up a report covering problems experienced by water suppliers and asking for Community-wide action on a number of issues (ref. 4). In the United Kingdom a joint working group of the water industry and the government also considered the issues. The Prime Minister's initiative to set up a national response plan for accidents outside the UK was another consequence. Some of the results of these discussions are covered in the later sections of this paper.

DRINKING WATER STANDARDS

8. Drinking water quality standards in Member States are largely circumscribed by the Directive 80/778/EEC relating to the quality of water intended for human consumption (ref. 5). This lays down Community-wide maximum admissible concentrations for 42 parameters and requires national limits to be specified for a further 12. Radioactivity is not included and Member States need not set limits in national legislation. Only Spain has chosen to include radioactivity in its latest proposals revising the national regulations for drinking water. The limits proposed are the WHO guideline values of 0.1 Bq/l for gross α activity and 1.0 Bq/l for gross β activity (ref. 6). In normal circumstances it would be expected that water supplies in all Member States would be below these levels since background values are low. The Drinking Water Directive includes, under Article 10, provisions for the supply of water during emergencies. Maximum admissible concentrations may be exceeded provided this does not lead to an unacceptable risk to public health.

9. Water consumers are unlikely to be in a position to make judgements on safety regarding radioactivity due to the complexity of the subject but reassurance from experts is being challenged increasingly on environmental matters.

10. In other Member States separate legislation covers total ingestion of radioactivity from food, including drinking water. Only in France, Luxembourg and Italy have separate limits been derived for drinking water as part of total ingestion. These are based ultimately on the Community directives in 1959, 1976 and 1980 which laid down the basic safety standards for the health protection of the general public and workers against the dangers of ionizing radiation (ref. 7-9). They were promulgated under the EURATOM treaty of 1957 (ref. 10).

11. The Commission itself agreed limits in December 1987 for foodstuffs and feedingstuffs which would be applied following a nuclear accident or any other case of radiological

Table 1. Release of radionuclides from nuclear accidents (ref. 1,2)

Accident	Principal nuclides released	Half life	Total activity released Bq.10^{15}
Windscale 1957	Iodine-131 Caesium-134 Caesium-137 Tellurium-132	8.04 d 2.065 y 30.2 y 78.2 h	1.2
Three Mile Island 1979	Iodine-131	8.04 d	6.10^{-4}
Chernobyl 1986	Strontium-89 Strontium-90 Zirconium-95 Molybdenum-99 Ruthenium-103 Ruthenium-106 Iodine-131 Caesium-134 Caesium-137 Barium-140 Cerium-141 Cerium-144	50.5 d 29.12 y 63.98 d 66.00h 39.28 d 368.2 d 8.04 d 2.065 y 30.00 y 12.74 d 32.50 d 284.3 d	2000

Table 2. Maximum permitted limits for drinking water and liquid foodstuffs*. Commission proposal COM (87)281 Final (ref. 11)

Nuclide	Limit Bq/l
Isotopes of iodine and strontium notably I-131, Sr-90	400
Alpha-emitting isotopes of plutonium and transplutonium elements, notably Pu-239, Am-241	10
All other nuclides of half-life greater than 10 days, notably Cs-134, Cs-137	800

* Liquid foodstuffs as defined by Chapters 20 and 22 of the Common Customs Tariff

emergency. The Commission in its proposal to Council (ref. 11) applied political and technical considerations to revise downwards values put forward by an expert group. The values for drinking water in this proposal are shown in Table 2.

12. After considerable debate in Council values for liquid foodstuffs were not included in the final regulation (ref. 12). It is stated that values are to be established and would be calculated taking into account consumption of tap water. The same values should be applied to drinking water supplies at the discretion of competent authorities in Member States. It would be quite surprising if in time the European Parliament did not challenge the decision to allow this discretionaryy approach and there are also likely to be pressures for more stringent limits.

13. In the United Kingdom, derived emergency reference levels (DERLs) have been drawn up to provide guidance for acceptable levels of radioactivity in drinking water following a nuclear incident (ref. 13).

14. Table 3 shows the lower limits for individual nuclides against the time of exposure. Substitution should be considered after the time interval given and should definitely be implemented at 10 times the values. It should be stressed that the limits given would provide the maximum allowable dose from each individual nuclide and allowance must therefore be made for the presence of more than one nuclide. Equally no allowance has been made for intake from other routes such as food. The EC foodstuffs regulations on the other hand do allow for these factors.

15. The public might well be confused by the existence of so many limits which they will always regard as values not to be exceeded. There is likely to be difficulty in understanding why they vary by almost 7 orders of magnitude, even though a scientific basis can be put forward for this range.

16. There is, however, a real scientific question. The basic limit of 1 mSv per annum over a lifetime used by ICRP gives a whole body risk to the first and subsequent generations of approximately 116 additional cancers for 100,000 population. This is two orders of magnitude greater than that deemed as acceptable for chemical carcinogens in drinking water. Even the seemingly stringent WHO guide levels give risks over a lifetime 5.5 times the values used for chemicals. In comparison with other risks in life these are small but it does point to some disparity in approach.

IMPACT OF NUCLEAR DISCHARGES ON WATER RESOURCES
Normal operation
17. The very presence of installations handling radioactive substances presents some risk to water supplies at all times. In the UK alone there are 12 nuclear power stations producing 20% of the total electricity demand. In addition there are 4 fuel processing factories. Each modern reactor core may contain over 100 tonnes of enriched uranium oxide fuel. When fully operational the total activity content may be 10^{20} Bq. In Member States the extent of nuclear power production varies

Table 3. Derived initial concentration in drinking water (Bql^{-1}) for substituting fresh supplies at various times

Radio-nuclide	Water substitution times			
	2 day	7 day	14 day	100 day
Sr–89	$2.3\ 10^5$	$6.9\ 10^4$	$3.6\ 10^4$	$8.5\ 10^3$
Sr–90	$2.8\ 10^4$	$8.1\ 10^3$	$4.1\ 10^3$	$5.7\ 10^2$
Ru–103	$8.5\ 10^5$	$2.6\ 10^5$	$1.4\ 10^5$	$3.6\ 10^4$
Ru–106	$7.3\ 10^4$	$2.1\ 10^4$	$1.0\ 10^4$	$1.6\ 10^3$
I–131	$1.1\ 10^4$	$3.7\ 10^3$	$2.4\ 10^3$	$1.7\ 10^3$
I–133	$8.3\ 10^4$	$6.7\ 10^4$	$6.6\ 10^4$	$6.6\ 10^4$
Cs–134	$4.3\ 10^4$	$1.2\ 10^4$	$6.2\ 10^3$	$9.1\ 10^2$
CS–137	$5.1\ 10^4$	$1.5\ 10^4$	$7.3\ 10^3$	$1.0\ 10^3$

Note : These concentrations are associated with 'lower' dose equivalent levels at which 'consideration' shall be given to substitution of water supplies. They are based on either an effective dose equivalent of 5 mSv or a dose equivalent to an organ of 50 mSv, whichever is limiting.

Table 4. Nuclear power stations under construction or in operation in Member States (1987)

Country	Sites	Gross output MWe
Belgium	3	5,759
Denmark	–	–
France	12	65,351
Federal Republic of Germany	14	24,269
Great Britain	12	13,967
Greece	–	–
Ireland	–	–
Italy	3	3,348
Luxembourg	–	–
Netherlands	2	531
Portugal	–	–
Spain	4	7,838

as indicated in Table 4. Taking Europe as a whole it is estimated that more than 300 nuclear power stations are in operation or under construction.

18. Under normal operation the release of radioactivity in gaseous and liquid effluents is controlled by national regulations which are required by the EC directives adopted under the EURATOM treaty. The total authorised annual releases from the ten power stations in England and Wales amount to 5700.10^{12} Bq for hydrogen-3 (tritium) and 126.10^{12} Bq for other radionuclides, predominantly caesium-137, sulphur-35 and strontium-90 (ref. 14). In fact the recorded discharges seldom exceed in total around 10% of the authorised levels.

19. With the exception of one installation, Trawsfynydd, the plants discharge to the sea. It is instructive to calculate the impact which typical effluents would have if they discharged to inland water courses as might be the situation in some Member States. Tritium is not considered here because of its low health risk factor. The published figures for caesium show that discharges in liquid effluents equate to between 10^9 Bq and $1.4.10^{12}$ Bq annually, depending on the station. Meeting the 100 day DERL requires a dilution of between 3,000 l/d and 4 Ml/d. To meet the WHO limit of 1 Bq/l gross β activity the dilutions required would be between 3 Ml/d and 4,000 Ml/d, a much more difficult task but probably a more realistic target based on the continuous nature of the discharges and the principle of ALARA.

Accidental discharges

20. The difficulty in predicting the impact of nuclear accidents on water resources stems from the number of variables involved. Table 5 gives the main ones to be considered and these are discussed in turn below.

21. Risk of accident. The principal risk is assumed to be from nuclear power stations. It has been estimated (ref. 15) that the risk of plant failure leading to an uncontrolled release at a modern power station lies in the range 1 in 10^5 to 1 in 10^6. With 20 power stations projected in the UK the annual risk is estimated as 1 in 50,000. This should be reassuring to water suppliers but three incidents in the last 30 years have raised some question marks. At the assessed risk level it is doubtful whether water suppliers require comprehensive contingency plans at all.

22. Acceptable standards for drinking water. This is more complex than is the case for chemical substances because acceptable risk is related to time of exposure, nuclide type and concentration. Water suppliers would need to depend on expert advice based on detailed analytical results. However, convincing the public that water is safe to drink is not entirely a scientific matter. This could be the most crucial factor in any future incident.

23. Important radionuclides. Chernobyl demonstrated that a wide range of nuclides could be released as listed in Table 1. In their assessment of the dose effects of Chernobyl on the

145

Table 5. Principal factors influencing impact of accidents on water supplies

Factor	Possible components
Risk of accident Acceptable drinking water standard	1 in 10^5 to 1 in 10^6 Derived emergency reference levels (DERLs) EC limits WHO guideline values National standards
Important nuclides	Iodine-131 Caesium-134 Caesium-137 Strontium-90 Ruthenium-106 Hydrogen-3
Extent of release Distance between accident and water source	Amount Period of discharge
Meteorological conditions	Wind speed and direction Precipitation
Type of water source	Rainwater Surface water Groundwater
Effect of treatment	Treatment type Radionuclide
Alternative supplies	Uncontaminated sources Tanker supplies Bottled water

Table 6. Decreasing vulnerability of water sources

Rainwater
Directly abstracted river water
Stored surface water
Groundwater from fissured strata
Water from bank infiltration, artificial recharge
        and deep surface water impoundments
Groundwater from deep unfissured aquifers

population within and outside the Soviet Union, the World
Health Organisation (ref. 2) concluded that iodine-131,
caesium-134 and caesium-137 were the most important nuclides
for ingestion and that radiocaesium alone was significant
beyond the first year. Within the USSR strontium-90 was also
significant and there is some uncertainty about hydrogen-3,
but environmental measurements indicate low concentrations.
The short half-life of iodine-131 indicates that only directly
consumed rainwater or water from short retention time supplies
should give rise to significant doses. This was the reason
for the UK government advice not to drink rainwater at the
time of Chernobyl.

24. Extent of release. Figures in Table 1 show that the
total release of radioactive material from Chernobyl was three
orders of magnitude greater than the previous highest at
Windscale and the period of release extended to 10 days before
containment measures were successful. Considering the
circumstances it is unlikely that this scale of accident will
re-occur. However, as part of the public enquiry into the
proposed Sizewell B plant the effect of an incident beyond the
normal reference accident was required and levels of fall-out
were calculated. Data exist therefore for estimating the
impact of this scale of accident.

25. Distance between accident and water source. This factor
is important not just because of the obvious reduction of
impact as distance from the accident increases but also
because distance has an effect on public reaction. As part of
the emergency planning arrangements zones are designated
around each nuclear installation within which a series of
measures would be taken depending upon the severity of the
incident. The measures include evacuation, issuing of
potassium iodate tablets, banning of milk and some foodstuffs
and radiation monitoring. The scale of measures in the USSR
can be judged by the fact that in excess of 23,000 people have
been permanently evacuated following the initial movement of
130,000 people in a 30 km zone around the plant, and over
300,000 are subject to health checks. Potassium iodate
tablets were distributed to the evacuees in the USSR and an
estimated 10 million young people and 8 million adults in
Poland (ref. 16).

26. Within the emergency zone water supplies are unlikely to
be a major consideration and food contamination, particularly
the iodine content of milk, would be a first concern followed
by caesium levels in other foodstuffs. Immediately outside
the emergency zone where the population is unlikely to be
evacuated, water supplies could be contaminated sufficiently
to justify full analysis to allow estimates to be made of the
likely dose to consumers. It is certain, however, that
reassurance monitoring would be required at much larger
distances, as evidenced by the UK experience where the
accident took place some 2000 Km away. One concern, which was
the case in Chernobyl, is where water supplies to areas
outside the critical zone are fed from waters which can be
contaminated from within the zone. The water supply for Kiev

comes from a reservoir fed by the rivers Pripyat and Dnieper which were at high risk from fall-out and run-off. It was also possible that groundwater outside the zone would become contaminated from the affected area. Extensive measures were taken to prevent this contamination taking place including the construction of below-ground containment walls for groundwater and embankments to prevent contaminated rainfall washing into the river Pripyat. Alternative supplies were provided for Kiev by transfer of water by pipeline from the river Desna, some 10 km away.

27. Meteorological conditions. Wind strength and direction and rainfall are critical factors in determining the local intensity of fall-out and the extent of spread of the plume. During the Chernobyl accident the wind initially directed the plume to the north-west but later this changed successively to west and south-west, north-west then north-east. The scale of the incident meant that contamination rose vertically to above 1200 m but later reduced to about 200-440 m. Deposition, however, was greatly influenced by precipitation in the areas of the plume and this gave considerable differences even within distant countries such as the UK. Due to this combination of factors highest levels of deposition outside the USSR occurred in north-east Poland, Romania, parts of Scandinavia, southern areas of the Federal Republic of Germany, northern Italy and Greece. Models have been developed to assist with the prediction of effects but this is clearly a complex subject.

Table 7. Percentage of water from surface and groundwater in Member States

Member State	Percentage surface water
Belgium	33
Denmark	1
France	36
Federal Republic of Germany	28
Great Britain	72
Greece	72*
Ireland	75*
Italy	12
Luxembourg	30
Netherlands	30
Portugal	75*
Spain	74

* provisional estimate

28. <u>Type of water source</u>. Contamination levels measured in the Member States following Chernobyl indicated the relative vulnerability of different types of water source. Table 6 shows sources in declining order of vulnerability. The type of water available for supplies varies within and between Member States. Table 7 indicates the percentage of water taken from surface and groundwater sources in the Member States. Clearly the United Kingdom and Spain overall are the Member States most vulnerable to contamination from a nuclear incident. However this over-simplifies the situation because within Member States there can be regions where surface water predominates. Supplies which are directly abstracted from rivers are at greatest risk because dilution and the decay of activity afforded by storage are not available.

29. <u>Effects of treatment</u>. Comprehensive studies have not been carried out to measure the effectiveness of treatment for removing those radionuclides typically released from accidents involving nuclear reactors. More work has in fact been done, particularly in the United States, on processes for removing naturally occurring nuclides such as radon, radium and uranium.

30. Work on nuclides of interest, such as caesium-137 and iodine-131, is limited and much of it has been carried out in the laboratory. Full scale investigation is limited due to the low level of radioactivity normally present in water abstracted. The increased activity resulting from Chernobyl led to some measurements being made on full scale plant but, although the activity levels were increased, they were still comparatively low, thus requiring long counting periods. The calculation then involved the subtraction of one very small number from another.

31. The results of studies so far indicate that the degree of removal depends very much on the type of treatment, the radionuclide concerned and whether it is in solution or associated with particulate matter. Conventional chemical treatment can give removals of between 0 and 90% the figure very much depending on the presence or absence of particulate matter. Results from full scale plant suggest figures of 30% – 80% removal for caesium-137 and 26% to 40% for iodine-131. Removal of total activity is of the order of 20-30% from all the results examined. As a result of Chernobyl further investigations are now in hand in a number of Member States.

32. One complication of the chemical treatment process is the build-up of radioactivity in the sludge produced during sedimentation and in deposits removed by filtration which subsequently are transferred to the backwash water. Where granular activated carbon beds are used activity also increases with time of filtration. Even at the relatively low levels of activity encountered in raw waters following Chernobyl, sludges in a number of Member States became sufficiently active to require special attention before disposal. If activity levels in raw water began to approach DERLs the risk to plant operators would be significant.

33. Use of alternative supplies. One possibility for water suppliers in the event of a nuclear accident is the use of uncontaminated sources in place of those affected by fall-out. This possibility will depend completely on local circumstances. The most desirable remedy would be to supply consumers from deep groundwater sources in place of surface supplies. This may be more possible in some regions within Member States than others. It is sometimes used to combat chemical pollution of surface supplies. In many areas, however, this would not be possible, for example where large urban populations are supplied from surface sources. The provision of temporary pipelines or mobile tankers is unlikely to be practicable and reliance would therefore have to be placed on the beneficial effects of dilution and storage on existing supplies to maintain activity levels below the DERLs. Stocks of bottled water would only be sufficient to replace supplies to fairly small populations.

Concentrations of nuclides likely to be reached in water sources

34. In view of the large number of variables affecting the likely concentrations in water it is only possible to estimate order of magnitude levels under assumed conditions and to compare these with concentrations found after Chernobyl.

35. Accident scenarios assume different degrees of failure and the related total release of individual nuclides. Using assessments of meteorological conditions it is possible to estimate deposition of nuclides under dry and wet conditions. Taking caesium-137 as a nuclide of concern for water supplies, a severe accident might lead to depositions of 10^4 Bq/m^2 over a significant area. By comparison the severe accident at Chernobyl led to depositions in Sweden of 30-80 10^3 Bq/m^2 over considerable areas and, in Cumbria, UK, a maximum of 17,000 Bq/m^2. Assuming uniform deposition on a water surface 1 m deep, a fallout of 10^4 Bq/m^2 would give, under uniformly mixed conditions, a concentration of caesium-137 of 10 Bq/l. Large variations would be expected because deposition would not be uniform and the concentrations would be affected by catchment conditions and run-off. Concentrations found after Chernobyl reflected this. Values were found in Cumbria in the UK in rainfall as high as 2600 Bq Cs-137/l. The bulk of reported levels in surface waters in the UK were below detection limits. However, detection limits varied from 0.01 Bq/l to 100 Bq/l caesium-137 thus making it difficult to determine the range of true values. Figures reported above detection limits ranged from 0.1 to 183 Bq Cs-137/l. Groundwater activities were below limits of detection at <0.28 Bq Cs-137/l.

36. Figures reported from other Member States include few results for specific nuclides. Caesium values for surface waters ranged from 0.2-19 Bq Cs-137/l, the highest levels being detected in the Federal Republic of Germany closer to the scene of the accident.

37. Treatment plants did not close their intakes following the Chernobyl incident except in one or two cases where

alternative groundwater resources were readily available.
However, many raw water sources reached levels where WHO
guidelines were breached and full nuclide analysis would have
been justified. The accompanying media publicity certainly led
to many enquiries from consumers seeking reassurance that
drinking water supplies were safe.

DEVELOPMENTS SINCE CHERNOBYL
38. A pertinent question to ask is whether, if another
incident happened tomorrow, circumstances would be very
different from those at the time of the accident on 26 April
1986. On some questions it is difficult to be sure, on others
new measures have been put in place.

Information exchange
39. Under the Council decision adopted on 14 December 1987
(87/600/Euratom) Member States are obliged to notify the
Commission and other Member States likely to be affected if
they are proposing to take action to protect the public as a
result of a nuclear incident or the detection of abnormal
levels of radioactivity within or outside its territory. A
schedule of appropriate information is included in the
measures which should be provided as long as this does not
jeopardise national security. The Commission is also to
participate in the IAEA convention on early notification of a
nuclear accident. These measures, if effective, should ensure
that members of the Community are better informed.
40. Within the UK full implementation of the RIMNET system
with 45 monitoring stations should ensure better internal
communication in the event of an accident outside the UK.

Emergency planning
41. Emergency plans for areas surrounding nuclear
installations are required by law in the UK and existed prior
to the Chernobyl incident. Because of the low incidence of
emergencies all regions were not fully trained to react at
that time. This aspect has now been improved. The particular
difficulties of Chernobyl were the distance between the
location of the accident and the areas affected together with
the lack of available information. The scale of effort and
mechanisms required to provide public reassurance had also not
been appreciated.

Education and training
42. The subject of radioactivity is a complex specialist
subject and reliance is normally placed on the provision of
expert advice from the nuclear industry, government
departments and other sources. The Chernobyl accident made
clear, however, that some knowledge is required by water
suppliers in order to provide reassurance to the public on the
safety of their water supply. A simple reassurance passed on
from experts proved not to be sufficient when questions were
raised by the media and informed pressure groups. EUREAU

therefore raised the need for training and education of water supply personnel in its report to the Commission (ref. 4). Some utilities in the UK have instigated training of this kind.

Monitoring

43. Monitoring programmes exist in the United Kingdom as part of the legislation controlling the release of radioactive substances to the environment. The major objective is to assess the doses of radiation likely to be received by the public. Monitoring of discharges and the local environment is carried out by the dischargers of radioactive wastes and independent checks are also made by government agencies. Part of this programme involves measurements on raw waters used for public supplies. This programme has been intensified following Chernobyl. Extensive reports are published regularly.

44. Monitoring by utilities has also been reviewed. Chernobyl showed a short-fall in available facilities for measuring radioactivity in water due to high demands for measurements on other foodstuffs. One conclusion of suppliers was that some arrangements are needed, either in-house or by contract, for ensuring adequate monitoring after an event. The need was seen for measuring total β activity as a screening test with more extensive nuclide analysis if trigger levels are exceeded. In order to maintain expertise and equipment in-house a regular monitoring programme is desirable. Utilities are therefore developing plans for implementation.

Public relations

45. The importance of contact with the public, the media and environmental groups was clearly brought out by the Chernobyl incident. The ability to understand the units of measurement used and to set the results in the context of public safety is paramount. With other substances this is easy to achieve normally by reference to national or international standards. For radioactivity this is much more complex and suitable yardsticks have yet to be developed. Provided doses are a fraction of those from natural sources the problem is not difficult but when figures move above WHO guideline values and towards DERLs conviction about safety becomes a much greater task. The water industry clearly hopes that such situations will not occur.

CONCLUSIONS

1. The Chernobyl incident served to awaken interest in the importance of radioactivity when judging wholesomeness of drinking water.
2. The accident by any standards was a major catastrophe which is unlikely to be repeated.
3. Routine operation of power stations appears to pose little threat to water sources used for potable supplies although

long-term discharges to inland river systems cannot be
ignored.
4. Chernobyl showed a lack of expertise on radioactivity
within water supply utilities and the absence of adequate
information systems for major accidental releases. Measures
are now in hand to improve this situation.
5. The wide range of published figures for protection of the
public from excessive doses of radioactivity from drinking
water is confusing for them even though most of these are
based on sound scientific principles.
6. Predicting the impact of accidental releases of
radioactivity on water supplies is a complex matter due to the
large number of factors involved.
7. From measures made following Chernobyl there seems to be
little risk to water supplies outside the immediate accident
zone but public reassurance is a major task.
8. Water suppliers see the need for monitoring facilities,
either within their own organisation or outside.
9. It is important that some staff in water undertakings are
trained in the fundamental aspects of radioactivity.
10. Insufficient is known about the removal of specific
radionuclides during treatment and the hazards to operators
from accumulations in sedimentaion tanks, sand filters and
granular carbon beds.

REFERENCES
1. HABERER K. Wasser Abwasser, 1987, 128 (7) 396–403.
2. WORLD HEALTH ORGANISATION. Chernobyl: health hazards from
radiocaesium. Environmental Health Series No. 24, Copenhagen,
1987.
3. NATIONAL RADIOLOGICAL PROTECTION BOARD. Living with
radiation. Third edition. HMSO, 1986.
4. EUREAU notice about the problem water suppliers would have
to face in the event of an accident happening in a nuclear
power station. EUREAU, Brussels, 1987.
5. EUROPEAN COMMISSION. Directive of 1 July 1980 relating to
the quality of water intended for human consumption
(80/778/EC). Official Journal L229/11, 30.8.1980.
6. WORLD HEALTH ORGANISATION. Guidelines for drinking water
quality, vol. I and II. Geneva 1984.
7. EUROPEAN ATOMIC ENERGY COMMUNITY. Council Directive of
2 February 1959. Standards for the protection of the health
of workers and the general public against the dangers arising
from ionizing radiations. Official Journal. L011, 221.
20.2.1959.
8. EUROPEAN COMMISSION. Council directive of 1 June
1976(76/579 Euratom) laying down the revised basic safety
standards for the health protection of the general public and
workers against the dangers of ionizing radiation. Official
Journal .L187,1. 12.7.1976.
9. EUROPEAN COMMISSION. Council directive of 15 July 1980
(80/836 Euratom) amending the directives laying down the basic
safety standards for the health protection of the general

public and workers against the dangers of ionizing radiation. Official Journal L246, 1. 17.9.1980.

10. EUROPEAN COMMISSION. Treaty establishing the European Atomic Energy Community signed in Rome 25 March 1957. Chapter III.

11. EUROPEAN COMMISSION. Proposal for a council regulation laying down maximum permitted radioactivity levels for foodstuffs, feedingstuffs and drinking water in the case of abnormal levels of radioactivity, or of a nuclear incident. COM(87)281 final. Official Journal C174/6 2.7.1987.

12. EUROPEAN COMMISSION. Council regulation (Euratom) No 3954/87 of 22 December 1987 laying down maximum permitted levels of radioactive contamination of foodstuffs and of feedingstuffs following a nuclear accident or any other case of radiological emergency. Official Journal L 371/11. 30.12.1987.

13. NATIONAL RADIOLOGICAL PROTECTION BOARD. Derived emergency reference levels for the introduction of countermeasures in the early to intermediate phases of emergencies involving the release of radioactive materials to atmosphere. NRPB, Didcot, England, 1986.

14. MINISTRY OF AGRICULTURE FISHERIES AND FOOD. Aquatic Environment Monitoring Report No.14. The Ministry, Lowestoft 1985.

15. GITTUS J. In perspective. Safety and nuclear power. The Chemical Engineer, May 1988, 12.

16. WORLD HEALTH ORGANISATION. Nuclear accidents and epidemiology. Environmental Health series No. 25. Copenhagen 1987.

17. AIETA E.M. et al. Radionuclides in drinking water: an overview. Journal American Water Works Association, 1987, 144. 79.

12. Different soil characteristics in Denmark and the Faroe Islands influence the radiological contamination of water resources

H. J. M. HANSEN, DSc, and A. AARKROG, DSc, Risø National Laboratory, Denmark

SYNOPSIS. A comparison between Denmark and the Faroe Islands of the contamination of water resources with strontium-90 from nuclear weapons fallout and cesium-137 from the nuclear accident at Chernobyl has shown that Danish ground water used as drinking water was nearly totally protected by morainic surface soils, while Faroese drinking water from streams that run along a peaty soil surface had a 30 times higher contamination level and made up about 3% of the total contamination of the human diet with cesium-137 after Chernobyl.

INTRODUCTION

1. The sensitivity of the biosphere to contamination by radioactive fallout depends on soil characteristics. The biological consequences to man of a given surface deposition will vary with the ion-exchange capacity and further chemical composition of the soil.

2. Strontium-90 and cesium-137 are the two main fallout nuclides that affect the human food chain. Both have a physical half-life of about 30 years. Strontium-90 is accumulated in our bones with a biological half-life of about 5-10 years. Cesium-137 enters all our cells together with potassium. It has a biological half-life of about 100 days.

3. The relatively large ion radius of Cs^+ (1.69 Å) enables its' fixation by entrapment in the lattice structure of clay minerals (ref. 1). In this, it contrasts with Sr^{++} (ion radius 1.13 Å) which remains predominantly in exchangeable forms (ref. 2). The ion-exchange capacity of clay minerals is reduced by any organic matter present in the soil (ref. 3).

4. Calcium affects the movement of strontium-90 in the soil apparently by enhancing the displacement of bound Sr^{++}. Although Sr^{++} is an easily exchangeable cation, it moves through the soil by diffusion and not just by simple mass flow in water (ref. 2).

5. Morainic clay and sand dominate the surface geology of agricultural Denmark; in contrast to the basalt rock and shallow surface soils, covered mainly by grass, of the Faroe Islands. Beneath the glacier deposits in Denmark there is limestone.

Nuclear contamination of water resources. Thomas Telford, London, 1990.

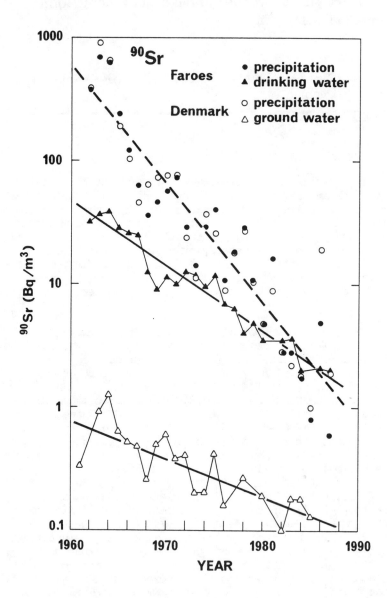

Fig. 1. Strontium-90 measurements in various water resources presented as geometric means of values from individual sites.

6. Danish drinking water is predominantly ground water, while Faroese drinking water comes from surface streams. The present report compares the radioecological sensitivity of Danish and Faroese water resources to contamination by radioactive fallout, based on the results of strontium-90 measurements from nuclear weapons fallout during the years 1962-1987 and recent cesium-137 measurements after the Sovjet reactor accident in Chernobyl in April 1986 (refs 4-6).

7. Methods are presented in the respective references.

STRONTIUM-90 FROM NUCLEAR WEAPONS
Drinking water

8. A direct comparison of the degree to which Danish and Faroese drinking water is contaminated with strontium-90 is presented in Fig. 1. Although there is a clear systematic variation in both the Danish and Faroese precipitation values from 1962 up to about 1975 - an initial maximum about 1963 is followed by further maxima about 1970 and 1975 - one can nevertheless picture the overall trend with time as an exponential decay of strontium-90 fallout concentrations in the rain, common for Denmark and the Faroe Islands. The systematic variation in the beginning is not larger than a more random fluctuation of the results after 1975.

9. A regression analysis shows a half life of 2.9 years for the precipitation concentrations as a whole. This reflects first of all the decreasing intensity of nuclear testing. A closer examination of the periods 1963 to 1968, 1971 to 1973 and 1975 to 1976 reveals a short-term half life of about 10 months, in agreement with theoretical considerations (ref. 4).

10. The common Danish and Faroese precipitation values enable a simple comparison of drinking water contamination. The strontium-90 concentrations in Danish ground water are a factor 30 lower than in Faroese drinking water. Regression analyses show corresponding half lives of 9.1 and 5.7 years, respectively.

11. Both the much lower Danish contamination levels and the corresponding somewhat longer overall half life of strontium-90 in ground water must be attributed to the large amount of clay minerals in Danish soils (paragraph 5) and, on the other hand, the high contents of organic matter in Faroese grass pastures, which reduce their ion exchange capacities (paragraph 3); together with the fact that groundwater resources as such do not exist on the rocky Faroe Islands. In contrast to the morainic soils of Denmark, the shallow Faroese surface soils have little water storage capacity. Faroese stream water is filtered mechanically before use as drinking water, but this leads to no substantial reduction of fallout contamination.

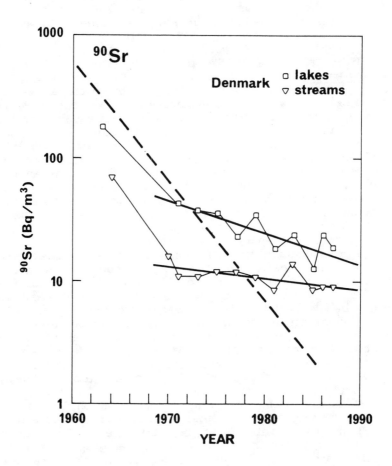

Fig. 2. Further strontium-90 measurements presented relative to the precipitation curve from Fig. 1.

Danish streams and lakes

12. Fig. 2 shows an interesting long-term affect on Danish stream water. Apart from an initial result in 1963, we see a very flat decay of the strontium-90 concentrations from 1970 and onward. A regression analysis shows a half life of 33 years, i.e. slightly longer than the physical half life of strontium-90. This means that we are nearly dealing with a state of equilibrium, where strontium-90 is released to stream water at a constant rate together perhaps with a small extra input from fallout precipitation.

13. Thus, while Danish stream water concentrations are about the same as Faroese drinking water (stream water) concentrations in 1970 (cf. Fig. 1), during the following years they become relatively higher. The ion exchange capacity of Danish surface soils seems to act as a reservoir or "memory" of accumulated strontium-90 fallout; in contrast to the peaty Faroese surfaces that allow strontium-90 to pass through and become unavailable to surface streams. Results from soil profiles have indeed shown (ref. 4) that strontium-90 penetrates much deeper into the ground on the Faroe Islands than in Denmark.

14. Danish lake water concentrations (Fig. 2) are higher than the corresponding stream water concentrations and show a half life of 12.6 years. They act as something between streams and direct precipitation, depending both on accumulated fallout levels and on acute fallout deposition rates. By way of comparison, the water supply of New York City (USA), which depends mainly on surface water, showed about half the strontium-90 concentrations of Danish lakes and a half life of about 9 years during the period 1966-1981 (ref. 7).

15. Why are Danish ground water concentrations (Fig. 1) not as constant (half life 9.1 years) as the corresponding stream water concentrations (half life 33 years)? They too are derived from precipitation that has passed surface soils. We would suggest that it is due to a lack of equilibrium during the vertical passage of rain water through the relatively shallow fallout deposition layer, on the way down to ground water; while the corresponding horizontal passage along the surface soil and into the streams is much more in contact with the accumulated fallout deposition, and thus in an overall state of equilibrium even with a shallow surface deposition layer.

CESIUM-137 FROM CHERNOBYL

16. Cesium-137 measurements in water samples are not available to the same degree as strontium-90 measurements, due to analytical difficulties during the period of fallout precipitation in the sixties. The latest results after the Chernobyl accident are not yet sufficient to enable the study of any comprehensive time sequence.

Table 1. Cesium-137 measurements in Danish water resources. Bq/m^3 (geometric means, $\overset{\times}{\div}$ SEM).

	Precipitation[c]	Streams	Lakes	Drinking water
May 1986	12000	30 $\overset{\times}{\div}$1.3	61[a]	
June	3200	15 $\overset{\times}{\div}$1.7	84 $\overset{\times}{\div}$1.3	0.31 $\overset{\times}{\div}$1.6
July August	607			
Sept. Oct.	137	5.3 $\overset{\times}{\div}$1.4	31 $\overset{\times}{\div}$1.3	
Nov. Dec.	84			
Jan. 1987 Febr.	99	2.7 $\overset{\times}{\div}$1.2	18 $\overset{\times}{\div}$1.4	
March April	81			
May		2[a]	2[a]	
June	36			0.06[b]±0.01
July Aug.	29			
Sept. Oct.	19			
Nov. Dec.	12			

a) Single values
b) Arithmetic mean
c) Mean SEM = $\overset{\times}{\div}$ 1.30

Table 2. Cesium-137 measurements in Faroese water resources. Bq/m^3 (geometric means, $\overset{\times}{\div}$ SEM).

	Precipitation	Streams	Lakes	Drinking water
Jan. 1987 Febr. March	169 $\overset{\times}{\div}$1.5			
April				3.3 $\overset{\times}{\div}$1.3
May June	69 $\overset{\times}{\div}$1.7			
July		7.1 $\overset{\times}{\div}$1.2	6.1 $\overset{\times}{\div}$1.6	6.3 $\overset{\times}{\div}$1.3
Aug. Sept.	16 $\overset{\times}{\div}$7.1			
Oct.				2.7 $\overset{\times}{\div}$1.2
Nov. Dec.	4 $\overset{\times}{\div}$4.7			

17. <u>Water resources in Denmark</u>. Table 1 shows the contamination of Danish water resources with cesium-137 after the accident at Chernobyl, April 26 1986, presented as geometric means so that SEM is expressed as $\overset{x}{\div}$ a factor rather than as ± a constant value. There is no clearcut pattern relative to precipitation. The two drinking water values are about a factor 50 lower than stream water (note that here we regard drinking water, not ground water, which was below the detection level) and lake water values seem about a factor 6 higher than stream water.

18. <u>Water resources on the Faroe Islands.</u> The corresponding Faroese results are shown in Table 2. They are mainly characterized by the similarity of stream, lake, and drinking water, at least in July 1987 when a special sample collection was carried out. Precipitation values are about the same as in Denmark but vary a great deal from place to place. The values in Table 2 reflect much fewer samples than in Table 1.

CONTAMINATION OF HUMAN DIET

19. Table 3 puts the contamination of Danish drinking water into perspective relative to the rest of the food chain (refs 4-5). One sees that it was of minute importance both in connection with nuclear weapons fallout and after Chernobyl. The total contamination of drinking water with cesium-137 from nuclear weapons fallout was calculated from the corresponding strontium-90 values assuming a ratio of 1:5 (ref. 7).

Table 3. Total[a] contamination of human diet per capita in Denmark.

| | Nuclear weapons fallout | | | | Chernobyl | |
| | strontium-90 | | cesium-137 | | cesium-137 | |
	Bq	%	Bq	%	Bq	%
Dairy products	2470	30	4175	17	386	31
Grain	3470	42	9680	39	359	28
Fruit and vegetables	2140	26	2400	10	203	16
Meat and eggs	170	2	7905	32	215	17
Fish	30	0	620	3	102	8
Drinking water	10	0.1	2	0.0	1	0.1
Total	8290		24782		1266	

a) 1962-1987 for nuclear weapons fallout and 1986+1987 for Chernobyl.

20. Measurements of the contamination of human diet on the Faroe Islands (ref. 6) showed a mean contribution from drinking water of about 3%, i.e. about 30 times higher than in Denmark, yet still of relative minor importance.

CONCLUSION

21. When drinking water is obtained from the ground beneath deep glacier deposits as in Denmark, it can be concluded that the water is nearly totally protected from any contamination by nuclear fallout. In a relative sense, this would apply even in the event of a nuclear war. There is no need of any restrictions on the consumption of ground water due to the radioactive contamination of morainic clay and sand.

22. It is only when surface water is used directly as drinking water that one needs to consider whether any extra precautions should be taken after a major nuclear event.

REFERENCES

1. SQUIRE H.M. and MIDDLETON L.S. Behaviour of Cs-137 in soils and pastures; a long term experiment. Radiation Botany 6 (1966) 413-423.
2. SQUIRE H.M. Long-term studies of strontium-90 in soils and pastures. Radiation Botanny 6 (1966) 49-67.
3. BARBER D.A. Influence of soil organic matter on the entry of cæsium-137 into plants. Nature 204 (1964) 1326-1327.
4. AARKROG A. Environmental studies on radioecological sensitivity and variability with special emphasis on the fallout nuclides Sr90 and Cs137. Risø Report No. 437, Risø National Laboratory, DK-4000 Roskilde, Denmark, June 1979.
5. AARKROG A., BØTTER-JENSEN L, CHEN QING JIANG, DAHLGAARD H., HANSEN H.J.M., HOLM E., LAURIDSEN B., NIELSEN S.P. and SØGAARD-HANSEN J. Environmental radioactivity in Denmark in 1986. Risø Report No. 549, Risø National Laboratory, DK-4000 Roskilde, Denmark, November 1988.
6. AARKROG A., BUCH E., CHEN QUING JIANG, CHRISTENSEN G.C., DAHLGGARD H., HANSEN H.J.M., HOLM E. and NIELSEN S.P. Environmental radioactivity in the North Atlantic region including the Faroe Islands and Greenland, 1986. Risø Report No. 550, Risø National Laboratory, DK-4000 Roskilde, Denmark, July 1988.
7. HARDY, JR. E.P. and TOONKEL L.E. Environmental report, May 1 1982. Environmental Measurements Laboratory, U.S. Dept. Energy, New York N.Y. 10014, 1982 (EML-405 UC-11).

13. Models and data to predict radionuclide concentrations in river basin systems

G. FLEMING, BSc, PhD, FEng, FICE, FRSA, and G. G. RUFAI, MSc, Strathclyde University, Glasgow, UK

SYNOPSIS. Radioactive contamination of land may result from the detonation of nuclear weapons or nuclear accidents, such as Chernobyl. The deposition of fallout on soil and/or plants, and subsequent erosion by rainsplash and overland flow, could introduce radioactive isotopes into the water and soil resources of the environment. A model to simulate the transport and deposition of concentrated pollutants and radionuclides within the river basin is proposed. The proposed model is built on an existing Strathclyde River Basin Model (SRBM), which has the potential to simulate runoff and erosion and the distribution of eroded soil particle sizes. An algorithm of the processes of concentration of pollutants and radionuclides can be developed based on the current understanding of the process of radionuclide attachment to soil particles.

1. The accident at Chernobyl introduced into the environment a plume of radioactivity, well defined in space and time. Barely 2 weeks after the accident, levels of Caesium -134 and 137 measured in soil and vegetation in the United Kingdom were 6670 Bqm^{-2}, 2390 Bqm^{-2} and 1780 Bqm^{-2} in Cumbria, Shetlands and North Wales, respectively (Ref 1). It was further claimed that, the half-lives of the nuclides found after the accident were 2 and 30 years for Caesium-134 and 137 respectively. To buttress this discovery, studies undertaken in Scotland a year after Chernobyl (Ref 2), revealed that surface deposits of Caesium -137, determined by aerial radiometric survey, were greater than 10,000 Bqm^{-2} on the Mull of Galloway, Isle of Whithorn, and North and South Uist.

2. Table 1 shows samples of rainwater collected after the accident from major catchments of U.K (Ref 3). Furthermore, radionuclide activity recorded in soil samples taken from the western slopes of the Penines, in U.K were 2400 $Bqkg^{-1}$ for top soil less than 2cm deep and 1000 $Bqkg^{-1}$ on grass.

3. Data from other countries show that durum wheat was contaminated after heavy fallout of radionuclides in Greece, during Chernobyl, and in Turkey, the large teacrop in the north of the country was also heavily contaminated (Ref 4).

Table 1. Levels of radioactivity recorded in sample of rainwater taken in UK (after Jones and Casle, 1987)

LOCATION	CONCENTRATIONS OF RADIOISOTOPES ($Bq l^{-1}$)						
	I-131	Cs-137	Cs-134	Te-132	I-132	Ru-103	Ru-106
DUMFRIES AND GALLOWAY (BNFL)	1250	250	130	1200	770	510	500
CUMBRIA (ICI)	784	845	77	-	-	203	-
HIGHLANDS (UKAEA)	4540	770	-	-	-	-	-
LANCASHIRE (CEGB)	1942	361	189	761	921	357	-
STRATHCLYDE (NRPB)	9400	2560	1650	10000	7600	[1050 Ba-140]	

BNFL   -   BRITISH NUCLEAR FUELS plc

ICI   -   IMPERIAL CHEMICAL INDUSTRIES

UKAEA   -   UNITED KINGDOM ATOMIC ENERGY AUTHORITY

CEGB   -   CENTRAL ELECTRICITY BOARD

NRPB   -   NATIONAL RADIOLOGICAL PROTECTION BOARD

4. Tests in garden soil in south western Ohio, U.S.A, prior to the Chernobyl event showed contamination with enriched Uranium 235 (Ref 5). This trend of radionuclide concentration in soils is buttressed by recent studies of plutonium concentration in surface sediments of the Ligurian Sea (Ref 6). They revealed that the concentrations of plutonium are about ten times higher in adjacent river sediments and are highly correlated with sediment porosities.

5. Evidence of current literature (Refs 7, 8), demonstrates that soil particles act as pollutant and radionuclide vectors. It is also widely accepted that, concentration of radionuclides is highly correlated to the porosity of sediments, which in turn is related to the grain size (Refs 6, 1, 7). There is some evidence to indicate that pollutants and radionuclides transported in estuaries, rivers and in oceans adhere to the fine sediments and the organic matter which is often associated with them (Refs 8, 9).

6. Hakonson, (Ref 10) in his evaluation of field studies of plutonium, reiterated that processes which transport soil within ecosystems, are paramount in the transport of environmental plutonium.

7. Understanding the soil/water/pollutant and radionuclide relationships within the environment is essential for the prediction of the effects and fate of the pollutants and radionuclides. A schematic diagram showing the soil and water continuum within the hydrological cycle is presented in Figure 1.

8. The interaction between rainfall, runoff, erosion, and pollutant/radionuclide concentration, and the evaluation of the pollutants and radionuclides adsorbed by the soil,requires the estimation of the overland flow volume, amount of soil eroded and the particle size distribution of the eroded soil. However, it is extremely difficult, expensive and highly inaccurate task to measure sediment processes.

9. Our aim in this paper is to explore the potential of the existing Strathclyde River Basin Model in combination with a proposed Quality Simulator, to simulate the movement of pollutants and/or radionuclides in the river basin due to atmospheric deposition or spillage.

10. The evaluation of the behaviour of specific pollutants or radionuclides as a function of the soil particle sizes, can be embarked upon in relation to surface erosion and subsequent deposition in valleys, river beds and reservoirs. An expansion of the Strathclyde River Basin Model to include the Quality Simulator is based on the physical and chemical properties of pollutants and radionuclides, e.g. Caesium-137 and Strontium-90, and their interactions with the hydrological cycle which include dynamic processes of rainfall, runoff,and erosion and transport of soil particles.

MATHEMATICAL MODELLING CONCEPT

11. A model is a simplified but coherent representation of

165

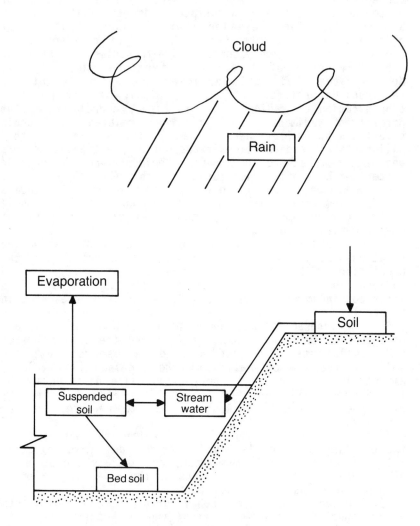

Fig. 1.   Schematic diagram showing soil-water continuum (modified after Salomons, 1984)

a real system (i.e. a river basin, river reach, a reservoir or a lake, etc). The general objective of a model is to simulate the system to obtain a global understanding of the behaviour of the system and of the different processes involved, and to undertake sensitivity analysis which provides information for decision-making. Models are vital when the system presents a high degree of complexity and offers alternate paths for action.

12. Fleming (Ref 12), describes a mathematical model as an abstract system interrelating a sample of input, cause, or stimulus of matter, energy or information, and a sample of output, effect or response of information, energy, or matter in a given time reference. Although mathematical models can be divided into various categories, there are at present no generally accepted rules regarding these divisions. As a result, several researchers have proposed different approaches such as Fleming (Ref 13) and Clark (Ref 14). In the course of this paper, the categories suggested by Fleming will be adopted.

13. The Strathclyde River Basin Model (SRBM) is a modified version of the Stanford Watershed Model IV (Ref 15). The flowchart of the SRBM is shown in figure 2.

14. In the SRBM, each basin is divided into segments by topography. Land surface representation by the model is shown in figure 3B. The representation of land surfaces in the model involves routing the overland flow, interflow and groundwater flows into their respective storages in a series of segments. At each segment boundary (i.e. an altitude contour) a proportion of this outflow enters the channel. Each segment is distinguished by width, length, and slope. The Watershed Model forms the entire basis of the SRBM and generates input files for further use by the Land Erosion and Routing Models. For the Land Erosion Model, these include throughfall and overland flow, and for the Routing Model, total flow reaching the channel network. In practice some parameters are evaluated by calibration, and others are evaluated from maps, surveys, or existing hydrometeorologic records and remote sensing data. The Watershed Model has been successfully tested throughout the world on a number of river basins (Refs 12, 16, 17, 18, 19). A typical output showing a comparison of recorded flow against simulated flow using the Strathclyde Watershed Model is depicted in figure 4.

15. The erosion model is a physically-based model capable of simulating the land and channel erosion for a field scale catchment. The effects of land use changes can also be undertaken using the erosion model. The erosion model computes the erosion from the land surface due to precipitation and overland flow, using a mixture of empirical and scientifically based algorithms.

16. Each of the primary processes of the erosion phase is modelled in a separate component. For instance; rainfall detachment is modelled by the momentum force of raindrops on the soil with the effects of vegetation cover, canopy density

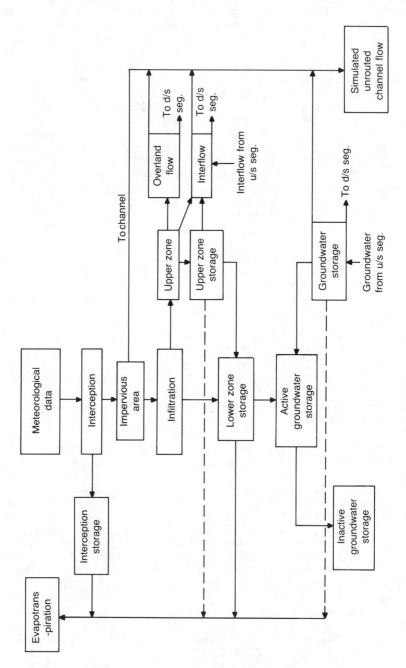

Fig. 2. Flowchart of modified Stanford Watershed model

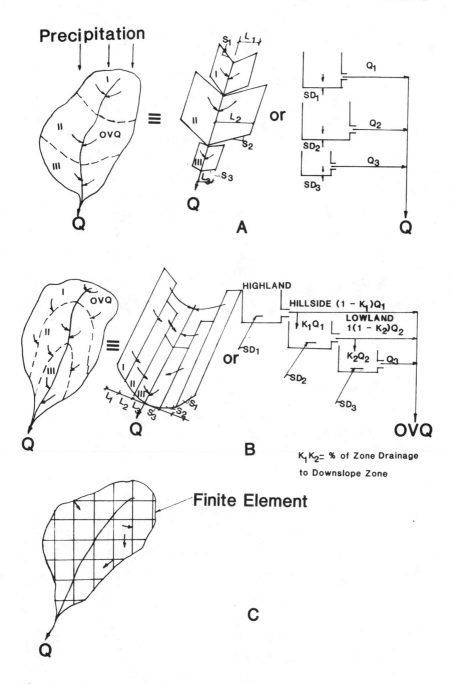

Fig. 3. Catchment area representation

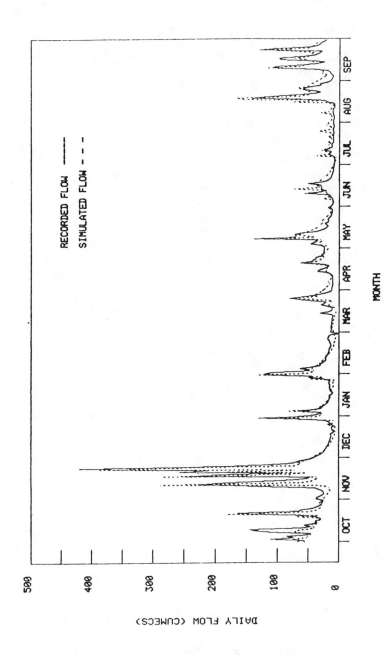

Fig. 4. Typical output of Strathclyde river basin model, comparing recorded flow against simulated flow (River Clyde at Daldowie, flow calibration 1963–64)

and the depth of overland flow on the soil surface, (Ref 20).

17.   When modelling overland flow detachment, use of critical shear stress method, utilising the modified Shield's relationship is made, (Ref 21). Overland flow transport capacity is modelled by unit stream power theory, (Ref 22). Armouring, by geometric deviation method, (Ref 23). Top soil exposure, particle size distribution of eroded soil and deposition storages are all modelled, (Ref 17). The erosion model produces daily and monthly summaries of erosion rates for the catchment and is capable of also producing hourly erosion rates for the period of simulation. If sediment in the channel network is of importance, the model can output the sediment reaching the channel network laterally.

18.   The channel routing model uses this data to route both water and sediment entering the river network. Flow routing is similar to the land surface routing which uses the St. Venant equations and the modified Manning's equation. Sediment transport capacity is also modelled using the unit stream power theory, (Ref 22). Sediment routing, by the kinematic routing technique.

19.   The erosion and the channel phase models have been used to calibrate and verify the effects of land use changes in Malawi, Central Africa (Ref 20). These are shown in figures 5 and 6 for basin erosion and particle size distribution of the eroded soil and the top soil layer, respectively.

SURFACE SOIL/RADIONUCLIDE INTERACTION

20.   The fallout from a particular nuclear event can be classified in four categories - dropout, close-in, tropospheric, and stratospheric (Ref 24). These categories differ in distance and time from the point of source. Dropout occurs at or very near ground zero, where the immediate effects of the burst are large. Close-in fallout consists of solid particles settling to earth under gravity within a few hours after the explosion. It may extend several kilometres downwind from the site of a large nuclear emission. Tropospheric and stratospheric fallout consists of very minute particles which may remain suspended in air for a long time. The scavenging action of rain drops is vital in bringing these particles to earth (Refs 24, 6).

21.   High concentrations of radioactive materials are found in areas receiving close-in fallout, and their subsequent distribution in soils is therefore of special importance. Less than 25 to 50 per cent of the fission products formed in a nuclear explosion at or near the ground surface may return to earth as close-in fallout (Ref 25). If early rain is associated with the fallout cloud, the amount of the fallout increases (Ref 24).

22.   The adsorption of cations by soil particle surfaces can occur by several processes; ion exchange is one of the most important. It has been discovered that ion exchange increases the sorption of calcium and strontium by a volume

171

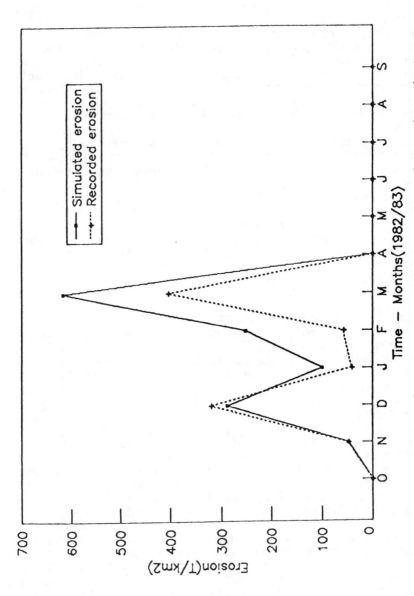

Fig. 5. Erosion model run for Mindawo 1, comparing recorded erosion against simulated erosion

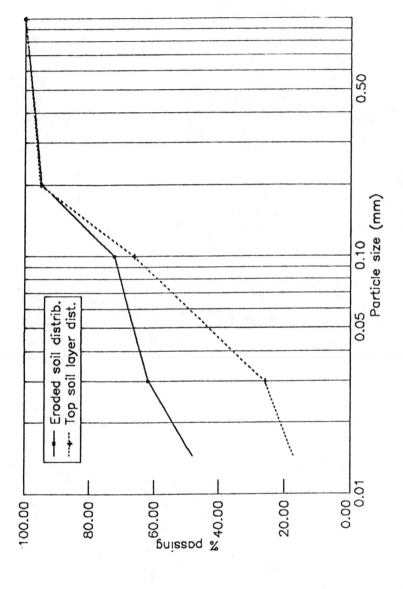

Fig. 6. Particle size distribution of eroded and top soil for Mindawo 1, 1982–83 calibration

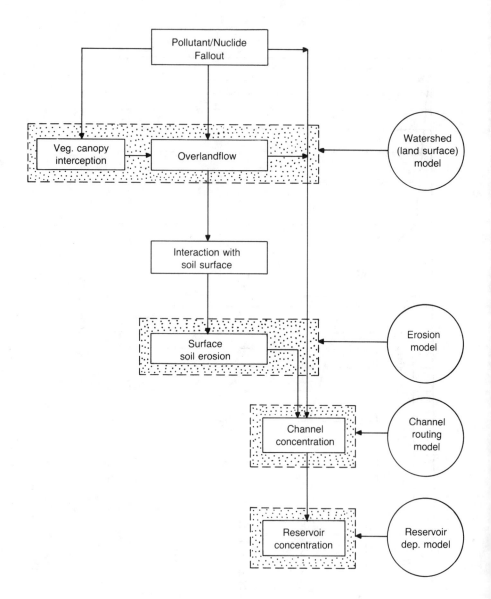

Fig. 7. Flowchart of river basin simulator

of soil 10 times larger than that held in solution in the pore space (Ref 26). The adsorption of plutonium, caesium, strontium, yttrium, and cerium ions from solution is reported to be nearly complete up to amounts equal to 0.01 times the saturation capacity of the soil (Refs 27, 28).

23. Strontium has a slightly higher adsorption energy than calcium (Ref 29). Leaching and uptake experiments indicate sites of differential adsorption (Refs 30, 29). The rate of exchange from solution to surface is rapid. for soils of high ''cation exchange capacity''(CEC), e.g. clays and silts (Ref 31), the relation is mainly complete in one minute, whereas for soils of lower CEC there is a significant rise in adsorption over a longer period of time (Ref 24).

24. With the current understanding of the attachment of radionuclides to soil particles, it is therefore possible to develop a model representing this link in the soil/water system.

THE QUALITY SIMULATOR (QS)

25. A schematic diagram showing the proposed Quality Simulator to simulate the movement of pollutant/radionuclides in a river basin is depicted in Figure 7. Superimposed on the Quality Simulator, is the River Basin Model divided into sub-models as follows; watershed, erosion, channel routing and reservoir sedimentation models. The Quality Simulator segregates the fallout of a nuclear event into various storages. These are; vegetal interception, soil surface and channel surface.

VEGETAL INTERCEPTION EFFECTS   26. Vegetal interception is the first point of contact in the movement of airborne pollutants/radionuclides through the river basin. Mechanical trapping of dry fallout, leaf absorption of specific nuclides, and retention of large amounts of debris in rainfall by wetting constitute the most significant vegetal mechanisms affecting the mobility of radionuclides. Each of these should be considered individually in computing the net effect that vegetation will exert in the over-all hydrologic transport process. The vegetation interception amounts estimated by the watershed model is a vital input to this process.

SOIL AND SEDIMENT EFFECTS

27. Soil-pollutant/nuclide interactions constitute the most important deciding process of the rate of radionuclide debris movement within the basin. Due to the adsorbing power of soils and to the large amount of soil available for exchange reactions, a pollutant/nuclide may become completely adsorbed by the soil, so that transport only occurs if the soil itself is transported. By estimating or measuring the soil sorption parameters under dynamic conditions for the specific soil, it is expected that the segregation of the nuclide between runoff water and soil during storm may be

predicted (Ref 32). The exclusion of the deep water
penetration from the Quality Simulator is justified because
measurements of Strontium-90 concentration in surface flow
and groundwater flow at Stanford University during 1963-1964
showed Strontium-90 surface water concentrations as much as
100 times greater than the Strontium-90 concentration in the
groundwater (Ref 33). They further conclude that, their data
supports the hypothesis that base flow is less important than
surface flow in determining concentrations of pollutants and
nuclides i.e. Strontium-90 in stream flow during storm
runoff.

29.   The sediment model and the quality simulator could
well be adapted for use with a physically-based distributed
models, e.g. the SHE model (Ref 33). The SHE is a distributed
model in a sense that the catchment parameters and the
rainfall input are spatially distributed. This type of land
representation by the model is illustrated in figure 3C. The
hydrological response in the SHE model is achieved in the
horizontal by an orthogonal grid network and in the in the
vertical by a column of horizontal layers at each grid
square. However, the large data requirements of this type of
model, sets a limitation for its use.

30.   Use can be made of remote sensing technique in spatial
coverage for the distribution and concentration of pollutants
and radionuclide in a basin. The following gives an example
of the potential of the Quality Simulator.

31.   Environmental studies using remote sensing radiometric
survey technique, revealed the distribution of surface
deposits of Caesium-137 on the southwest coast of Scotland
(Ref 2). An extensive 10km x 10km grid soil survey of the
area shows that major source of Plutonium-239 and 240 to the
area is from weapons fallout. Concentrations of Caesium-134
and 137 were highly influenced by Chernobyl nuclear reactor
accident. Near shore the effect of airborne sea-to-land
transfer of nuclides was insignificant. This type of survey
can reveal the deposition patterns of nuclear event and
natural distribution of uranium, thorium and potassium to a
high level of accuracy. (Ref 2).

32.   Using the proposed River Basin Quality Simulator and
the pollutants/radionuclides concentration information (e.g.
Ref 2), the movement of the nuclides within the catchment
might be simulated. Coupling this method of prediction with a
regular mapping of the basin using remote sensing techniques,
a comprehensive assessment and monitoring of the basin's
radioactivity or pollutants in any future nuclear event or
nuclear reactor accident could be achieved.

DATA REQUIREMENT OF THE MODEL

33.   Table 2 shows the data requirement of the River Basin
Quality Simulator. The table subdivides the requirements for
the watershed, erosion, channel models and the quality
simulator.

Table 2. Data requirements of river basin quality
simulator (RBQS)

Model Component	Description of Data
Land Hydrology Phase	Physical data Topography Meteorological data Vegetation area Canopy density Model parameters Runoff rate
Erosion Phase	Vegetation area Canopy density Vegetation height Vegetation roughness equiv. Drainage parameters Soil particle sizes Organic content of soil Rainfall rate Overland flow rate Top soil store Recorded erosion rate
Channel phase	Manning's roughness coeff. Overland and river flows Topography Channel cross-sections Sediment concentrations
Quality phase	Topography Leaf intercepted poll/nucl. Land surface concentr. Stream channel concentr. Type of pollutant/nuclide Physical/chemical info. of soil on land and channel. Remote sensing maps showing pollutants/nuclides concen- tration.

177

SUMMARY AND CONCLUSIONS

34. An evaluation has been undertaken of the more vital parameters involved in the proposal of a physically-based quality simulation model for numerically predicting pollutants and radionuclide movement on the land surface, in stream channels, and in a reservoir.

35. Incorporated into the proposed Quality Simulator are parameters which could be obtained from remotely sensed maps of pollutant and radionuclide concentrations and their interactions in the hydrologic cycle. These interactions include interception and drip-off by vegetation, exchanges with soil particle sizes, erosion by rainsplash and overland flow, transport to main streams by overland flow, transport and deposition in stream channels, and finally, deposition in reservoirs.

36. The proposed model could be used to predict the concentration of pollutants and nuclides in surface water, and in reservoirs at intake points where water will be utilised for domestic purposes. The model could also be used for monitoring the movement of radionuclides within a river basin.

37. Last but not least, the Quality Simulator could be used for forecasting the distribution and movement of pollutants and radionuclides in a nuclear event, in the same manner as routine weather forecasting.

38. This paper identifies the availability of hydrologic models and the understanding of the radionuclide and hydrological process interactions. It also proposes that a physically-based distributive quality model can be developed using remote sensing data as input.

39. Finally, the authors believe that this is a vital area for future research and the lack of such modelling techniques requires appropriate funding. We have developed the technology to generate power by nuclear fission, yet we have neglected to develop the necessary tools to predict the movement of emissions given an accident situation. For a society so conscious of health and safety, where seat belts are mandatory in cars, it is difficult to understand the lack of commitment to developing assessment and predictive models for radionuclide and pollutant movement within the environment.

REFERENCES

1. HOWARD B., LIVENS F. May sheep safely graze?. New Scientist, 1987, April, 46-49.
2. BAXTER, M.S. Scottish Universities Research and Reactor Centre, 1987-88 Annual Report, compiled by Whitley, J.E., produced by Thomson, G.M, 1988.
3. JONES F., CASTLE R.G. Radioactivity monitoring of the water cycle following the Chernobyl accident. Journal of the Institution of Water and Environment, No.2, 1987, vol.1, 205-217.

4. MACKENZIE D., GLEMY M. From Polish potatoes to Turkish tea. New Scientist, 1987, April, p48.
5. ED MAGNUSON, They lied to us. Time Magazine, October, 1988, 27-35.
6. JENNINGS C.D., DELFANTI R., PAPUCCI C. The distribution and inventory of fallout plutonium in sediments of the Ligurian Sea, near La Spezia, Italy. Journal of Environmental Radioactivity, 1985, vol. 2, 293-310.
7. KOURIM V. The role of sediments as related to radionuclide movement in surface waters. Nuclear Research Institute, Czechoslovak, Atomic Energy Commission. Role of sediments in the accumulation and transport of radionuclides in the waterways. Final report of a co-ordinated research programme, International Atomic Energy Agency, 1985.
8. The role of sediments in the accumulation and transport of radionuclides in the waterways. International Atomic Energy Agency. Final report of a co-ordinated research programme, 1985.
9. REYNOLDS T.D., GLOYNA E.F. Uptake and release of radionuclides by stream sediments. Environmental Health Engineering, 1961, University of Texas, Austin, Texas.
10. HAKONSON T.E., WATTERS R.L., HANSON W.C. The transport of plutonium in terrestial ecosystems. Health Physics, 1980, vol. 40, 63-69. Pergamon Press, USA.
11. SALOMONS W. Sediments and water quality. Symposium on micro-pollutants in sediment water systems, Delft, the Netherlands, 1984, Dec.11.
12. FLEMING G. Computer simulation techniques in hydrology, Elsevier, New York, 1975.
13. FLEMING G. The Clyde Basin: Hydrology and sediment transport, PhD thesis, 1969, Civil Engineering Dept., University of Strathclyde, Glasgow.
14. CLARK R.T. A review of some mathematical models used in hydrology with observations on their calibration and use. Journal of Hydrology, 1973, vol. 19, 1-20.
15. CRAWFORD N.H., LINSLEY R.K. Digital Simulation in Hydrology - Stanford Watershed Model, Technical report No. 39, 1966, Dept. of Civil Engineering, Stanford University, USA.
16. DONIGAN A.S., CRAWFORD N.H. Modelling pesticides and nutrients on agricultural lands. U.S. Environmental Protection Agency Report, EPA - 600/2 - 76 - 043, 1976.
17. WALKER J. A regional soil erosion model. PhD thesis, Department of Civil Engineering, Univ. of Strathclyde, Glasgow, 1979.
18. McKENZIE R. The effects of snow processes and land-use changes on hydrological response. PhD thesis, 1982, Department of Civil Engineering, Univ. of Strathclyde, Glasgow, 1982.
19. RUFAI G.G. The effect of hydrology on reservoir sedimentation. Unpublished MSc thesis, 1984, Department of Civil Engineering, Univ. of Strathclyde, Glasgow.
20. RUFAI G.G. Modelling the processes of erosion and land

use changes (provisional). PhD thesis (in preparation), 1989, Department of Civil Engineering, Univ. of Strathclyde, Glasgow.

21. PARK S.W. Modelling soil erosion and sedimentation on small agricultural watersheds. PhD thesis, 1981, University of Illinois at Urbana-Champaign, USA.

22. YANG C.T. Unit stream power and sediment transport. Proceedings of ASCE, Journal of Hydraulics Division, No. HY10, 1972, vol. 98, October, 1805-1826.

23. LITTLE W.C., MAYER P.G. Stability of channel beds by armouring. Proceedings of the ASCE, Journal of Hydraulics Division, No. HY11, 1976, vol. 102, November, 1640-1661.

24. FRERE M.H., MENZEL R.G. The behaviour of radioactive fallout in soils and plants. National Academy of Sciences - National Research Council, publication number 1092, 1963. Washington, D.C., p32.

25. LARSON K.H., NEEL J.W. Summary statement of findings related to the distribution, characteristics, and biological availability of fallout debris originating from testing programs at the Nevada test site. U.S Atomic Energy Commission, 1960, UCCLA.

26. ORCUTT R.G., NAOR I., KHAIN G., KAUFMAN W.J. Hydraulic and ion-exchange phenomena in the underground movement of radio strontium. U.S. Atomic Energy Commission, 1956, TID - 7517 (part 1a).

27. McHENRY J.R.,RHODES D.W., ROWE P.P. Chemical and physical reactions of radioactive liquid wastes with soils. US Atom. Energy Commission, 1956, TID - 7517, (part 1a).

28. McHENRY J.R. Ion-exchange properties of strontium in calcareous soil. Proceedings of the Soil Science Society of America, 1958, vol. 22, 514-518.

29. HEALD W.R. Characterisation of exchange reactions of strontium or calcium on four clays. Proceedings of the Soil Science Society of America, 1960, vol. 24, 103-106.

30. CLINE J.F., HUNGATE F.P. Effect of strontium and calcium in soil on uptake of Sr^{90} by barley plants, Biology Research - Annual Report, 1955, Hanford Atomic Production Operations, Richland, Washington, US Atomic Energy Commission, HW - 41500, 1956.

31. SHIH C., GLOYNA E.F. Radioactivity transport in water - Transport of Sr^{85} and Cs^{137} in an aquatic environment. Center for Research in Water Res., Technical Report No. EHE 01 - 6602, CRWR - 10, 1977, The Univ. of Texas at Austin.

32. HUFF D.D., KRUGER P. Simulation of the hydrologic transport of radioactive aerosols. Radionuclides in the environment, chapter 27, 1970, 487-505. Freiling, E.C (Ed), Amer. Chem. Soc., Washington, D.C.

33. BATHURST J.C. Physically-based distributed modelling of an upland catchment using the Systeme Hydrologique European. Journal of Hydrology, 1986, vol. 87(1/2), 89-102.

14.   Evaluation of the impact of the Nogent nuclear power plant on the Paris area water supply system

D. LEGUY and Y. RETKOWSKY, Seine Normandy Basin
Financial Agency, France

INTRODUCTION

The starting up of a nuclear power plant in NOGENT S/SEINE upstream of the main Paris area surface water intake stations led the Seine Normandy Basin Agency and the main water utilities involved to pay attention to the eventual consequences of this nuclear plant on the drinking water supply system of the area. Indeed, the river Seine itself represents one half of the drinking water resources of the area, and even more if the intake from the alluvial water table, downstream from the capital is taken into account.

Therefore, a working group, run by the Basin Agency and associating the town of Paris, the Ile de France Waterboard, the Compagnie Generale des Eaux, and the Société Lyonnaise des Eaux, was created in 1983, to study the possible impact of the nuclear plant. The main preoccupations which this study highlighted led to the studies and equipments programme that this paper intends to present.

I - A CONCISE PRESENTATION OF THE WATER SUPPLY SYSTEM OF THE PARIS AREA

The administrative region "Ile de France" consists of eight counties where over 10 million inhabitants live (1/5 of the French population). The urban area, Paris and its surburbs, which include 500 towns, is positionned in the geographical center and represents about 8.5 million inhabitants.

Within this area eighteen drinking water supply networks can be considered among which the main six supply 300 towns concentrated within a radius of 25 km around Paris. They ensure 90 % of the total consumption.

Towns or waterboards	Private water supply companies	Supplied Population
VILLE DE PARIS	Société Anonyme de Gestion des Eaux de Paris Compagnie des Eaux de Paris Société Parisienne des Eaux	2.170.000
SYNDICAT DES EAUX D'ILE DE FRANCE	Compagnie Générale des Eaux	3.980.000
SYNDICAT INTERCOMMU-NAL DE LA PRESQU'ILE DE GENNEVILLIERS	Compagnie des Eaux de Banlieue	540.000
SYNDICAT POUR LA GESTION DU SERVICE D'EAU DE VERSAILLES ET SAINT CLOUD	Société des Eaux de VERSAILLES et SAINT CLOUD	310.000
COMMUNES ET SYNDICATS DES BANLIEUES OUEST ET SUD/EST	Lyonnaise des Eaux	1.170.000
COMMUNES ET SYNDICATS DES BANLIEUES EST ET NORD/OUEST	Société Française de Distribution d'Eau	660.000

These networks which are now, fairly well interconnected are all run by private or mixed sector companies. The groundwater production capacity supplying them is about 1.2 Mm³/day. A considerable quantity comes by gravity flow from areas located over 100 km from the capital by means of aqueducts built during the last century. These groundwaters only need a sterilization treatment. On the other hand, the treatment in considerably more extensive when water comes from the alluvial tables downstream of Paris.

The other resources, that is to say, the main ones, come from the three principal rivers of the region ; the river Seine and its two tributaries : the river Marne on the East and the river Oise on the North-West. The total nominal production located on these three rivers is 3.3 Mm³ /day shared out over about 15 production units of various sizes. However, the river Seine is still the most frequently used source (about one half of the total). It should be pointed out here, that the intake from these rivers is possible thanks to :

- the dams upstream on the Seine and Marne basins which enable the rise of low water flow in particular

- the efforts made to cope with most industrial and urban pollutions

- the development of more and more efficient facilities in water treatment plants.

Nevertheless during a drought periode (i.e. Summer 1976) or in case of a massive accidental pollution of a river the quantity and quality of water would only be just sufficient to cope with the demand.

II - THE STUDIES AND EQUIPMENTS PROGRAMME WHICH WAS INITIATED PRIOR TO THE STARTING UP OF NOGENT POWER STATION

From the beginning, as a result of the announcement of the opening of NOGENT nuclear power plant, the working group, already mentionned, successively considered the possible chemical, thermal and radioactive impact of the nuclear plant, according to a studies programme divided into seven themes :

- a continuous observation of the quality of water in the Seine and drinking water intake,

- radioactivity alarm devices were installed upstream of the main waterworks,

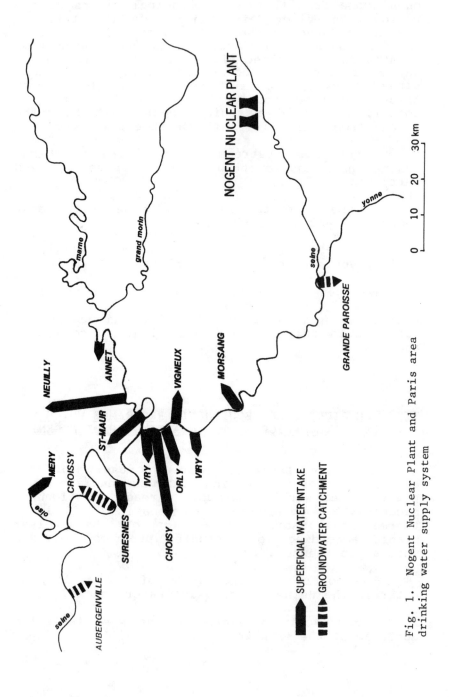

Fig. 1. Nogent Nuclear Plant and Paris area drinking water supply system

- studies of the feasability of treating radioelements in the water treatment plant facilities,

- radioecological synthesis of the main regional rivers,

- evaluation of the risks for the catchment area according to incident and accident scenarios drawn up by the nuclear security services,

- impact of a rise in temperature of the water on algae population and Seine physico-chemical quality around the actual intake-points,

- prevention of classical accidental pollution (adequate precautions when stocking and handling non radioactive toxic products) within the nuclear plant.

The conclusions of the working group given in 1984, have especially shown the water suppliers and basin agency's concern to know about and follow the evolution of the radioactivity of the Seine and the capacity of the area's water supply system to cope with all the foreseeable working situations of the nuclear plant (up to and including a highly improbable major accident).

These concerns were taken into account and led them to think harder about the accident situation themes, that is to say :

1 - The definition and setting up of a proper analysis structure for the water utilities, in addition to the Service Central de Protection contre les rayonnements ionisants network including:

a β total radioactivity analysis device for each of the three largest waterworks on the Seine (MORSANG, ORLY, CHOISY),

a more sophisticated radioactivity measurement laboratory at the ORLY plant, enabling selective γ radiation measurements,

a continuous measurement and alert station for β and γ total radioactivity at NANDY upstream of all the urban area's waterworks.

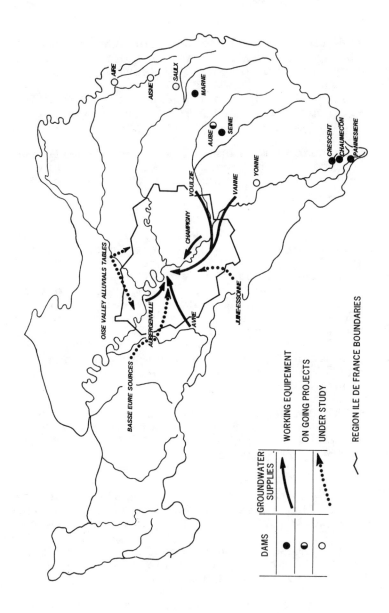

Fig. 2. Dams and groundwater supplies for the urban Paris area

Today, all these devices are operational and a study of the measurements shows no impact of the nuclear plant on the global radioactivity of the river Seine.

2 - Evaluation of the feasability of treating Seine water tainted with radionuclides according to two complementary methods :

- doping of Seine water with radionuclides (concentrations from 400 to 800 Bq/l) and treatment in an experimental station copying the CHOISY LE ROI treatment plant facility. These tests will allow us to examine on one hand the ability to reduce the radioactivity in various working conditions and on the other hand, to study the accumulation of the radionuclides in the clarification and filtration sludges,

- neutronic activation measurement of Seine water throughout the CHOISY LE ROI treatment plant. The method of analysis consists in bombarding a water sample with neutrons so as to transform the elements capable of being activated it contains, into γ emitters whose concentration can then be measured by spectrometry.

The first results of these experiments show, in the main, that the clarification and filtration stages would bring the Cs 134 count significantly down, while at the same time the I 131 seems to pass through all the different stages intact.

We must however be careful when we look at these results which are still only partial.

3 - Evaluation of the consequences of a nuclear power reactor accident on the Paris area water supply system

The methodology used with the collaboration of the Nuclear Safety Protection Institute was the following

* Analysis of the different types of discharges and natural environment contamination :

- direct atmospheric discharge after a failure of the confinement envelope

- discharge due to a leak or a burst of a storage tank containing contaminated water

- passage of the molten core throught the cement floor of the barrier wall.

Among these three scenarios, the first was selected as being the most worrying for an eventual contamination of the Seine river water intake. The second one would have merely led to a lesser contamination and the third one would have implied an important transfer time thus making it less crucial than the first one.

* Determination of the "source term" (radionuclides discharged during a major nuclear accident)

In the scenario, the faulty reactor is supposed to discharge a level of radioactivity represented by the "source term" S_3. It corresponds to a melting down of the core given that, during the first 24 hours following the melt down the barrier wall remain air tight. The discharge during this period are therefore limited to the "natural leaks" from the barrier wall. Beyond this time, as a result of the rise in pressure, the engineer in charge is compelled to discharge the radioactivity over 48 hours through the sand filters system which has a minimal capture efficency for aerosols of 90 %.

* Development of models of :

- atmospheric diffusion and dry and wet deposits on the soil,

- wash off, run off and transfer to the Seine of the source term.

In particular, the data which we choose were :

. Meteorology :

- wind speed : 5 m/s, normal diffusion

- wind direction : West (local prevaling winds) blowing from 270 $\pm$ 30 °

This direction is the one which will lead to maximal fallout in the Seine basin upstream of NOGENT.

. Raingauging : two hypotheses

- no rain during the radioactive discharge,

- 1 mm/h rain during the radioactive discharge

. Hydrology :

- Rate of flow in the Seine at NOGENT 40 m³/s (= 100 m³/s in MELUN, i.e. the average low water flow)

- soil retention of the radioactivity deposits : two hypotheses :

* 95 % (run off, wash off coefficient = 0,05)

* 80 % (run off, wash off coefficient = 0,20)

(the sedimentation phenomena in the river haven't been taken into account, which is pessimistic).

The calculations have therefore been made for the following three hypotheses :

- dry weather

- 1 mm/h rain, run off wash off coefficient = 0,05

- 1 mm/h rain, run off wash off coefficient = 0,20.

The results are expressed in terms of activity discharge of the Seine at NOGENT, bearing in mind the number of the most important isotopes at different times. It then became quite evident that the main isotopes in terms of radiological consequences are I 131 and I 132. In dry weather, the activity discharge of the Seine in I 131 would reach 4.10^8 Bq/s about 36 hours after the beginning of the accident.

In wet weather the maximum reached is clearly higher (10^9 Bq/s in I 131) and there is a considerably longer contamination duration.

The contamination in C_s, particularly 134 and 137 is about one tenth of the contamination level of I 131. The level for S_r 90 is about one hundred times weaker.

* The routing in the Seine of the pollution from the nuclear plant to 40 km downstream of Paris

This phase of the study enabled us with the help of the simulation model Disperso (developed by the basin agency, the Compagnie Generale des Eaux and the Ile de France waterboard) to determine the evolution in the Seine of the concentrations in major elements C_s 134 and I 131 after a nuclear accident.

The calculations showed, with the most infavourable hypotheses chosen as follows :

- rainfall on NOGENT = 1 mm/h

- run off wash off coefficient = 0,2

- radionuclides periods I 131 = 8,05 days

C_s 134 = 750,00 days

that the I 131, though disappearing quite quickly, involves the most important constraints.

Indeed, between the 8 th and 16 th days after the accident (that is to say during 8 days) the concentration in I 131 would be above 400 Bq/l in the raw water supplying all the water intake stations (from MORSANG to SURESNES). The concentration would either exceed 400 Bq/l at the important ground water catchment areas of CROISSY and AUBERGENVILLE further downstream but the transfer time from the river to the alluvial table would put off the appeerence of the radioactivity in the water of the wells for several days.

For Cs 134, the concentration in the raw water would exceed 800 Bq/l at all the water intake stations but for a shorter time (3 days) between the 10 th and 13 th days following the accident.

In these conditions and given that the security rules that the water suppliers adhere to (to abstract raw water only when its activity level is below the crisis thresholds to be applied for drinking water), the whole superficial water intake of the Seine would be closed down for 8 continuous days.

* Consequences on the Paris area's drinking water supply system

. On one hand, the important investment programmes which has been undertaken for several years now, by all the water utilities in the area, with the financial help of the basin agency :

- development of the nominal capacity of the main waterworks and increase in the usage of ground-water resources,

- modernisation of treatment plants facilities,

- development of : emergency interconnections (including link Marne-Seine),

- Creation of : raw water storages and drinking water reservoirs

. And on the other hand the most recent on-going projects :

- emergency supply for the IVRY plant with water from the Marne basin (SAGEP),

- emergency intake in the Essonne for the Morsang plant (Lyonnaise des Eaux),

- increase of the intake and treatment capacity of the NEUILLY S/MARNE plant (SEDIF),

will soon enable the Paris area's drinking water supply system to cope with the consequences of the accident described above without harm to the consummers (it should, however be noted that the calculations have been made with a consumption level equal to the daily average consumption plus 10 %).

III - <u>CONCLUSIONS</u>

In current working conditions, the discharge of the NOGENT nuclear power plant, located on the river Seine 150 km upstream of the main Paris area waterworks does not in any way harm drinking water production.

As well, in the case of a major accident which we should stress is a highly improbable event and which would prevent any water intake in the Seine for a whole week, the Paris area's drinking water supply system would be able to go on supplying the consummers correctly.

This would be no longer true, if an accident occured closing down simultaneously other resources especially the river Marne which becomes in this scenario the backbone of the regional water supply system.

Consequently the principal efforts to be made in the future, to increase the safety of the Paris region's water supply system would concern :

- the construction of a new dam on the river Marne and a better control of all accidental pollution,

- and the maximal development of the ground-water intake especially with the laying of water supply pipes from the resources still available (Basse Eure, Juine Essonne sources and Oise Valley alluvial tables) towards Paris.

Discussion

Dr J. Sinnaeve, *Commission of the European Communities, Brussels*
It has been mentioned several times that ingestion by water is a minor
pathway. However, drinking water quality in general and
contamination with radionuclides is a matter of outspoken public
concern. In the case of an accident, for surface water uses the zero-risk
approach is not applicable. What can be done by the utilities to improve
the information for and communication with the public, and what would
be the efficiency of additional filtering?

Dr P.A. West, *North West Water*
Despite intensive monitoring by government and the water industry of
water supplies in the event of a nuclear event, some members of the
public will probably desire greater reassurances over water safety, and
will seek this by purchase and use of 'point-of-use' filtration devices.
The water industry can anticipate that enquiries will need to be handled
from local government and the public over the efficiency of these devices
for removal of radionuclides. Is there any evidence that these
off-the-shelf devices could be effective in providing additional protection
of water supplies, and is there a possibility that their use could be
adverse in resulting in a moderately radioactive filter which may pose
problems of disposal?

Dr I. Gans, *Institute of Water, Soil and Air Hygiene, Federal Health Office,
Berlin*
I should like to comment briefly on removing radionuclides by means of
simple filter devices. One has to bear in mind that the chemical mass of
radionuclides in water is very, very small. Therefore, the removal
mechanism is associated with the stable isotapes. Radionuclides can be
removed only if one removes the corresponding stable element to the
same degree. There is no way to remove just the radionuclides by
conventional water treatment.

Mr A. Barber, *Engineers for Nuclear Disarmament*
Since the major proportion of radioactive contamination of the food
chain is from animal products, do we know how the radionuclides are
taken into the animal? Is it by one or all of the following: dry deposition

Nuclear contamination of water resources. Thomas Telford, London, 1990.   193 of fall-out on ground/grass; fall-out contained in rain falling on grass; fall-out in drinking water consumed by the animal?

Mr R. Clayton, *Crowther Clayton Associates*
With reference to Paper 12, we are experiencing an increase in pesticides in groundwater as a result of the increasing use of pesticides over the past two to three decades; there is a significant time-delay between cause and effect. Can Dr Hansen be certain that the radionuclides with much longer half-lives will not eventually appear in groundwater - even in the excellent Danish groundwater which he described?

Professor S. Bergström, *Swedish Meteorological and Hydrological Institute*
Papers 13 and 14 represent two fundamentally different approaches to the problem of modelling the hydrological consequences of a nuclear event. Paper 13 suggests the use of relatively advanced modelling techniques, while Paper 14 is based on a very simple description of the climatological and hydrological conditions.

The problem has much in common with that of modelling the long-term consequences of acid rain, when it comes to a combination of traditional runoff models and advanced hydrochemical considerations. This requires more physically correct models than does traditional runoff modelling, in particular as concerns water pathways and transit time distribution of the water in the ground. For example, studies of the concentration of oxygen-18 in precipitation and runoff have shown that the transit time of water is grossly underestimated in most rainfall-runoff models in use today. Another common feature of the two disciplines is the difficulty of verifying the models against reliable field data. We have as yet very little data available to support models of long-term acidification, and we have few nuclear events as well.

As concerns the two papers, there are some questions on the hydrological modelling, which should be of general interest. Paper 13 suggests relatively advanced hydrological modelling, although all modelling is a crude simplification of nature. Different hydrological models can often give almost identical runoff simulations, while their potential for hydrochemical simulation varies greatly on account of the different descriptions of water pathways. Is the physical foundation of the suggested hydrological models stable enough for application to radionuclides? Have the models been sufficiently verified against field data other than runoff? For example, what is the physical interpretation of the interflow component of the modified Stanford watershed model? What about the transit time distribution? Table 2 shows quite extensive data requirements. Can these be fulfilled in the normal case? Although a model is classified as physically correct, belief in the model requires model verification. This is especially the case when we try to model complex processes, such as the migration of different kinds of radionuclides in a heterogeneous environment. How shall we be able to verify the models so that we can trust them in the case of a nuclear accident? What use can we make of data from the Chernobyl disaster?

Paper 14 describes a very crude way of estimating the contribution of radionuclides to the river. Has a more complete hydrological model been considered and, if so, why was the idea abandoned? The two climatological and hydrological scenarios suggested do not seem to represent very extreme conditions. What are the probabilities and what is the rationale for using these probabilities? The results are, of course, sensitive to both choice of model and assumed hydrological and climatological conditions. Has this sensitivity been analysed, and what were the results?

Dr V. Dubinchuk, *International Atomic Energy Agency, Austria*

In the IAEA, several programmes are being implemented relating to environmental problems. Some of them, for instance the VAMP programme, are dealing with modelling of radionuclide migration in terrestrial, aquatic and urban systems. Another study, being undertaken by the Isotope Hydrology Section, is on nuclear techniques in pollutant transport and is concerned with interaction between solute and rock (methodological aspects). In the framework of the programme, isotope tracer techniques are being developed and used in order to evaluate the residence time distribution function of water and pollutants (including radionuclides) in field and laboratory conditions. The techniques are really a general way to get information for forecasting goals. For example, data on the concentration of tritium in atmospheric precipitation (onput to all hydrological systems) and in surface and groundwaters (output) are widely used to estimate the mean residence time of water as a carrier of pollutants (radionuclides). Then it is possible to use any independent or isotope tracer data on retardation factors (effects) for water in the given system to obtain the residence time of given pollutants. For instance, if the mean residence time is 1 year and the retardation factor is 5, then, evidently, the mean residence time of the radionuclide will be 1 x 5=5 years. It means that on average any sudden impact will be reflected in concentration variations in 5 years.

If we had models (such as those described in Paper 13 and in Paper 10), with known residence time in each compartment, the migration of radionuclides could be forecast. In such estimates, a number of isotope tracer techniques mentioned above would be very useful as well as the concept of residence time distribution. The Isotope Hydrology Section has made and is trying to make relevant efforts in this field to achieve mutual co-operation with national and international communities. International and national efforts in this direction should be continued.

Mr R. Castle, *North West Water*

I agree with Professor Flemming (Paper 13) that modelling of water supply systems for the movement of radionuclides would provide a useful means of managing water resources in the event of a nuclear event. However, I should like to stress that the monitoring of water supplies to produce actual figures for the level of contamination is the best way to reassure the general public. To this end I believe all water service comparisons etc. should have access to a means of measuring gross alpha and gross beta activity in water supplies.

Dr Miller, *Paper 11*

Public reassurance is a matter of prime importance following a nuclear accident. There will be a need to respond to water consumers with little background in radioactivity, and to the more informed sector including environmental groups and the media. Consumers will simply need to be told whether the water is safe. It is important for water suppliers to have some simple yardstick to use with which to provide reassurance. In the UK, it is proposed that utilities should have means of measuring activity on their major sources to provide a basis for this reassurance. Environmental groups and sections of the media will seek more detailed information and are likely to have greater familiarity with the subject. It is important, therefore, that some members of staff in the utilities have a good background in this field in order to deal with the technical aspects raised. One problem in this area is the increasing tendency to challenge the view of 'the expert'. Therefore, it is important that water utilities build up confidence in their consumers by adopting an open approach at all times so that assurance given during times of emergency is more readily received.

On the question of point-of-use devices, it is unlikely that significant removal would be achieved by simple mechanical filters, as the activity is unlikely to be present in a particulate form. Ion exchange units are likely to be more effective and there is some evidence that activity from radioiodine could be reduced significantly by activated carbon. Where the activity level is high enough to cause concern, units which give effective removal would give rise to an additional hazard on account of the accumulation of nuclides with longer half lives. Disposal of the spent cartridge would in this case require special advice.

Dr Hansen, *Paper 12*

With regard to the uptake of radionuclides in the food chain, we do know a great deal more about this process now, thirty years after the nuclear weapons fallout in the late fifties and early sixties. Both dry and wet deposition, as well as both root uptake and direct uptake through plant surfaces are involved in food contamination. Table 3 gives an overall view. The fact that we have assayed groundwater for such a long period does give us a substantial guarantee against any unpleasant surprises in the future from new and so far unheeded radionuclides.

Professor Fleming and Mr Rufai, *Paper 13*

Professor Bergström touches the heart of the problem of mathematical modelling; he is correct when he states that all rainfall runoff models are a simplification of nature. However, it is important to remember that the quantification of hydrological processes, because of the highly dynamic variation, is not an exact science. The second point to be remembered is that the modelling approach recommended in our paper is intended for application before a nuclear event, in order to determine the response of river basins to different scenarios of rainfall and runoff. For this reason, sensitivity analysis can be applied, and the response of these river basins to input can then be analysed. The transit time of water is indeed a most important process to get correct in the simulation, but this will depend very much on whether we are trying to model iodine or caesium radionuclides. Each has a different half life.

The physical foundation of the suggested hydrological models is, in our opinion, stable enough for application in order to research the ability to simulate the movement of radionuclides. The paper stresses, however, that a considerable amount of research is essential in this area, in order to verify the runoff models and to show that they are stable for the purpose intended. Research at the present time is not of the highest national priority, but, in our opinion, it must take a high priority in the future if the movement of a number of pollutants, including radionuclides, is to be fully understood and hence counteracted by engineering.

The database required for such models is extensive, but it can be obtained, particularly now that we have further data on radionuclide concentrations in soils obtained by remote sensing. This type of additional data makes the problem of simulation and the interpretation of inputs much more accurate, although not absolute.

A more complete hydrological modelling approach would invariably use a distributed system, and such a distributed system would require considerably more data. The argument which we have put forward is that as the problem becomes complex, the database to be used in the analysis will become equally complex. If we are unwilling to take an analysis to this depth of understanding, then we will not in the future be in a position to mitigate the effects of such contaminations. It must be remembered that Chernobyl has occurred and the engineers at that time were not in a position, either to use models or to understand the distribution of the radionuclides in the system. Indeed, three years after the event, we still do not know the distribution of the radionuclides throughout the soil water systems of the river basin draining from the contaminated areas and elsewhere in Eastern and Western Europe. Hence, the modelling approach is one which must be deployed to increase our understanding of the problem.

We fully agree with Dr Dubinchuk that the current research into isotope tracer techniques will be extremely valuable in estimating and understanding the residence times and transit times of water and the pollutants which it carries. This will go some way to improving our modelling techniques, and the research on model development must be integrated with research using isotope tracer methods.

We also fully agree with Mr Castle that the best way to reassure the public is to measure the actual contamination in the water supplies and to make these publicly known. However, the modelling techniques proposed by us are to enable us to predict in advance and, it is hoped, in real time, what the response scenarios might be to a nuclear event which takes place on a particular river basin. The two methods are complementary and should be developed as such in the future.

Mr Leguy, *Paper 14*
The development of a finer model of hydrological processes implicated

in the calculation of outflow to the Seine has not, for the moment, been considered. The aim is to encompass the order of magnitude of the duration of non-availability of intake of potable water into the river, not to approximate better the physical phenomena.

It is true that the climatic and hydrological scenarios held do not represent the most extreme conditions, but rather the more probable ones, in terms of climatology as much as of hydrology. Sensitivity tests are currently being set up, with much harsher scenarios. First results appear, nevertheless, to confirm the length of time that the Seine is not available for the production of potable water.

15. Public water supply sources — the practical problems

E.G.W. CHAMBERS, MBA, BSc, MICE, MIWEM, Strathclyde
Regional Council, Glasgow, UK

SYNOPSIS. A complex system of reservoirs, streams, treatment
works and pipe networks is used to provide the public water
supply to consumers in Strathclyde. The manner in which a
nuclear event would affect the quality of water available from
this supply would depend on a wide variety of factors. The
extent to which the quality from each source could be
maintained or improved if found to be unsatisfactory would
depend on the extent of contamination and the particular
characteristics of each source. Development of contingency
plans will incorporate monitoring of supplies and development
of effective communications both internally and externally.

WATER SUPPLY ARRANGEMENTS IN SCOTLAND
1. Within Scotland, local services are provided by three
forms of local government organisations, Regional, District
and Island Councils.
2. The mainland of Scotland is divided into nine Regions.
Within each of these Regions, a Regional Council of elected
Regional Councillors is responsible for the provision of major
services including education, social work, strategic planning,
industrial development, roads, water and sewerage.
3. Each Region is sub divided into a number of Districts.
Each District Council is responsible for the provision of more
locally based services including housing, cleansing,
environmental health, detailed planning and leisure and
recreation.
4. Islands Councils are single purpose authorities
providing all the services required by the limited populations
resident on the offshore islands of Orkney, Shetland and the
combined Western Isles.
5. Thus Regional and Island Councils are the authorities
responsible for the provision of water supply, sewerage and
sewage disposal functions to the domestic population and
industry located within their Regions. As water authorities,
these Councils are statutorily obliged by the provisions of
the Water (Scotland) Act 1980. The principal duty imposed by
this legislation is the provision of an adequate supply of
wholesome water for domestic purposes throughout its area of
supply where this can be provided at reasonable cost.

Nuclear contamination of water resources. Thomas Telford, London, 1990.

6. Following the introduction of the European Commission Directive 80/778 on Quality of Water Intended for Human Consumption (ref. 1) the standards specified in that Directive have become to be accepted as the definition of the term wholesome. These standards are likely to be enforced more rigorously as a consequence of the promotion of Water Regulations for Scotland under the mainly English orientated Water Act 1989.

7. In respect of standards for the radionucloid content of supplies, this Directive is silent. As reported by previous presenters Jones (ref. 2) and Miller (ref. 3) considerable attention has been given to the setting of standards but as yet no definitive agreement has been reached. In view of the emotive nature of radioactivity, it would be very beneficial if widely accepted standards could be established at an early date.

WATER SUPPLY ARRANGEMENTS IN STRATHCLYDE

8. Strathclyde Region covers an area of 13851 square kilometres in west central Scotland including the islands of the Clyde Estuary and a number of islands in the Inner Hebrides.   There is a resident population of some 2.3 million people within the Region and a wide variety of agricultural, commercial and industrial activities.

9. Strathclyde Regional Council is water authority for this area except for a small area in the Cumbernauld and Kirkintilloch areas of the Region. At the present time, in excess of 99% of the population are connected to the public water supply system.   The balance are isolated individual or groups of properties remote from the existing public supply network and which cannot be connected at "reasonable cost". These properties have to rely on private wells or stream intakes for their water supplies.

10. The Regional Council's Water Department supplies daily some 1080 Ml of treated water to its distribution system. Consumer and other studies have shown that each domestic consumer uses on average 130 litres per day and that this is used for the following purposes:-

Activity	Actual Use (litres/person/day)	Percentage Use
W.C. Flushing	42	33
Dishwashing & cleaning	29	23
Personal washing & bathing	26	20
Laundering	21	16
Drinking and cooking	11	7
Gardening and car washing	1	1
Total	130	

11. Some 340 Ml. is supplied daily to non domestic
consumers.   This water is used for the wide variety of
commercial, industrial and agricultural activities found in
the mixed urban/rural economy of Strathclyde.   Water is
used by non domestic consumers:-

- in major water using industries e.g. chemicals, paper
  making, electronics;
- in shops, offices and non water using industries for
  "domestic" purposes;
- in food processing and manufacturing industries;
- in food preparation etc. associated with cafes,
  restaurants and hotels;
- in agricultural and horticultural activities;
- in schools, colleges and universities;
- in leisure based industries and activities.

12.   These supplies are provided from a network of:-

        10   Natural lochs
       139   Impounding Reservoirs
             (Local intakes on streams
        93 -(Springs
             (Boreholes

13.   Traditionally water supplies in Strathclyde have been
developed on the basis of discrete sources supplying local
communities.   Consequently, a wide range of size of supplies
is currently in use reflecting the large number of former
water authorities.   One of the major benefits derived from
the Regional water supply system created in Strathclyde has
been the opportunity to rationalise supplies and interconnect
major supplies. Although an extensive programme of
rationalisation and modernisation of supplies is presently
underway to ensure that they all meet the Directive's
standards it will be necessary to continue to utilise many of
the very small supplies currently in use for the foreseeable
future.

14.   The largest supply for which the Regional Council is
responsible is the reservoirs in the Loch Katrine complex -
Loch Katrine, Glen Finglas, Loch Arklet, Loch Drunkie and Loch
Vennachar.   This complex is capable of maintaining a daily
supply of 450 Ml per day while discharging a compensation flow
of 227 Ml per day to the River Teith which itself flows into
the River Forth.

15.   Similarly, supplies are made available to consumers in
Strathclyde from the Loch Lomond Regional Scheme.   This
scheme is operated by the Central Scotland Water Development
Board and can supply some 403 Ml per day to consumers
throughout the Central Belt of Scotland from the 87,000 Ml. of
water made available for water supply purposes from the Loch's
top four feet of water.

16. By comparison, in Argyll, the smallest sources currently in use are at Claddich and Kilberry which serve some six and eight properties respectively. At both locations the system comprises of a burn intake, coarse screen, balancing tank and chloros disinfection plant and distribution pipework. On the Island of Arran in the Firth of Clyde, the Catacol source supplies 21 properties and the Kings Cross supply 35 houses from similar systems to those in Argyll

17. As the vast majority of supplies are derived from upland reservoirs or streams, the water abstracted for distribution through the public water supply system tends to be coloured and acidic and thus requires treatment before supply to consumers. As noted in paragraph 13, a programme of treatment works rationalisation and modernisation is underway. Works are being, or will be, undertaken at some 138 sources to ensure full compliance with the standards specified in the E.C. Directive.

18. In the interim, a wide variety of water treatment processes are in use. The simple and inadequate nature of many of these facilities again reflects the historical development of supplies by small authorities lacking the necessary expertise in water supply provision and the standards then accepted by consumers. These facilities include:-

1. Coarse screening followed by disinfection;

2. Fine screening followed by disinfection and lime addition;

3. Slow sand filtration followed by disinfection;

4. Single stage chemical treatment involving rapid gravity filters or pressure shell filtration followed by disinfection and normally final ph correction;

5. Complex two stage treatment involving primary settlement followed by secondary filtration in rapid gravity or pressure shell filters followed by disinfection and final pH correction;

6. Ozonation of one supply.

19. The opportunity presented by the formation of the single water authority for Strathclyde Region to develop a Regional water supply system has been taken. Progress made during the life of the former Water Boards to link supplies has been continued by Strathclyde and considerable progress achieved with the further linking of major supplies. This interlinking of supplies enables water to be introduced from alternative sources in the event of operational difficulties being experienced with one particular supply or it becoming necessary to undertake major maintenance on a supply. It is also of particular importance during periods of reduced

rainfall, as has been experienced this summer, when available water can be redistributed to minimise the effects of reduced rainfall in particular areas or inadequate supply provision.

20. The availability of an adequate and safe water supply is thus of critical importance to the continuation of the normal life cycle of the inhabitants of Strathclyde. The majority of consumers do not appreciate the complexity of the public water supply system. It is taken for granted that a supply of colourless water of sufficient volume and pressure to meet individual needs will be available as and when required. The disruption which can result from a failure to meet this requirement only becomes apparent to consumers when their supply has to be interrupted or its quality deteriorates following operational difficulties with some aspect of the system.

FACTORS AFFECTING SIGNIFICANCE OF NUCLEAR EVENT ON WATER RESOURCES OF STRATHCLYDE

21. The particular effects of a nuclear event involving the release of radionuclides on the quality of water available from the public water supply system within Strathclyde will depend on a wide variety of factors. These factors can be summarised by the following headings:-

1. Source of event
2. Nature of event
3. Rainfall pattern following the event
4. Wind pattern
5. Time of year
6. Source of water supply

Source of Event

22. The effects of a particular incident would clearly be significantly influenced by the source of the event. Within Strathclyde itself, there are two types of installation having the potential for creating difficulties. The S.S.E.B. operates two nuclear power stations at Hunterston near Largs on the Clyde estuary. Both the British and United States navies operate bases servicing their submarine fleets within the Clyde estuary. A number of nuclear powered submarines operate from these bases including those equipped with polaris and poisidon ballistic missiles. In the near future, trident missiles are to be introduced.

23. Although outwith Strathclyde, the nuclear power stations at Torness and Chapel Cross are situated within 50 and 20 miles of the Region's boundaries. British Nuclear Fuels facilities at Sellafield are also located only 40 miles south of the major sources at Bradan and Daer.

24. However, as the Chernobyl incident illustrated, it is not only nuclear events at "local" installations which may pose threats to the water resources within the Region. It must be recognised that the effects of an incident at any nuclear facilities within the United Kingdom or the majority of Western Europe could have an effect on the Region's water resources.

Nature of Event

25. As recognised by previous speakers there are several pathways by which radioactive contamination can enter water resources. The simplest route is the direct discharge of radioactive effluent into water courses subsequently used as the source of the public water supply.

26. An alternative route involves the discharge of gaseous and fine particulate material into the atmosphere. These discharges may subsequently settle by gravity or be washed to the earth's surface by rainfall.

27. The final route would result from an accident involving the spillage of radioactive fuel or material in transit within the Region leaking into a source of the public water supply.

28. Within Strathclyde, there are no direct discharges into water courses used to supply the public water supply system. Similarly as the vast majority of water sources are situated in remote upland areas, the potential for a transit orientated incident is considered to be small.

29. Consequently, the implications of an incident involving the aerial pathway is the situation which requires greatest consideration. The magnitude and location of any discharge would clearly influence the possible effects on the water supply system.

Rainfall Pattern

30. As noted in the previous paragraph, the aerial pathway route is the most likely manner in which the effects of a nuclear event would lead to the water supply system in Strathclyde becoming affected. Consequently, the rainfall pattern experienced during the period following an incident would be critical in determining the nature and extent of any effects experienced. Total rainfall, its intensity and distribution will be of importance. As has been experienced during this summer, significant differences in rainfall pattern can occur throughout the Region. During the early summer, parts of the Region received only 50% of long term average rainfall as compared to other parts receiving the average level of rainfall.

Wind Pattern

31. As for the rainfall pattern the direction and strength of wind experienced following an incident would be significant in determining the extent and distribution of radionuclide material deposited on water sources. The prevailing wind pattern in the west of Scotland is broadly westerly.

However, reflecting the cyclonic pattern of the weather experienced winds from all aspects of the compass from south to north west cannot be considered to be unusual.

32. An easterly wind does tend to be unusual and tends to occur only for short periods during the winter. This situation clearly has significant implications for the situation which would arise in respect of the Torness facilities.

Time of Year

33. The effects of a particular event would depend on its date of occurrence and the weather conditions experienced during the previous three months. As the water supply system within Strathclyde is largely serviced from upland sources, reservoirs and streams tend to have excess water available during the winter months. Throughout most winters reservoirs are full and overflowing and streams are passing flows many times in excess of that to be abstracted. In that situation the dilution effect of radioactive deposits is likely to be very considerable. However, in these circumstances, the catchment areas of reservoirs and stream intakes tend to be saturated so that run off will be relatively rapid.

34. By contrast, during the summer months and as particularly experienced during the past summer, the volume of water available in reservoirs and streams can be seriously depleted and catchment areas can become dried out and stream flows reduced to trickles. In that situation, it could be anticipated that contamination would be retained within the catchment area but that the effects on reservoirs could be more significant when run off occurred due to the reduced opportunities for mixing with uncontaminated water stored in the reservoir.

Source of Water Supply

35. As noted in earlier paragraphs, a wide variety of sources are used to service the public water supply system within Strathclyde. The particular effects of a nuclear event on individual sources would be influenced by the nature of that source. Whereas the effects on a stream intake could be expected to be reasonably rapid; the effects on a major reservoir could be expected to exhibit completely different effects both in respect of timing and extent.

36. The differential effects would be further exacerbated by the nature of treatment available. While doubt exists about the efficiency of water treatment processes in reducing the level of radionucloids in water, clearly no reduction in the level of contamination would be possible at these sources provided with minimal treatment. Those sources with treatment could expect to reduce contamination although the extent will depend on the nature of the treatment facilities, the quality of the raw water available and the operating efficiency of the particular facilities.

DEVELOPMENT OF ROUTINE AND CONTINGENCY PLANS

37. As has been described in previous paragraphs, due to the geographical size of the Region, the public water supply system serving Strathclyde is a complex network of reservoirs, stream intakes, springs, treatment works and pipe networks. The water resource consequences of a nuclear event on the operation of this complex system would depend on a wide variety of factors.   Before considering what steps could be taken to ameloriate the effects of these consequences, consideration has to be given as to what the Council as water authority would be expected to achieve in the event of a nuclear event insofar as the provision of public water supplies is concerned.

38. In the event of a catastrophic accident similar to that at Chernobyl occurring within or in close proximity to the Region, it would not be possible to sustain normal lifestyle in the area surrounding the source of the incident Consequently a different set of criteria would have to be considered but would involve detailed consideration of the implications of the factors detailed previously.

39. Water supplies are used for a wide variety of purposes.   It is my belief that except in the event of a catastrophic local incident, present knowledge indicates that the only problem which might arise from the radionuclide contamination of public water supplies in Strathclyde would be associated with the ingestion of drinking water containing radionuclides or the use of this water in the manufacture or preparation of food.   Consequently, it is likely that the public water supply would continue to be of a standard suitable for all the purposes detailed in paragraphs 10 and 11 particularly the maintenance of toilet and washing provisions and the vast majority of non domestic purposes as normal except for those associated with dietetic needs.

40. The measures to be taken must be aimed at trying to ensure that water of acceptable quality was available for drinking and food manufacture and consumers clearly understood the extent to which supplies could be utilised.   The extent to which supplies for dietetic purposes are considered a risk or unsatisfactory will depend on the standards ultimately set for the radionuclide content of drinking water and water in food.

41. On this basis, the features being incorporated into my Department's operating procedures and contingency plans include:-

- monitoring of supplies on a routine basis and at increased levels following a nuclear event.
- alterations to operating practices at reservoirs, treatment works and throughout the water distribution system.
- communications with consumers, elected members, specialist agencies, regional and government departments and committees.

Monitoring

42. Three of the atmosphere monitoring sites established under the United Kingdom government's RIMNET scheme are located within Strathclyde at Tiree, Oban and Machrihanish. Reflecting the prevailing pattern of westerly winds, it is advantageous that these sites are along the western periphery of the Region. It is anticipated that the equipment installed at these sites will provide the first warning and information on the extent of increased radionucloides whether or not details of any future nuclear event are made known.

43. The radionuclide content of water samples collected from major reservoirs throughout the system is also being monitored on a routine basis under a programme co-ordinated by the Scottish Development Department (S.D.D.). The S.D.D. is the central government department responsible for overseeing water supply in Scotland. This national programme has been augmented by a Strathclyde programme under which the Council's Regional Analyst measures the radionuclide content of water drawn from other sources. This latter programme ensures that every source in use throughout the Region will be sampled annually and sources supplying in excess of 16Mld^{-1} quarterly. As experience gained nationally during the Chernobyl incident showed the radionuclide content of waterworks sludge increases more significantly than that of the final water, sludge from a number of treatment works will also be monitored under this programme. It is anticipated that these arrangements would highlight any increases in the radionuclide content of water resources throughout the Region.

44. In the event of increased activity being detected or information received of a nuclear event, sampling of sources will be rapidly increased. The Government's National Response Plan (ref. 4) identifies the additional sites to be included in the national programme of monitoring. The choice of sources to be sampled by Regional staff would be made after assessment of the factors identified in paragraphs 21 to 36 as being critical to the likely effects of an event. The sampling programme to be followed will be a balance reflecting the need to monitor the low risk supplies serving the Region's large population centres and the potentially high risk sources serving small populations.

Alterations to Operating Practices

45. In the event of this monitoring identifying that the radionuclide content of individual or groups of sources has increased significantly limited alterations could be made to operating practices to try to reduce the effects on the quality of supply at consumer taps. The opportunity to make alterations would obviously depend on the characteristics of the particular source.

46. If the effects were confined to a small number of sources, the first factor to be considered would be whether the pipe distribution system could facilitate the introduction of unaffected or less affected water from another source.

If the substitution of supplies was possible, arrangements would be made to withdraw the affected supply and introduce the alternative source. The radionuclide content of the withdrawn supply would continue to be monitored and only reintroduced when it was found to be satisfactory.

47. If substitution of supplies is not practicable, consideration would then have to be given to the operation of the affected sources. For supplies using water abstracted from impounding reservoirs opportunities may exist to minimise the radionuclide content of the raw water abstracted. Where raw water can be made available to a treatment works from different reservoirs, the quality of water may vary from reservoir to reservoir. Use of the reservoir with lowest radionuclide content and withdrawal of the other reservoir or reservoirs would clearly be beneficial in that situation.

48. Most large reservoirs and many small have been provided with draw off arrangements which allow raw water to be abstracted from different depths of the reservoir. Consequently, the radionuclide content of supplies may be reduced by changing to another draw off level. Initially, it is likely that the lowest draw off would be the most appropriate but as the initial radioactive runoff settled into the depth of the reservoir, the highest draw off may give the lowest levels of radionuclides. Determination of the best draw off level would require the monitoring of the radionuclide content of the water throughout the depth of each affected reservoir.

49. Evidence available suggests that the water treatment processes in use in Strathclyde may be effective in removing proportions of radionuclides from raw water supplies. The removal efficiency will, however, vary depending on the type of treatment, nature of the raw water and the radionuclides present. Alexander (ref. 5) has estimated that the removal efficiences of the processes in use in Strathclyde could be:-

WATER TREATMENT Process	Chemical coagulation, Settling and/or filtration	Slow sand filtration
Removal Efficiences of Radionuclides by Water Treatment Processes	(%age reduction)	
^{51}Cr	10–98	
^{32}P	68–99	80–99
^{90}Sr	0–70	0–5
^{91}Y	80–91	
^{106}Ru	77–96	
^{131}I	0–44	50–99
^{137}Cs	0–6	50
^{144}Ce	80–94	99

50. Some confirmation of the improvements possible has been gained from studies of treatment works performance during the Chernobyl incident (ref. 6) and from very limited measurements taken at the Bradan source in the Region.

51. Within Strathclyde, detection of significantly increased radionuclides in raw water would immediately result in an appraisal of the operating practices at treatment works associated with the affected sources. At those few sources still relying on slow sand filtration, the only opportunity available to improve performance would be to reduce the rate of filtration. This could only be achieved by reducing demand at the works either by partially replacing supplies from another less affected source or persuading consumers to reduce their consumption.

52. At those works with single stage chemical treatment, performance could be improved by reducing throughput particularly where this allowed optimisation of chemical dosing. Performance could also be improved by increasing the frequency of backwashing of filters. This would, however, reduce the quantity of water available for supply to consumers, could lead to difficulties with the disposal of the backwash water and sludge and would have significant manpower implications.

53. The most significant reductions in radionuclide content would be achieved in the two and three stage chemical treatment plants in use and being provided under the programme of rationalisation and modernisation underway. This type of plant removes both the natural impurities present in the raw water and chemicals added to improve the treatment process. Their performance in respect of radionuclide impurities could be improved in a number of ways.

54. To obtain the maximum possible yield from each source treated, supernatant water collected from backwash water is normally returned to the plant inlet and retreated. If the radionuclide content of the raw water increased, this recirculation would be stopped as evidence available (ref. 6) confirms that the sludge processes concentrates the radioactive impurities. This situation could expose employees at treatment works to risk of increased exposure and difficulties with the safe storage and disposal of this washwater and sludge. Arrangements would consequently also have to be made to resolve these ancillary problems. As for the previous filtration systems, removal efficiencies could be further reduced by reducing throughput and ensuring that chemical dosing is maintained at optimum levels. The reduction in throughput could again only be achieved if surplus quantities of water from less affected sources could be introduced into the supply area or consumption reduced.

55. No improvements to the levels of radionuclides present would be possible in those treatment works relying on coarse or fine screening. These are mechanical processes which aim only to remove debris and particulate matter. If the quality of raw water available to those sources could not be improved

to an acceptable level, consideration would have to be given to the practicability of providing consumers with non piped supplies for dietetic purposes.

56. As noted earlier, the quantities of water used for drinking and dietetic purposes are very limited. In the Civil Defence plans formulated for implementation in the event of nuclear war, current thinking indicates that the population would be asked to store some 1.2 litres of water per person per day.

57. Experience of the maintenance of non-piped supplies for dietetic purposes has been gained by this Department during the execution of major maintenance programmes on water mains. During this work it is necessary to interrupt normal supplies for periods of 48-72 hours. Throughout the period of the work supplies are delivered to individual consumers in 20 litre containers fitted with a small tap. On any one day upto 250 homes can be supplied and this level of activity can be sustained for upto six months.

58. The maintenance of supplies is, however, a very labour intensive activity. The extent to which non piped supplies could be provided to consumers would depend on the availability of suitable quality of water, containers and labour to deliver the water on a regular basis. While the Water Department's existing resources could sustain the maintenance of non-piped supplies to two or three of the smaller sources, extension of the arrangement to further small sources or any of the large sources would require very considerable external assistance with the provision of labour and containers.

Communications with Interested Parties

59. There has never been a greater need than presently exists for the maintenance of good communications between employees of the Water Department, consumers, elected members and representatives of the press, interested bodies and agencies. This need would be exacerbated following a nuclear event because of the level of experience and knowledge amongst Water Department staff, elected members, consumers and representatives of the press about acceptable levels of radionuclides and the potential risk from their presence in public water supplies. Consequently, the issue of good communications and training will be addressed in the contingency plan being prepared.

60. To avoid unnecessary confusion and duplication it is envisaged that if an event occurred co-ordination of communications will be carried out by one senior member of staff. Lines of communication will have to be established with the groups detailed in the following paragraphs:-

61. The Scottish Office's incident control centre to be established under the National Response Plan arrangements. This would ensure that the latest information is available on the known or anticipated extent, spread and nature radionuclide contamination and the advice being offered by the

Technical Co-ordination Centre on water supply matters. It would also facilitate the flow information to these bodies on the situation within Strathclyde and any needs for information or assistance with labour or specialist materials or equipment.

62. Water Department staff engaged on the operation of reservoirs, treatment works and distribution systems. This would be necessary to co-ordinate the execution of measures considered necessary to maintain the supply of adequate quality water or improve any supplies identified as not being satisfactory. Reassurance may have to be provided to employees as to their own safety and any precautions to be taken particularly with the handling of washwater and sludge in treatment works.

63. Another important aspect of communications with staff will be the provision of clear and unambiguous information to allow them to answer enquiries from members of the public. No matter how comprehensive or specific the advice issued direct to consumers, inevitably individual consumers will seek clarification of their own particular circumstances.

64. Communications with individual consumers will also be of particular importance. During the Chernobyl incident, limited numbers of enquiries were received seeking reassurance about the safety of water supplies. However, in any further incident, it is anticipated that the level of enquiries will be of a different magnitude due to the post Chernobyl debate and provision of information. Consequently, public relations arrangements with consumers will have to be co-ordinated and unambiguous.

65. In the very unlikely event that consumers have to be advised to stop drinking water from the public supply system, it would be desirable to issue each household or business affected with a letter. This letter would outline the extent of the problem, indicate those activities for which water could and could not be used and advise of the arrangements to be made to maintain alternative supplies.

66. Communications through the media - radio, television and newspapers would provide another route to consumers. It would be imperative that information issued to the press was consistent as experiences gained during periods of operational difficulty have shown the confusion which can arise if all statements made by staff are not consistent. In order that local managers can deal with press enquiries concerning local situations, the adequacy of the internal communications with staff previously referred to will be of critical importance.

67. Reflecting that the Regional Council is water authority, good communications will also have to be maintained with the Chairman of the Water and Sewerage Committee and elected members. These communications will be maintained on the basis of informal briefings, issue of copies of press releases and staff information sheets and formal reports to Committees. Communications would also have to be maintained with the Council's Emergency Planning Officer and Regional

Analyst as they would be undertaking specialists roles and providing liaison, information and advice.

CONCLUSIONS

1. Strathclyde Regional Council supplies some 1,080 Ml of treated water to domestic and non domestic consumers daily through a complex system of reservoirs, stream intakes, treatment works and pipe networks.

2. The effect of a nuclear event on the quality of water available from each source will depend on a wide variety of factors including the source, nature and date of the event, the pattern of rainfall and wind following the event and the facilities provided at each source.

3. Except in the case of a local catastrophic incident, on the basis of present knowledge and standards, water of acceptable quality will be available for all purposes except possibly the provision of drinking water and water used in the manufacture or preparation of food.

4. The extent of problems to be experienced with the provision of drinking water will depend on the acceptable standards ultimately agreed and the nature of any future incidents.

5. Monitoring of all Regional sources is now being undertaken on a routine basis and would be increased in the event of a nuclear event occurring or an increasing radionuclide content being detected in water supplies.

6. The extent to which the radionuclide content of raw water could be reduced during the water treatment process will depend on the nature of the contamination, the overall quality of the raw water, the treatment facilities provided and opportunities available to reduce the demand on the particular works.

7. In the very unlikely event that it become desirable to provide alternative supplies for dietetic purposes, existing resources would only cope with very limited demand. Large scale provision of alternative supplies would require external assistance with the provision of labour and equipment.

8. Provision of effective communciations would be of paramount importance during the period following a nuclear event if standards were to be maintained at the highest possible level and public confidence maintained in the safety of the public water supply.

REFERENCES
1. EUROPEAN COMMISSION. European Community Council Directive No. 80/778/EEC Relating to the Quality of Water Intended for Human Consumption. Official Journal of the European Communities, No. L229.11.
2. JONES M.W. The UK national response plan for nuclear accidents overseas. Paper 6 to Conference on Water Resources Consequences of a Nuclear Event, University of Strathclyde, Glasgow, UK September 1989.

3.   MILLER D.G.   The consequences of a nuclear event on water resources - the UK and other European countries.   Paper 11 to Conference on Water Resources Consequences of a Nuclear Event, University of Strathclyde, Glasgow, UK September 1989.

4.   DEPARTMENT OF THE ENVIRONMENT   The National Response Plan and Radioactive Incident Monitoring Network (RIMNET) Phase 1, Her Majesty's Stationery Office, London, 1988.

5.   ALEXANDER B.   New Tasks of Water Undertakings with Regard to Environmental Problems, I.W.S.A. Congress, Rio de Janeiro, September 1988.

6.   JONES F. and CASTLE R.   Radioactivity Monitoring of the Water Cycle, October 1986 I.W.E.M.

16. Safety of drinking water supplies to suburban Paris: analysis and control of radioactivity at Choisy-le-Roi

M. RAPINAT, Compagnie Générale des Eaux, Paris, and
J. M. PHILIPOT and J. L. CADET, Compagnie Générale des
Eaux, Choisy-le-Roi, France

SYNOPSIS. In order to anticipate the nuclear power plant set up at Nogent/S/Seine 150 Km upstream the Choisy-le-Roi water treatment plant (800.000 cubic meter per day) and more generally to assume the safety of water distribution and cope with the risk of casual pollution the Syndicat des Eaux d'Ile de France and the Compagnie Générale des Eaux have undertaken several stringent actions.

- founding in 85 a new laboratory branch for radioactivity measurement.
- adding new elements to the existing alarm network (automatic analysis of the raw water quality).
- studies for the treatability of radioelements.
- using protected resources (ground water).
- set up of a second treated water feeder between the river Seine and the river Marne areas.

Others projects are under study, as the creation of a raw water reservoir and increasing the capacity of treated water stockage.

INTRODUCTION

The Ile de France water board supplies drinking water to some 4,5 million subscribers in the suburbs of Paris. The annual volume distributed via the system is in the region of 350 million cubic metres. The water Board derives its feedstock mainly from the rivers Seine, Marne and Oise and, in view of the deterioration of the raw water, has been pursuing a stringent policy to protect the quality and safety of production ever since the early seventies.

On the river Seine, the largest of the Water Board's production units in capacity (800,000 m³/day design rate), the Choisy-le-Roi waterworks, has seen its initial treatment train drastically altered in order to reach and maintain the highest possible quality level. This facility, is of the biological type. It consists of ozonation prior to the injection of reagents in a tank specially designed to permit optimized

contact times and the addition of emergency products when
necessary (pH adjustment, reducing agents, powdered activated
carbon), followed by clariflocculation, biological filtration
on sand, an ozonation stage combined with secondary biological filtration on granular activated carbon plus final chlorination. The substitution of ozonation instead of prechlori-
nation, on the one hand, and the combination of ozonation and
GAC filtration, on the other, ensures the biological removal
of both ammonia and organics. the fact of switching chlorination to the end of the treatment has greatly improved the quality of the water produced : less organo-halogen compounds
and unpleasant tasting substances are generated.

This sytem reproduces at an accelerated rate the phenomena
that contribute towards self-purification in a natural environment ; like any state of biological equilibrium, it is sensitive to the effects of toxic matter that may be acciden-
tally discharged to the river due to pollution hazards.

THE PHENOMENON OF ACCIDENTAL POLLUTION

Every year, we record on the Seine, upstream of
Choisy-le-Roi, fifteen or so cases of accidental pollution,
some of which may involve adjustments to the treatment, a
slowing down of operations on the waterworks and perhaps even
the shutdown of the pumping station. In their awareness of
this situation, the Water Board and its tenant operator,
Compagnie Générale des Eaux, have undertaken a series of
actions at different levels.

1 - Surveys

- Identification of hazardous areas : these surveys conducted
by Compagnie Générale des Eaux in close collaboration with
the Classified Installations Department, the Directorate of
Industry and Research and industrialists themselves have
resulted in improved knowledge of existing hazards, the identification and location of dangerous stocks, improvement in
preventive measures and in the awareness of those concerned.

- Modelling the behaviour of the different pollutants on being
spilt in the natural environment : DISPERSO model, effective on
soluble and pseudosoluble products, is bidimensional. It gives
accurate information as to the time a sheet of pollution is
liable to flow perpendicular to the water intake, as well
as the concentration of the product and the time the distur-
bance is likely to last in order to anticipate the emergency
measures required.

- Participation in drawing up a regional and district emergency
procedure and in the engineering of an internal alarm system.

2 - <u>Safety investments</u>

- Creation of a raw water storage basin,
- Interconnection of networks between the Seine, the Marne
ant the Oise and intercommunications with neighbouring distri-
butors,
- diversification of resources,
- creation of alarm station networks upstream of the water
intakes.

Since the nuclear power station of Nogent-sur-Seine was commissioned in 1985, the pace of investments on safety has been
stepped up.

HAZARDS DUE TO NUCLEAR POWER PLANTS

1 - <u>Products and analysis</u>

Since 1978, the natural dose equivalent attributable to drinking water has been limited by the W.H.O. to a maximum of
(0.05 mSv) 5mrem.

On this basis, the Maximum Admissible Concentrations adopted
for total alpha, and total bêta radioactivity respectively are
3 pCi/l (0.1 Bq/l) and 20 pCi/l (0.8 Bq/l).

In anticipation of the installation of the Nogent-sur-Seine
nuclear power plant, a radioactivity control laboratory was
set up at Choisy in 1985.

<u>Total alpha and total bêta radioactivity control</u>

The alpha radionuclides likely to be found in water are mainly
U (238 235 234) Th (232 231) and daughter products.

The bêta generating isotopes that one is most likely to en-
counter in water are Sr (90), Cs (134), Cs (137), K (40),
Co (60), Mn (54), Na (24) and C (14).

Total alpha and bêta radiation control is done by means of a
gaseous current meter.

The alpha and bêta rays ionize the gas in the meter and the
ionization is then detectable.

The results obtained on the Suspended Solids and filtrate of
water sampled before and after the power station went into
action in September 1987 have been below the metering detection threshold i.e., approximately :

- 0,01 Bq/l on S.S.
- 0,20 Bq/l on filtrate.

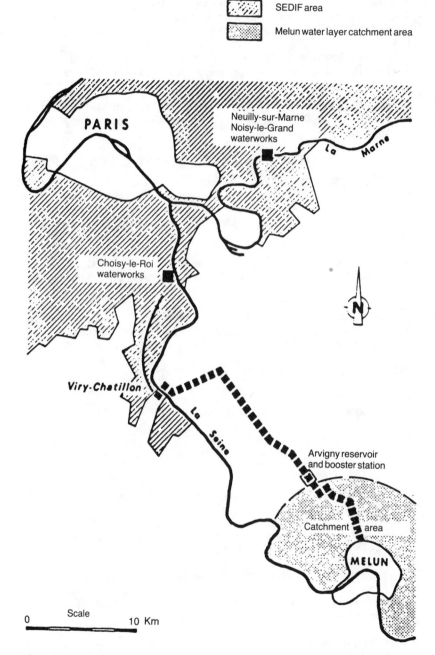

Fig. 1. Feed from Melun water layer (Champigny limestone)

Control of total gamma radiation

The gamma generating radionuclides the most often found in water are : Be,Cs,Co,Mn, and Ce.

In order to monitor the impact of the liquid effluents discharged by the nuclear power plant (especially) those composed of Co (60) and Cs (137), a continuous detector measures the total radioactivity at the Choisy-le-Roi water intake point. The instrument used is a scintillator consisting of a Nal crystal probe and signal transmitter.

The alarm threshold was set at 400Bq/l, which is the current emergency threshlod under project as a European standard for drinking water.

If this limit is overshot, the analyzer automatically samples the water, by means of a hydrocollector, and this sample is sent to a concerned laboratory.
Until today, no alarm signal has been triggered by this detector.

Preventive radioactivity monitoring in the Seine waters is combined with complementary measuring by an official organisation. The procedures for prompt transmission and analysis of the samples are now perfectly tuned, which should guarantee optimum application in the event of emergency occur.

Lastly, we should like to point out that special watch is kept on the impact of the liquid effluents discharged by the power plant into the river.

Boron, sulphates and chlorides are regularly analyzed (use of boric acid used for nuclear reaction and of sulphuric acid and sodium hypochlorinte used in the conditioning of coolants).

2 -Alarm system

Upstream of the Choisy-le-Roi intake structure, there is a network of alarm stations capable of detecting all the "usual" pollutants, such as those generated by organic or mineral spills including hydrocarbons, ammonia and heavy metals. These stations will be completed by continuous radiation measuring instruments as soon as reliable equipment appears on the market.

3 -Capability of treatment trains to treat radionuclides

The SEDIF and the C.G.E, with the assistance the Basin Authority, are conducting a series of pilot-scale tests faithfully reproducing the Choisy-le-Roi treatment system, in order to examine :
- possibilities of abating radionuclide activity in different operating configurations ;

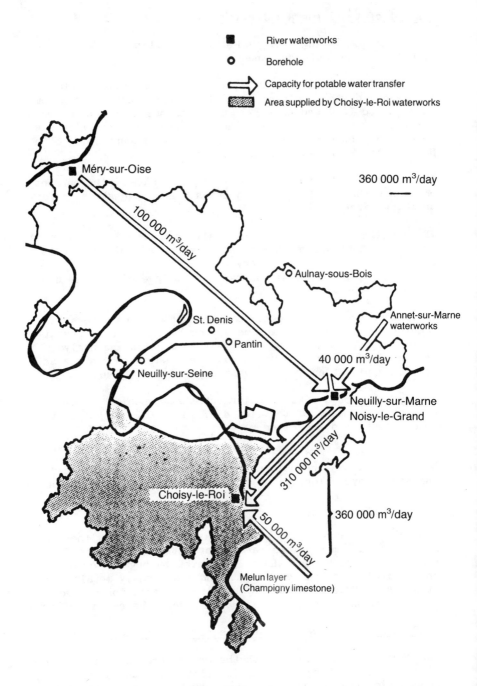

Fig. 2. Emergency feed for Choisy-le-Roi works as at July 1988

- the accumulation of these elements in the by-products generated in the course of potable water treatment : sedimentation
tank sludge and dirty wash water from sand and activated
carbon filters.

Those tests are not yet finished, but it already appears that
for water contaminated in some extent, significant abatements
are obtained.

This study will enable us to define the optimum operating
conditions for the treatment train and the most suitable
reagents to use in a crisis.

REINFORCED SAFETY EQUIPMENT

To stand up to pollution for any length of time with the
possible shutdown of the Seine intake structure, it is vital
to reinforce the safety equipment to avoid having to cut
off the water supply. Our solution was to increase transfert
capacities and the diversification of resources.

1 -Diversification of resources

One of the best methods of protection against nuclear hazards
is to draw on resources that are practically unexposed, such
as ground water. Compagnie Générale des eaux operates deep
wells on behalf of the SEDIF at Albien, Sparnacien,
Neuilly/S/Seine, Pantin, Saint-Denis, Aulnay and
Issy-les-Moulineaux.
Permits to tap fossil layers are strictly rationed and bring
only a margianl contribution compared with the volumes of
water delivred in the territory supplied by the water Board
(about 2.5%). Although this is indeed a marginal amount, it
would nevertheless be of capital importance, should there
ever be a regional disaster causing all intake from the rivers
to be stopped. With the help of exceptional emergency permits
to increase pumping and well-organized emergency measures, it
would enable the subsistence needs of the population to be
satisfied.

A further step in the direction of more diversified resources
was taken in 1988 with the commissioning of a feeder originating in the limestone layer of Champigny, tapped north of
Melun. This plant includes the catchment field and 8
drillings, a storage capacity of 500 m³, a booster station
and a 25 km feeder with a nominal diameter of 800 mm termina-
ting south of the network under the influence of Choisy-le-Roi.

This feeder supplies, in normal operating conditions,
33.000 m³/day and can deliver as much as 50.000 m³/day in an
emergency. Extension works are planned to bring this flow rate

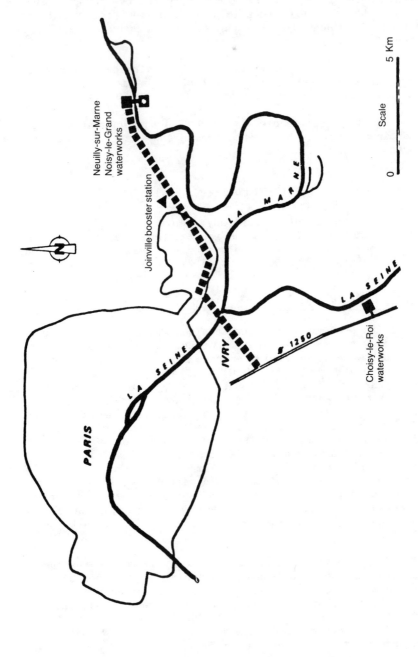

Fig. 3. Second feed of filtered water Marne–Seine

up to 80.000 m³/day. During its first 6 months in operation, this standby system was called into action four times for serious hydrocarbon pollution causing the operating rate of the Choisy-le-Roi waterworks to fall to two-thirds of its normal output.

2 -Increasing transfer capacities from the Marne to the Seine and vice versa

Since the end of the seventies, the first ND 1250 mm feeder linking the Neuilly-sur-Marne and Choisy-le-Roi water works was inaugurated. It operates in both directions and provides the transfert of 270.000 m³/ day at low pressure and 150.000 m³/day at high pressure i.e. in the case where the lifting pump of either of these plants is cut off. A similar interconnection exists between Méry-sur-Oise in the North and Neuilly-sur-Marne. Its transfer capacity is 100.000 m³/day.

In 1985, the SEDIF decided to construct a second link between the Seine and the Marne, in consideration of the start up of the nuclear power plant at Nogent-sur-Seine. Work began in March 1986 and the link was operational by the beginning of 1988. Fifteen kilometers long with a ND of 1250 mm, this pipe main is laid in a ditch in a densely built-up area and crosses numerous obstacles (the Seine, motorways A4 and A6, the R.E.R. and other railway tracks).

The amounts transferred are 200.000 m³/day from the Marne to the Seine and 150.000 m³/day in the opposite direction.

A booster station had to be built haf way accross, enabling the first lifting stage of the choisy-le-Roi network to be directly supplied from the Marne.

The possibilities of transfer from Marne to Seine and makeup supplied from the Melun water layer make it possible to close the Choisy-le-Roi intake in the event of an emergency without suspending the distribution of drinking water.

CONCLUSION

The best way to increase the safety of the drinking water supply system at all levels is of concern of the leading water distributor of France (3rd biggest in Europe). In the safety-investment programme to protect the water supply in the coming years, action is taken on two fronts :

- To increase Water Board reserves to 24 hours (average consumption). The present reserve is sufficient for approximately 17 hours. Two reservoirs are about to be built, one at Châtillon at the Ist lifting stage with a capacity of 50.000 m³, the other at Villejuif at the 2nd lifting stage with a capacity of 8.000 m³ ;

- to study the possibility of creating a raw reserve common to both the strategic water works i.e ; Choisy (Water Board) and Orly (SAGEP), whose intake structures on the Seine are very close together.

17. Impact of fall-out and management of removal by conventional water treatment

W. J. MASSCHELEIN, R. GOOSSENS and A. DELVILLE,
Laboratories of Brussels's Intercommunal Waterboard, Brussels,
Belgium

SYNOPSIS. Twenty isotopes were identified in Belgian waters
during the Chernobyl fall-out. The most significant were
^{103}Ru, ^{132}Te, ^{131}I, ^{134}Cs and ^{137}Cs. ^{90}Sr was not found.
At present, the data on their removal rate have been com-
pleted by the use of tracers on a full-scale plant. The tra-
cers used were : ^{58}Co, ^{103}Ru, ^{134}Cs, ^{131}I and ^{85}Sr. Even
though flocculation has been confirmed as the main removal
process, new evidence on the reversibility of the fixing in
the sludge has been produced. It is not possible to formulate
a single well-defined removal rate by the process, however
management options are presented. The removal of cesium by
sand filtration is very significant.

INTRODUCTION
1.   The potential impact of nuclear power plants on the
water resources is increasing with the steady increase of
the number of the units installed as well as the production
capacity of the latter. As far as the radioactive discharges
are concerned, several types must be considered : discharges
in normal operation, leakages during minor accidents, effluents of nuclear fuel processing units, dismantling operation
risks and consequences of major accidents. Most fortunately
it must be noted that during years the nuclear power stations
have known to be an industry with high operational security.
However, preliminary investigations indicate that if a significant or major accident did occur it would have dramatic
consequences on the available water resources, concerning
at least a zone defined by a radius of 16 to 20 km and in a
sector zone up to a distance of 80 km (1,2). If we apply
these assumptions to the Belgian area, the conclusion reveals
that no significant waterwork is out of danger (see Figure
n° 1).

2.   Consequently, the Brussels' Waterboard has made provision to face with radioactive discharges and has installed
all necessary control facilities. These facilities have been
proven to be operational at the time of the Chernobyl accident (3,4,5).

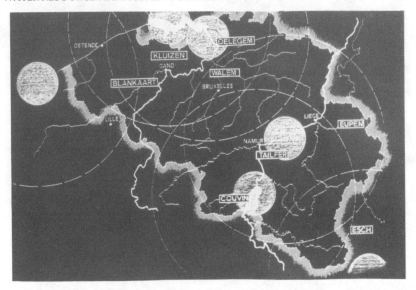

Fig. 1.   Location of nuclear power plants (Belgian area).

3.   During the fifties and sixties, several over-view
publications have summarized the investigations concerning
the removal of radioisotopes by coagulation-settling and
other treatment procedures, both in Jar Tests and pilot
investigations. Considering the most significant isotopes of
the Chernobyl fall-out and summarizing the data of that time
(6,15) we have as following :

Elimination by Jar Test treatment: 0-6 % for ^{137}Cs;
0-6 % for ^{89}Sr; 0-10 % for ^{131}I. Yields can be increased by
adding clay, except for iodine. Removal of iodine is improved
by adding activated carbon; in which case 60-75 % removal have
been claimed (8,11,12,14).

Elimination by sand filtration: up to 30 % removal of
^{137}Cs by filtration has been described (14). Dissolved
cesium was removed less than "adsorbed cesium".

Softening and ionic exchange: significant removal of
ionic isotopes e.g. 40-80 % for strontium and also for
iodine.
Thusfar no explicite data has been reported for ^{132}Te and
^{103}Ru in representative conditions of drinking water treatment. The fixing by adsorption on bottom sediments is often
considered as a determinant phase of removal (9,15).

4.   The purpose of this contribution is to report the behaviour of a classical water treatment plant, during the remote
Chernobyl fall-out, to complete the available data by results
of investigations on full-scale and to formulate management
options applicable in critical periods.

CONTROL FACILITIES AT THE BRUSSELS' WATERBOARD
5.   One of the important water resources of the Brussels'
Waterboard is a plant located on the River Meuse, about 45 km
downstream of the site of French-Belgian nuclear power plants
in Chooz. Therefore, the control and prevention of radioactivity of the water delivered from the plant is considered to
be a vital question. Falicities have been installed to evaluate and to control the importance of the radioactivity of the
water under normal conditions of operation.

6.   The laboratory of the Tailfer plant, is equipped with
two γ -detectors and a liquid scintillation counter.
(a) The first is a 3 inch Na I-cristal counter, surrounded
by 10 cm of lead and coupled to a 1000 multichannel analyser.
This detector is used only for semi-quantitative determination
on a raw water sample in the energy range of 340 tot 1340 keV.
These countings enable us to follow-up the γ -activity of the
River Meuse. The first detection of the Chernobyl fall-out
was carried out with this device.
(b) The second γ-detector is a 3 inch Ge cristal, surrounded
by 10 cm lead and coupled to a 8000 multichannel analyser
(Canberra, series 40). In normal operation, this counter is
used to control the activity of the suspended matter, the
sediments and the sludge provening from the treatment of the
water of the River Meuse. Water samples are counted in a 4
liter Marinelli Vessel. Solid samples are dried at 105°C and
counted in petri-disks.
(c) The tritium activity, released by the nuclear power plant
(16) is measured by the liquid scintillation counter (Pac-
kard Tri-Carb 1500).
(d) The central laboratory in Brussels is equipped with more
facilities (16).

CHERNOBYL FALL-OUT IN BELGIUM - IMPACT ON WATER - 1986
7.   The Chernobyl fall-out was detected in the water from
May 3rd on. A first peak value was observed on May 5th and
6th and a second, more important one on May 9th. Fig. 2.
gives the evolution of the gross β-activity in raw and
treated waters. The isotopes detected correspond to the
list of nuclides evidenced in aerosols during the same
period (16,17,18); furthermore, the concentration factor in
the sludge has enabled to complete the list. The most significant nuclides in the drinking water were ^{131}I, ^{103}Ru,
^{134}Cs, $^{99}Mo-^{99m}Tc$, $^{106}Ru-^{106}Rh$, ^{140}La, $^{132}Te-^{132}I$ and $^{95}Zr-$
^{95}Nb. Their removal by treatment ranges between 30 and 70 %.
The gross β -activity of the treated water remained below
1 Bq/l, with an average removal of 45 ± 12 %. The average
removal of γ -emittors attained 27 ± 12 %; the latter depends
on the nuclide. Unlike normal condition in which activity in
water is measured, the back-ground due to the activity of
the air was not neglectible.

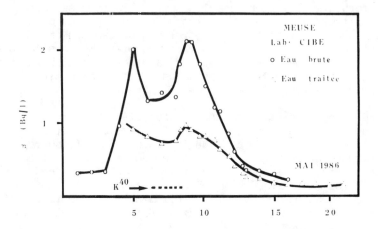

Fig. 2. Total β-activity of Meuse water (May 1986).

8. Regarding the long-term effects of the Chernobyl fallout, the adsorption on river sediments and the particulate
matter suspended in the river waters has proven to be significant. The main isotopes involved were ^{134}Cs and ^{137}Cs.
Fig. 3. shows the evolution of the radiocesium content of
the sludge at the Tailfer plant.

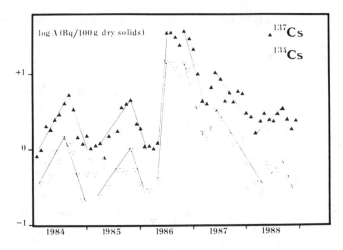

Fig. 3. Fixation of cesium isotopes on flocculated
matter.

FURTHER EXPERIENCE

9. In order to estimate to the efficiency of a conventional water treatment as used at the Tailfer works the following tracers were used : ^{58}Co, ^{103}Ru, ^{134}Cs, ^{131}I, ^{85}Sr. The major objective of this study was to determinate the concentration factor in the sludge and to formulate a model for the management of the operation accordingly (ref. 5). During the experimental period the raw river water quality was sufficiently constant in order to accomplish mass balance : 40,25 g dry solids are obtained in the sludge produced by 1 m^3 raw water.

It contains the following components.

- suspended matter from the River Meuse	12	g
- activated carbon	6,25	g
- activated silica	3,25	g
- organic compounds from the River Meuse	5	g
- Al (OH)$_3$ (partially hydrated))	13,75	g
	40,25	g

This balance relates the activity measured in 1 g dried sludge originated from 25 l treated water.

10. Experimental results are summarized in figures 4, 5 and 6.

The hatched areas on the figures correspond to the release of activity from the sludge after the injection was stopped.

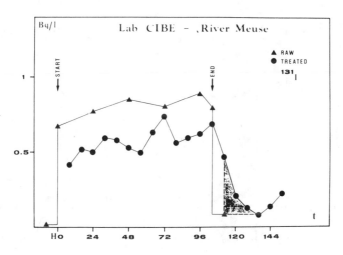

Fig. 4. Removal rate of ^{131}I (time in hours).

The activity measured in the settled water are the same as those in the filtered water except for Cs as indicated later. The removal efficiencies of individual isotopes are :
^{131}I = 17 %, ^{103}Ru = 73 %, ^{58}Co = 61 %, ^{85}Sr = 3 %.

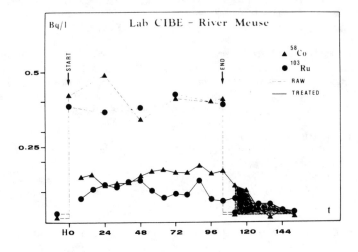

Fig. 5. Removal rate of ^{58}Co and ^{103}Ru (time in hours).

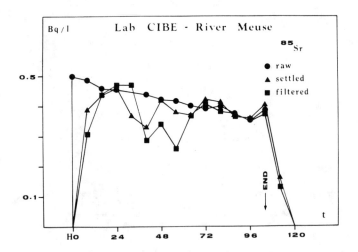

Fig. 6. Removal rate of ^{85}Sr (time in hours).

Table 1. Activity balance for individual isotopes.

Raw water flow : 1600 $m^3 h^{-1}$; sludge bleed : 45 $m^3 h^{-1}$; sludge load : 64,8 kg h^{-1} dry material.

Isotopes	^{103}Ru	^{58}Co	^{134}Cs	^{131}I	^{85}Sr
Activity injected Bq m^{-3} KBq h^{-1}	390 624	410 656	410 656	790 1264	421 674
Activity in sludge Bq g^{-1} KBq h^{-1}	7 454	6,17 400	3,17 205	3,25 211	0,08 8
Activity in settled water : Bq m^{-3} KBq h^{-1}	99 158	172 275	283 452	622 995	403 645
Activity in filtered water : Bq m^{-3} KBq h^{-1}	95 152	169 270	181 290	625 1000	408 652
Balance KBq h^{-1}	-18	+14	0	-53	-14
Excess - deficit (in percent)	-2,9	+2,1	0	-4,2	-2
Avg. removal rate (in percent)	73	61	56	17	3

ACTIVITY ON SLUDGE
    11.   After several hours of injection there occurs a
saturation of the sludge layer. This takes place approximately 64 hours after the beginning of the experiment.
The equilibrium activities reported on the basis of "dry
sludge" are : ^{103}Ru : 7   Bq/g
             ^{134}Cs : 3,17 Bq/g
             ^{131}I   : 3,25 Bq/g
             ^{58}Co : 6,17 Bq/g
             ^{85}Sr : 0,08 Bq/g
These values are typical for the settlers in Tailfer and
could be system-dependent.
The gradual saturation of the sludge layer up to the saturated activity level (As) can be described for the investigated
isotopes by classical mass transfer equation between phases.

231

$$- \frac{dA}{dt} = k (As - A) \text{ which on integration for } A=0$$

and t=0 gives $\ln \dfrac{As - A}{As} = - kt$

After a system-dependent period, related to the flow conditions, like sludge bleed-rates, mixing, etc., a decrease of activity fixed on the sludge was observed.

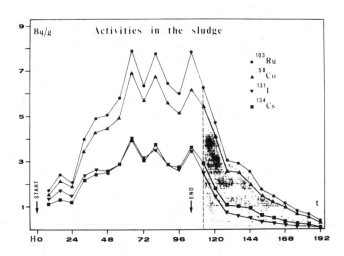

Fig. 7. Activities measured in Becquerel per gram dried sludge (time in hours).

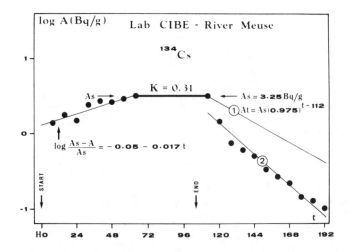

Fig. 8. Saturation of sludge by ^{134}Cs (time in hours).

The data converge to a generalisation which corresponds to a classical exponential model of the mass transfer.

$$^{103}Ru : \ln \frac{As - A}{As} = + 0,14 - 0,032 \ t$$

$$^{58}Co : \ln \frac{As - A}{As} = + 0,09 - 0,030 \ t$$

$$^{134}Cs : \ln \frac{As - A}{As} = - 0,12 - 0,039 \ t$$

$$^{131}I : \ln \frac{As - A}{As} = + 0,04 - 0,034 \ t$$

12. The first and most important mechanism of bleeding of the activity from the sludge layer is to be attributed to the sludge purge. In conditions of the experiment this purge was equal to 2,5 % bleed per hour of the total sludge blanket. This elution is described by the following equation :
$At = As (0,975)^{t-112}$. (The starting time of the elution phase was fixed at 112 h after the beginning of the tracing).
The experimentally observed elution was globally more important than the one predicted by the sludge bleed rate (line 2 on Fig. 8.). The difference in activity as measured and that calculated for the sludge bleed rate represents the elution of activity of the sludge layer by the water. The elution of activity "adsorbed" in the sludge blanket by the water transiting in the treatment is proportional to the activity in the sludge layer.
In our case, elution rates as measured are in the range of 1 % per hour for a water flow of 1600 m^3 h^{-1} through a sludge layer of 1800 m^3 th. e. a water transit time of about 1,3 h.

PARTICULAR CASE OF CESIUM
13. The removal efficiency for ^{134}Cs in the full-scale test gradually decreases from 65 % to 20 % in settled water and from 80 % to 50 % in filtered water (Fig. 9.).
The removal of cesium by rapid sand-filtration is very significant.
As a consequence, several tests were carried out in the laboratory to study the adsorption of ^{134}Cs on different sands.

LABORATORY "JAR TEST" ON SAND
14. 4 liter ^{134}Cs solutions were put into contact with increasing quantities of sand. After 7 hours of agitation with a velocity of 150 r.p.m., the solution was filtered and the liquid counted with the γ -Ge spectrometer.
Where the sand of the module 4 at the Tailfer plant is concerned, we observed a relationship between the amount of activity adsorbed and the amount of sand; contrary to the sand of the module 1 for which less or no adsorption was observed (Fig. 10.). Both sands are currently used since $\pm$ 10 years in the plant.

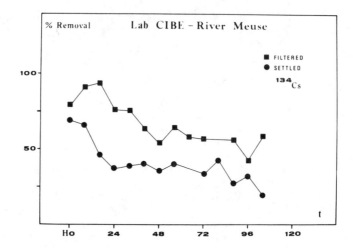

Fig. 9. Removal rate of ^{134}Cs by settling and by filtration (time in hours).

This may be related to the concentration of K (potassium).
  Module 4 ^{40}K = 0,30 Bq/g
  Module 1 ^{40}K = 0,09 Bq/g

LABORATORY "COLUMN TEST" ON SAND
  15. A glass column with a diameter of 32 mm, a height of 300 mm and a volume of 0,242 l was filled with sand provening from module 4 and fed continuously at controlled flow rate with a solution of ^{134}Cs. The filtrate is counted with the γ Ge-detector.
The adsorption rate is a function of the flow rate. With lower flow rates, more activity is fixed on the sand and the time required to reach saturation is longer.

CONCLUSIONS
  16. It has been possible to determine and measure the remote fall-out of the Chernobyl accident with the operational equipment installed by the Brussels' Intercommunal Waterboard. The board has cooperated closely with the sanitary authorities of Belgium and has assumed the responsability of control of the drinking water during that period. The most significant isotopes were ^{132}Te, ^{131}I, ^{103}Ru, ^{134}Cs and ^{137}Cs among about twenty different isotopes which could be identified in water resources. At all instances, the concentration measured in the raw water resources from May 5th to 20th 1986 ranged between 10 to 20 % of the total maximum permanent admissible concentration in drinking water. About half of the risk was due to ^{131}I. Long-term effects concern Cs isotopes.

  17. The management options for water-undertakings resulting from the study of the impact of the Chernobyl accident and analogous simulation experiments are the following :
234

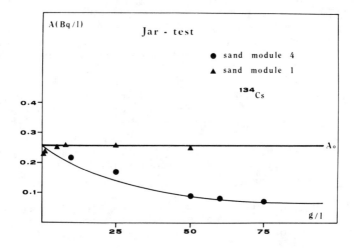

Fig. 10. Adsorption of ^{134}Cs on sand in "Jar Test".

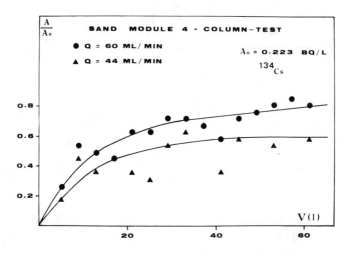

Fig. 11. Adsorption of ^{134}Cs on sand in "Column Test".

- the installation of counting facilities, preferably in different locations, seeing that the activity in local air is a background not to be neglected in critical situations, contrary to normal conditions.
- the permanent availability of sampling equipment as well as storage of bottles and containers can be determinant in critical circumstances.
- the intervention in the water treatment to optimize the removal rates depend on an adsorption-desorption model as the one developped in this study. The sludge bleed can be optimized to restore fresh adsorbing sludge through a sludge recycling system. No systematic removal yield can be claimed as typical for a unit process of water treatment. The elimination of cesium by fixation on sand is remarkable and is under further investigation.

18. The most important conclusion of this work and similar investigations is that communication and open exchange of information is the most important factor in critical circumstances.

REFERENCES
1. MASSCHELEIN W.J. and GOOSSENS R. Ressources en eau et centrales nucléaires. Water Supply, 1983, vol. 2, 201-213.
2. DAVIES Sh. and BUMSTEAD J.C.. Nuclear power reactor accidents and the role of water system managers. Journal of the American Water Works Association, 1982, vol. 74, 383-390.
3. MASSCHELEIN W.J., GOOSSENS R., GENOT J., HALLEUX R. and DELVILLE A.. Impact of Chernobyl fall-out on drinking water in Belgium - Letter to nature (in press).
4. MASSCHELEIN W.J., GOOSSENS R., DELVILLE A., GENOT J. and HALLEUX R.. Enseignements relatifs aux performances d'une filière classique de traitement d'eau potable lors des retombées de l'accident de Tchernobyl 1986. International Atomic Energy Agency - SM - 2991009, 1987, 507.
5. GOOSSENS R., DELVILLE A., GENOT J., HALLEUX R. and MASSCHELEIN W.J.. Removal of the typical isotopes of the Chernobyl fall-out by conventional water treatment. Water Research (in press 1989).
6. MORTON R.J. and STRAUB C.P.. Removal of radionuclides from water by water treatment processes. Journal of the American Water Works Association, 1956, vol. 48, N° 5, 545-558.
7. BERNHARDT H., HARTMANN H. and BAUMGARTEL F.. Möglichkeiten der Dekontamination von Wässern mit Schnellfilteranlagen. Vom Wasser, 1962, vol. 29, 341-417.
8. STRAUB C.P., MORTON R.J. and PLACAK O.R.. Studies on the removal of radioactive contaminants from water. Journal of the American Water Works Association, 1951, vol. 43, 773-792
9. HABERER K.. Über die Entnahme Radioaktiver Spaltprodukte bei der Trinkwasser - Aufbereitung - Kerntechnik, 1962, vol. 4, 377.

10. CLARKE J.H., CUMBERLAND R.F. and SMYTH M.J. Treatment of low-level radioactive effluent by a ferric hydroxide precipitation. U.K. Atomic Energy Authority, 1968, AERE-R5724.

11. MITCHELL N.T., EDEN G.E. and DUNCAN W.A.. Removal of certain radioactive isotopes during the primary sedimentation of sewage. Journal of the Institution of Sewage Purification, 1963, vol. 6, 581.

12. EDEN G.E., DOWNING A.L. and WHEATLAND A.B.. Observations on the removal of radioisotopes during purification of domestic water supplies. Journal of the Institution of the Water Engineers, 1952, vol. 6, 511.

13. CERRAI E. and TRIULZI C.. Decomtaminazione di acque contenenti Cs-137. Energia Elettrica, 1959, vol. 8, 746-753.

14. STRAUB C.P.. Limitations of water treatment methods for removing radioactive contaminants. Public Health Reports, 1955, vol. 70, 897.

15. SACHSE G. and WINKLER R.. Natürliche Ionenaustauschfähige Stoffe zur Entfernung Radioaktiver Verunreinigungen aus dem Wasser. Fortschritte der Wasserchemie und ihrer Grenzgebiete, 1964, 131-137.

16. GOOSSENS R., DELVILLE A. and MASSCHELEIN W.J.. Le contrôle préventif de la radioactivité de bas niveau par les sociétés de distribution d'eau. Sciences et Techniques Municipales, 1985, vol. 80, 23-34.

17. DEVELL L., TOVEDAL H., BERGSTROM U., APPELGREN A., CHRYSSLER J. and ANDERSSON L. Initial observations of fall-out from the reaction accident at Chernobyl. Nature, 1986, vol. 321, 192.

18. FRY F.A., CLARKE R.H. and O' RIORDAN M.C. Early estimates of UK radiation doses from the Chernobyl reactor. Nature, 1986, vol. 321, 193-195.

18. Water resources management strategy for Pakistan in case of nuclear disaster

A. M. KHAN, NED University of Engineering and Technology, Karachi, Pakistan

SYNOPSIS.   In Pakistan, no management strategy existed for combating major disasters. A nuclear disaster involves the emission of insidious radiations which can cause different cancers if ingested with water.   The water supplies in Pakistan are managed by local water boards or Water and Power Development Authority.   A plan called Karachi Emergency Relief Plan (K.E.R.P) has been formulated for overcoming natural and nuclear disasters in Karachi.   This plan does not consider the radioactive pollution of water supplies separately.   It can be made more effective with certain improvements and used as a model for managing nuclear disasters in other cities of Pakistan.

INTRODUCTION
1.   Pakistan is an agricultural country where water is used for irrigation purposes throughout the year.   It is served by River Indus and three other rivers Chenab, Jhelum and Sutlej.   Indus is the major river starting from the Himalayas and feeds a network of canals and meets the water supply and irrigation needs of most of the population.   Hence the population is overwhelmingly dependent on clean and unpolluted water.
2. Nuclear radiation can be the result of an accident similar to a Chernobyl type accident or it can be the result of aggression during a war similar to Hiroshima type atom bomb. The dangers resulting from an accident to a power plant like the one proposed on River Indus at Chashma (capacity 700 MW) must be analysed. Any pollution of the river will take the contamination downstream and affect biological life.   An existing plant Karachi Nuclear Power Plant (KANUPP, capacity 150 MW) is located 30 miles from Karachi, the biggest and most populated city of Pakistan.   Neighbouring countries like India have Nuclear Power Plants.   Depending on the size of accidents and with an East-West wind direction, effects similar to Chernobyl type disaster cannot be ruled out.   It is unfortunate that to cope with major disasters in the past due to earth quakes, epidemics, floods and bomb blasts no management strategy was deployed.   Emergency relief was provided mainly by special army units.

Nuclear contamination of water resources. Thomas Telford, London, 1990.

DAMAGE CAUSED TO WATER RESOURCES

3.   An accidental nuclear disaster is likely to be less severe than that due to an atomic bomb explosion. The latter type is beyond the scope of the strategy discussed in this paper.

4.   Open sources of drinking water would be contaminated limiting emergency ingestion levels when contaminated with 10 C/m of mixed fission products per day (ref. 2). Although the natural processes greatly clean up the water, but effects on water users are long term and include the following.

Damage Caused to Animal and Plant Life

5.   Contamination of water with fission products will irradiate the produce of the farms supplied by this water. The animals grazing on the grass and drinking the water will fall sick, plus the vegetation and cow's milk become unfit for consumption.

6.   Fishes and marine life like water ducks and birds feeding on water insects will also be effected. They are found to have many times more radioisotopes than the water in which they live (ref.l). They transfer radiations to people consuming them.

Damage Caused to Human Beings

7.   Radioactive material can enter the body due to consumption of food and water which gets contaminated directly with fission products. Alpha and Beta particles originating outside the body cannot penetrate the outer layers of skin, but if the sources of radiation e.g plutonium (which is α-particle emitter) are inside the body, they can dissipate their entire energy within a small volume of body tissue causing considerable damage (ref.2). Damage caused to human beings from internal radiation exposure will lead to cancers of different organs, gene mutation, blindness and even death, depending upon the nature and amount of radioactivity ingested.   Genetic effect of radiation may lead to severely handicapping diseases to the future generation.   Thus effects on public health owing to water contamination are the primary concern in case of nuclear disaster.

WATER RESOURCES SYSTEM IN PAKISTAN

Water Supply in Rural Area

8.   In rural areas, the water is supplied from the canals. Water obtained from domestic wells is limited.   The water supply from the rivers into the canals can be controlled at the headworks.   Water Treatment Plants generally do not exist.

Water Supply in Urban Areas

9.   In Pakistan, the houses in urban areas have underground water tanks, overhead water tanks or wells where a few days supply of water is stored.   In case of nuclear disaster such water is likely to escape initial contamination and can provide short term relief.   For long term supply, the contaminated water from the main sources which can be the rivers, lakes and

open reservoirs, has to be treated before it can be distributed to the public. In big cities treatment of water against radio-activity is possible at municipal water treatment plants, where easy and inexpensive treatment like alum coagulation can be effectvely given. At some municipal plants sand filtration facilities are also present which can make water safer.

ROLE OF GOVERNMENT AGENCIES IN PAKISTAN

10. The management of water supply, disaster relief, nuclear water disposal and environmental pollution monitoring is the responsibility of the following organisations.

Water and Power Development Authority (WAPDA)

11. The present management of water supply rests with the local water boards in the urban areas. WAPDA supervises the water supply and power in the country.

Environmental Protection Agency (EPA)

12. It has been set up recently by the Government and has yet to establish itself.

Directorate of Civil Defence

13. This organisation plays the major role in combatting disaster by providng rescue teams, first aid, fire fighters etc.

Pakistan Atomic Energy Commission

14. The scientists of Pakistan Atomic Energy Commission (PAEC) and Karachi Nuclear Power Plant (KANUPP) have the expertise to analyse the radiation, such as the source of release shape and size of nuclear cloud, its temperature and its physical properties. PAEC has been empowered by legislaton to deal with nuclear disaster.

Meteorological Department

15. The rate of atmospheric diffusion of radioactive material from a disaster depends to a large extent on the weather conditions. Atmospheric temperature profiles, wind speeds and direction, the months and season of the year, local terrain, presence of precipitating cloud and geographical location of the area would play a major role in deciding how far from the disaster site, the water resources would be polluted and to what levels. An estimation of rain fall intensities, drop sizes and distribution in air would be needed in case of washout which produces high concentration and deposition of radioactive material on ground. Hence Meteorological Department's services would be needed in nuclear hazard evaluation.

STANDARD FOR RADIATION LEVELS IN WATER

16. Once nature and amount of radioactivity in water has been determined, the next step is to decide as to what level of radiation would be acceptable in water and how much of it would be harmful. Tables have been formulated, such as one giving Maximum Permissible Body Burdens and Maximum Permissible Concentrations of Radionuclides in Air and in water for Occupational Exposure (ref. 4). These are recommended by United States National Committee on Radiation Protection and

Measurement (NCRP). The recommendations of International Commission on Radiation Protection (ICRP) also exist. National Regulations have been set up in the U.K and other countries as well. Hence either the International recommendations can be followed, or national standards can be formulated on the basis of International recommendations and experiences.

TREATMENT OF WATER FOR REMOVAL OF RADIOACTIVITY

17. The Water Engineers on advice from the Environmental experts may determine how the radioactivity could be removed from the open sources of water supply i.e the reservoirs of filtration plants, the canals or rivers, and to supply the public with alternate sources of drinking water, until the sources could be made safe.

Location of Radioactivity Monitoring Stations

18. Focal points of strategic importance will have to be set up in the water disribution system where radioactivity monitoring instruments are to be located, and as soon as emergency ingestion levels are reached the water supply should be stopped and either diverted downstream or diverted to treatment facilities.

Methods of Treatment

19. If radioactivity is found in water then depending upon the amount and nature of radioactivity and the size of the treatment facility the following treatments can be given (ref. 6).

  (a) Carrier Precipitation or Coagulation followed by Sedimentation
  (b) Storage
  (c) Adsorption
  (d) Sand filtration
  (e) Ion-Exchange
  (f) Electrodialysis
  (g) Evaporation
  (h) Metallic Displacement or Scrubbing
  (i) Biological Processes
  (j) Crystallization

20. Of these coagulation followed by sedimentation is the cheapest and the most widely used method of removing radioactivity from water. Repeated precipitation by addition of calcium chloride at successive points removed 99% of radioactivity (ref.   ).

Handling of Radioactive Waste

21. Special techniques, equipment and clothing are needed for handling of radioactive waste. Hence operators at the water treatment plants have to be pretrained.

Disposal of Radioactive Waste

22. The radioactive waste has to be disposed off in predetermined sites either by burning or by burrying beneath the ground or by sinking in deep-sea trenches (ref. 1).

Public Awareness

23.   While this whole operation is being carried out co-opera
tion with the local authorities and media will be necessary
to keep the public informed and to prevent them from using
contaminated water supplies.

MANAGEMENT STRATEGY

24. To combat the nuclear disaster or other emergencies
successfully, the city of Karachi is studied here as a model.
The application may be extended to other cities with similar
problems.

25.   An emergency relief plan known as   Karachi Emergency
Relief Plan (K.E.R.P) has been formulated.   This delineates
the Basic Plan which outlines the scheme for government-wide
organizational structure during periods of emergency, and major
lines of authorities.   It also presents the 'Response Activity'
concept of operations and outlines the guidance and assignments
to   agencies   and   officials   with   primary   functions,   secondary
functions   and   support   functions (ref.5). The   Basic   Plan   and   its
application to Nuclear Hazards is as follows.

Basic Plan of K.E.R.P for Nuclear Disaster

26.   The basic plan has been divided into three parts:
(a)   Pre-disaster
(b)   During disaster
(c)   Post disaster

27.   It will be activated through the Karachi Emergency Relief
Office (K.E.S.O), whose director is the Commissioner of Karachi.
He will be in close contact with the Provincial Governor
through the Chief Secretry of the Governor.   There are a
number of Response Activity Co-ordinators (RACs), each specifically assigned the task of overall co-ordination in a particular
area of response.   Each response activity co-ordinator is the
head of the agency with primary function and is responsible
for   preparing   Standard Operating   Procedure   (S.O.P)   for   that
particular response activity.   The response activities for combatting nuclear disaster are as under.

Environmental   Radioactivity Monitoring

28.   Karachi Nuclear Power Plant   KANUPP is the Primary
Agency responsible for providing initial assessment of the situation   by   continuously   monitoring   environmental   radioactivity
level, dose calculation and for transmission of this information
to other secondary and support Response organisations through
Director KESO.

Provision and Supply of Prophylactics

29.   The Primary Agency in this case is also KANUPP and
is responsible for supplying prophylactics (like KI) to the various
Response Authorities and to the general public when required.

Confiscation of Edible Items

30. The Karachi Emergency services Office (KESO) is the Primary Agency for this response activity. The Director KESO, i.e the Commissioner Karachi will be Response Activity Co-ordinator.

Alert and Notification

31. The Plant Manager of KANUPP alongwith the Director of KESO, shall be responsible for all matters regarding Alert and Notification during all phases of Nuclear Hazard. The Director of KESO shall make sure that all departments and agencies with primary, secondary and support functions respond adequately to accomplish this responsibility. The Plant Manager of KANUPP shall also inform the Director of Directorate of Nuclear Safety and Radiation Protection (DNSRP), of the possible inter-regional and international consequences.

32. The Director of DNSRP shall notify international agencies, such as the International Atomic Energy Agency, World Meteorological Organizations, etc., about the incident, under obligations of the Convention of Early Notification, and about the assistence required in case of a nuclear accident or radiological emergency.

De Contamination Services

33. The Director of KESO i.e Commissioner Karachi, shall be the Response Activity Co-ordnator for decontamination services, and will be responsible for directing, Co-ordinating and monitoring all decontamination services operations and their co-ordinators. He will also encourage all agencies of the government to develop the capability to provide assistance in manpower, equipment, logistics, chemicals etc. to accomplish this response activity.

Other Response Activities

34. In addition to the above five response activities for dealing with a nuclear disaster, the Karachi Emergency Relief Plan contains other response activities to combat all types of disaster like earthquakes, floods, cyclones etc. Most of these activities will also be applicable to nuclear disaster. These are
   (a) Disaster Protective Measures
   (b) Resource Identification
   (c) Public Education and Information/Warning Dissemination
   (d) Evacuation and Mass Care
   (e) Communication
   (f) Search and Rescue Operation
   (g) Public Safety
   (h) Emergency Health and Medical Services

REVIEW OF THE K.E.R.P PLAN

35. The K.E.R.P for handling nuclear emergency designates most of the Primary or main responsibility to the Plant Manager of KANUPP and Commissioner Karachi. They would be respon-

sible for co-ordination with other secondary and support organisations. How this co-ordination will be achieved is only given in vague terms and is not detailed.

36. The organisational chart shows that the Provincial Government will be involved through the Governor, Chief Minister, Chief Secretary and Relief Commissioner, but again their specific roles are not delineated and all the decision making has been laid on the shoulders of two persons. These two will be required to deal with the emergency situation in which millions of people will be involved.

37. The number of trained personnel at KANUPP would not be enough to combat the disaster both at the plant and in the whole city. No consideration has been given to the fact that the Plant Manager of KANUPP or his counterparts could themselves get effected being so near the disaster site. Who will take control then? Hence Co-ordination at national and international level is also necessary, as was deduced from Chernobyl.

38. The Basic Plan mentions that Standard Operating Procedures (SOPs) will be prepared by each Response Activity Coordinator for the respective response activity, containing all essential information and steps necessary for the effective implementation of these response activities. But no guidelines for the preparation and formulation of these procedures are included in the basic plan.

Provisions of Water Contamination in K.E.R.P

39. General management strategy to deal with nuclear disaster at KANUPP exists in the form of Karachi Emergency Relief Plan. This plan does not consider the radioactive pollution of water supplies separately. This is on the assumption that Karachi is at a safe distance of 30 miles from KANUPP whose nuclear fuel consumption is limited, the capacity of the plant being 150 MW only. Secondly the water for two or three days supply is usually stored in concrete or Alumnium tanks of houses. Hence in the basic plan of K.E.R.P., WAPDA has been completly ignored, while the local water board in Karachi, Karachi Water and Sewerage Board (K.W.S.B), has only been included as Secondary role agency in two of the response activities viz (Para 28) Environmental Radioactivity Monitoring and Decontamination Services (Para 33), without mentioning as to how its services will be utilized. In the other two activities i.e Confiscation of Edible Items (Para 30) and Alert and Notification (Para 31), K.W.S.B has not been included.

40. This approach is not safe for public, as there are open reservoirs at all the water treatment facilities in Karachi where water is purified before it is distributed to the city. The radioactive pollution of this water should be considered. A few changes are suggested in the Response Activities to combat nuclear disaster as under.

RECOMMENDATIONS

Inclusion of Utilities Dealing with Water Supplies within City

41. The Karachi Water and Sewerage Board (K.W.S.B) should be included as secondary Agency in the Response activites of Confiscation of Edible Items (Para 30) and Alert and Notification (Para 31).

42. The Karachi Development Authority (K.D.A) should also be included for checking, monitoring and removing of radio-activity from new water supply facilities being developed by it.

43. Similarly all the private, government semigovernment organisations with their own water facilities in and around the city should be included in response activities.

Co-ordination with National Agencies

44. There is always a possibility that a disaster might be too severe and complicated to be dealt with locally. A radioactive disaster can have serious national consequences, hence coordination at national level is necessary. It can be achieved by the appointed representative of the Governor of Province who can coordinate effectively with concerned national agencies serving directly under the Presidents or Prime Minister's representative. These national agencies can then work as support agencies for that particular response activity. One such agency can be the Pakistan Atomic Energy Commission which can act as support agency to suplment the effortsof KANUPP. Similarly WAPDA can supplement the relief work and help the staff of K.W.S.B in the management of water resources if needed.

Co-ordination with International Agencies

45. Chernobyl disaster has shown how countries far and near can be affected by radioactivity. There were reports in the Pakistani press that traces of radioactivity were found n the milk powder imported from European countries into Srilanka a few months after Chernobyl disaster. Hence International agencies should be incorporated in the Basic Plan. They can serve as support agencies and co-ordination with them can be achieved through the Central government's representative.

Response Activity Co-ordinators

46. The Commissioner Karachi being the director of Karachi Emergency Services Office (K.E.S.O), already has the overall responsibility to overcome the crisis. Hence instead of assigning him the work of Response Activity Coordinator. (Para 30,31, 32) as well, it can be given to the head of utility in the primary role, whose coordinating functions would be most important and whose services would be required round the clock.

Delineation of Responsibilities

47. An outline of the responsibilities or functions of secon-

dary role agencies and support agencies should also be included with the responsiblities of Response Activity Co-ordinators in the Basic Plan.

Application of Recommendations to Basic Plan

48. The Response Activity, Environmental Radioactivity Monitoring, Fig.1, has been taken as an example and suggested changes are shown in Fig. 2. Fig. 3 shows the Post Disaster Plan with inclusion of national and international agencies in support role. The functions and responsibilities of these agencies can be included in the Basic Plan as under.

Functions of Primary Agency

49. In this case KANUPP is the Primary Agency. The function of Response Activity Co-ordinator is the same as given in Para 28.

50. These are agencies within the city like the local water board, for monitoring Radioactivity in the environment, atmosphere, water food etc with the help or supervision of KANUPP. The agencies suggested, and their functions are

51. Directorate of Civil Defence. Civil Defence personnel can monitor radioactivity within the city.

52. Karachi Water and Sewerage Board (K.W.S.B). For monitoring radioactivity in the water supplies for the city, within the city, at water filtration plants and open reservoirs.

53. Karachi Development Authority (K.D.A). For monitoring radioactivity at its under construction and under implementation projects of water supply, water treatment and sewage treatment plants.

54. Civil Aviation Authority. For monitoring radioactivity within the areas under its jurisdiction, especially to see that no contaminated item leaves the city via air.

55. Karach Port Trust (K.P.T). For monitorng radioactivity in the seaport area especially for checking the contamination of edible items, and fishes brought in by fishing trawlers. These may be unfit for human, livestock and plant use if irradiated.

Functions of Support Agencies

56. These are national and international agencies whose co-operation is needed for monitoring of radioactivity in and around the disaster area. These can be the following.

57. Environmental Protection Agency. For monitoring radioactivity in the country.

58. Water and Power Development Authority (WAPDA). For monitoring radioactivity in the water resources of the councountry.

59. Ministry of Agriculture. For monitoring radioactivity in food and in farms around the city and in food being transported inland.

60. Meteorological Department. For monitoring radioactivity in atmosphere within city and country.

247

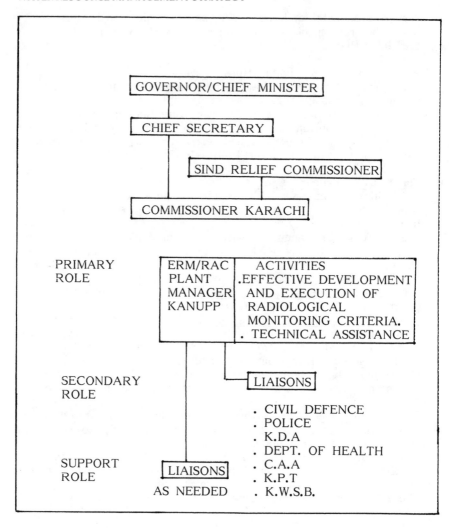

Fig. 1. Response Activity: Environmental Radio
Activity Monitoring (E.R.M) as suggested
by K.E.R.P.

61. World Meteorological Organisation (W.M.O). For monitoring radioactivity in neighbouring countries atmosphere and world-wide.

62. National Institute of Oceanography (N.I.O.C). For monitoring radioactivity in the Indian Ocean.

63. Pakistan Atomic Energy Commission (P.A.E.C). For supervising, advice and co-ordination of monitoring radioactivity within the city and country, and supplementing the work of KANUPP officials.

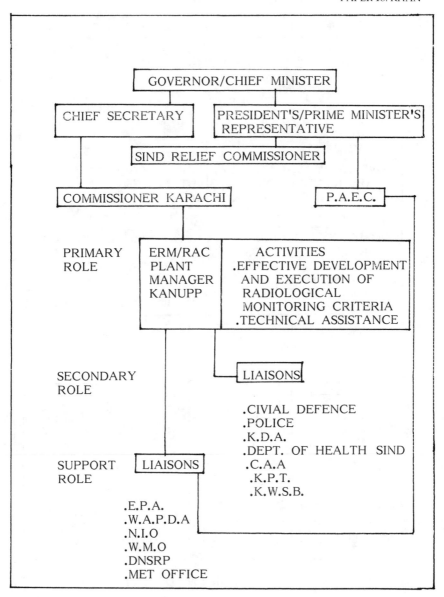

Fig. 2.   Suggested Changes in Environmental
Radioactivity Monitoring

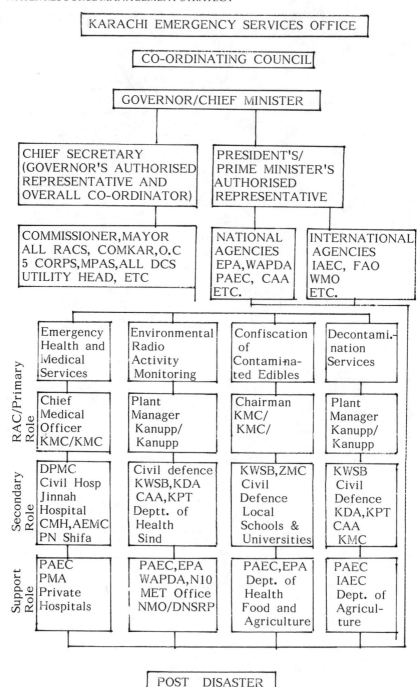

Fig. 3.   Suggested Changes in Post Disaster
K.E.R.P Plan

64.   Directorate of Nuclear Safety and Radiation Protection.
For co-ordination of radioactivity monitoring between national
and international agencies.
65.   Department of Health, Sind.   For monitoring radioactivity
within the province for possible harmful effects on public health.

CONCLUSIONS
66.   This paper proposes a Water Management Strategy for
Karachi in case of nuclear disaster.   A Basic Plan to combat
emergencies for the city of Karachi called K.E.R.P already
exists awaiting approval.   Essential features of the plan are
outlined, and the limitations of not including water resources
have been discussed.   In the Basic Plan, the local water board
K.W.S.B has only been included as secondary role agency in
Environmental Radioactivity Monitoring and in   Decontamination
Services without outlining its function.
67.   The inclusion of K.W.S.B in Confiscation of Edible Items,
inclusion of brief description of secondary agencies' functions
in the Basic Plan and inclusion of national agencies like WAPDA
and international agencies like IAEC as support role agencies
is suggested.   An example of recommended changes is shown
in Fig. 2 and Fig. 3.   Lastly it is recommended that approval
be given to the Karachi Emergency Relief Plan, so that it
can be followed if need arose.
68.   The Emergency Relief Plan for Karachi City can be
adopted as a model by other cities in Pakistan which are likely
to be affected by nuclear radiation in case of a nuclear disaster.

REFERENCES
1.   DRESNER L.   Principles of Radiation Protection Engineering,
Translation of Jaeger's Principles of Radiation Protection,
chap. 4 and chap. 17, McGraw-Hill, U.S.A, 1965.
2.   RUSSELL C.R.   Reactor Safegaurds, chap. 8, Pergamon
Press, Great Britian, 1962.
3.   FARMER F.R.   Nuclear Reactor Safety, U.S.A, 1977.
4.   Maximum permissible body burdens and maximum permissible
concentrations of radionuclides in air and water for occupational
exposures.   National Bureau of Standards Handbook, 69.
5.   Karachi Emergency Relief Plan, Nuclear Hazards, Vol-II,
THE PLAN.
6.   MURRAY R.L.   Introduction to Nuclear Engineering,
Chap. 10, Prentice - Hall, U.S.A, 1964.

ACKNOWLEDGEMENTS
    The co-operation shown by the Directorate of Civil
Defence (Sind) in providing detailed information on the
Karachi Emergency Relief Plan is gratefully acknowledged.

19. Evaluation of radioactivity measurements in Belgium and Dutch water supply facilities following the Chernobyl event

W. VAN CRAENENBROECK, PhD, Antwerpse Waterwerken nv, Antwerp, Belgium

SYNOPSIS. The results of a full scale plant experiment at the Oelegem Production Centre of the water supply company of Antwerp (Belgium) indicate that removal efficiencies for radionuclides in conventional water treatment plants, operated under normal working conditions, are rather low. After the fall-out of radionuclides caused by the accident at Chernobyl on April 26th 1986, removal efficiencies were recorded ranging from 34% up to 84%, with an average of 50±20% for different water treatment plants in Belgium and the Netherlands. The resulting values are compared and the determining factors discussed. Removal efficiencies appeared to be similar to those obtained before the Chernobyl event.

INTRODUCTION

Information about removal of radionuclides during water treatment processes is rather limited. Lowry and Lowry (ref. 1), and Masschelein et al. (ref. 2), had to base their review of data about the removal performance of man-made radionuclides on publications going back as far as the fifties and sixties. In this context, a report from 1954 of the Oak Ridge National Laboratory is still worthwhile to be mentioned (ref. 3). More recent publications are only available in relation to the removal from drinking water, of naturally occuring radionuclides such as radium (ref. 4), uranium (ref. 5), or radon (ref. 6). They have been reviewed by Aieta *et al.* (ref. 7).

From the above mentioned literature, it can be concluded that most of the cationic heavy radionuclides may be removed by the coagulation-flocculation process with an efficiency of 90% or more. This is the case for all elements which are fixed in or adsorbed onto solid particles, or co-precipitate with the coagulant. ^{32}P, occuring in the form of the phosphate-ion, may also be eliminated by this process, just as uranium which forms stable nagatively charged uranyl-carbonate complexes. The ^{131}I however, although present as the iodide-ion, is practically not eliminated. Only the addition of silver salts may improve the elimination efficiency, but it is obvious that this approach is only applicable on a small scale, because of the high working costs. Strontium and cesium activities are practically unaffected by the coagulation step. Sand filtration as such (slow or rapid) appears to be an unefficient elimination technique, unless radionuclides are presented in solid form, or in combination with a flocculent.

Softening by increasing the pH (e.g. lime softening) gives also rise to good decontamination for most of the radionuclides, strontium included, but not for cesium.

Ion exchange gives outstanding results : this technique is in fact used for decontamination of the primary coolant of nuclear power plants. Elimination of uranium or iodine with anionic resins gives efficiencies of more than 99%, while cationic resins remove strontium to the same extent. Clay particles have comparable properties, which implies that their addition to the coagulation-flocculation process, enhances its efficiency.

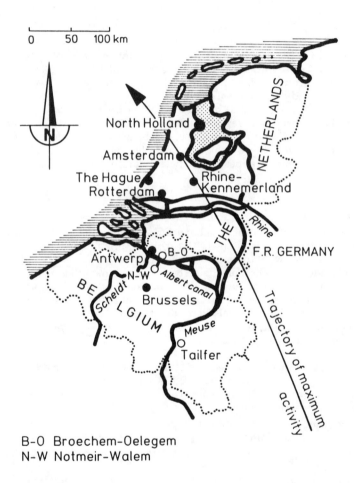

B-0 Broechem-Oelegem
N-W Notmeir-Walem

Fig. 1. Location of treatment plants of the water companies covered by the survey. The arrow indicates the trajectory of maximum activity on May 2nd.

In drinking water production plants in Belgium and the Netherlands, full scale plant data on radionuclide removal were hardly available before the nuclear accident at Chernobyl. Routine sampling and measuring on raw and finished water form the production Centre "Notmeir-Walem" of the water supply company of Antwerp, Belgium (coagulation-flocculation with alum, followed by rapid and slow sand filtration), had shown an overall removal efficiency of 76% for α-emitters, and 36% for β-emitters (including ^{40}K), over the period 1970-1980. Data from the Brussels water supply company at its production plant at Tailfer indicate that on the average, only 50% of the gross β- and γ-activity is removed under normal operating conditions (ref. 8).

DRINKING WATER PRODUCTION FOR ANTWERP

The water supply of Antwerp and its surroundings, is based essentially upon surface water, withdrawn from the Albert Canal system, which links the river Meuse with the river Scheldt, and is fed with water from the former river (Fig. 1).

The Oelegem production plant of the *Antwerpse Waterwerken* has a capacity of 120,000 m^3/d, and takes its water directly from the Albert Canal, where it is stored for about one month, after which it is submitted to a treatment consisting of coagulation-flocculation (alum), rapid and slow sand filtration. Another 250,000 m^3/d is taken from a canal branch, the Nethe Canal, 100,000 of which is submitted to the same type of treatment. The remaining quantity is treated by direct filtration and granular activated carbon filtration.

RADIONUCLIDE BALANCE FOR THE OELEGEM TREATMENT PLANT

During an experiment in the Oelegem Production Centre, a mass balance was made over the period September 7th-16th 1977 for a number of radionuclides occuring in detectable quantities. A volume of water equivalent to four days of production, that is about 400,000 m^3, was followed on its way through the different treatment steps. Samples were taken at regular intervals of 4 hours, at the strategical points : the water intake (total, centrifuged, solids), the coagulants (aluminium sulphate and activated silica), the effluent of the settling tanks after coagulation-flocculation (water and sludge), the effluent of the rapid sand filters, the influent and effluent of the slow sand filters. The individual samples were combined in order to make one single composite sample. At each sampling point, the zero sampling time was shifted in function of the residence time since the water intake, which was considerable after storage between rapid and slow sand filters (100 hours). Sampling of the coagulants enabled to evaluate any possible contamination with radionuclides from outside the treatment process.

From the experimental results, as summarized in Table 1, it follows that of the current α- and β-emitting radionuclides, only the activities of ^{226}Ra, ^{90}Sr, and ^{3}H were measurable. The removal efficiency in a conventional water treatment plant like the one at Oelegem, seems to be rather low. ^{226}Ra scored best with 50%, whereas ^{90}Sr appeared to be not eliminated at all, just like tritium, which is present in the form of tritiated water. The removal efficiencies for ^{210}Po and $^{228-232}Th$ however could not be assessed, because the activity levels for these two elements were too low to be quantified. Over-all elimination efficiencies are comparable to those after coagulation-flocculation/rapid sand filtration. This indicates that (slow) sand filtration is not efficient in removing radionuclides, as described by Valentine *et al.* (ref. 9). Hence, the coagulation-flocculation step must be the one responsible for the removal. The striking similarity of the over-all elimination efficiency on the one hand, and the part of solids bound radionuclide on the other hand, show that physical removal of suspended solids from the water phase is the major elimination mechanism.

Table 1. Elimination of radionuclides in the Oelegem Production Centre 7-16 September 1977 (activity in mBq/l).

nuclide	raw water total activity	%solid	after coagul.-flocc. and rapid filtration activity	%elim.	afterslow filtration activity	over-all elimination %
^{226}Ra	5.9±1,9	51	2.6±0.4	44	3.0±0.4	50
^{90}Sr	8.9±3.9	0.6	10.4±3.7	0	11.1±3.7	0
^{210}Po	≤9.3±0.7	≥76			≤3.7	(60?)
$Pu(\alpha)$	≤1.9	?			≤1.9	(0?)
$^{228-232}Th$	≤16.7±2.6	≥78			≤3.7	(78?)
^{3}H	40701				51800	0

CONSEQUENCES OF THE CHERNOBYL ACCIDENT FOR THE ANTWERP WATER SUPPLY

The accident in the nuclear power plant at Chernobyl, on April 26th 1986, has again clearly demonstrated that events happening at a distance of thousands of kilometers may have detectable consequences in our part of the world. The degree to which this happens, depends primarily on the meteorological conditions. In May 1986, these were such, that massive fall-out of radionuclides from the radioactive cloud passing above the eastern part of Belgium and The Netherlands, could take place.

The measurements indicated from the beginning that the major part of the radionuclides consisted of ^{131}I (half-life 8 days). γ-Spectrometry revealed also the presence of ^{132}Te, ^{134}Cs, ^{137}Cs and ^{103}Ru (ref. 2) . The α-activity was practically not influenced.

The evolution of the beta-radioactivity of air and water was followed intensively by the water supply companies or contracted laboratories. In the zone covered by the water intakes for the Antwerp water supply, the measurements indicated a steep drop in gross β-activity of the air, from a maximum of 25 Bq/m^3 to 0.01 Bq/m^3, following heavy rainfall (Fig. 2). Consequently, the activity in rain water reached high levels, resulting in daily mean values of 100 Bq/l at Antwerp on May 3rd, and even 550 Bq/l at Amsterdam, following instantaneous values of 2000 to 3000 Bq/l. This caused in his turn the values in surface waters to increase rapidly, especially in shallow rivers with higher run-off coefficients, such as in urban areas. The β-activity in the river Schijn, which crosses suburbs of Antwerp, reached 50 Bq/l on the 6th of May, while in the canal system serving as a raw water source for the Antwerp water supply, maximum values of 5 to 6 Bq/l were found. The river Meuse, which feeds these canals, showed somewhat higher values, reaching a maximum of 17 Bq/l on the 5th and 6th of May. All values normalized slowly afterwards, with some 2 Bq/l still after one week.

Striking was also the geographic effect, with decreasing activities from east to west in samples taken on the same day : 15-17 Bq/l in the river Meuse at the Belgian-Dutch border, 3 Bq/l in the neighbourhood of Antwerp, and about 1 Bq/l in the river Scheldt near the French border. Masschelein *et al.* (ref. 2) reported maximum values of 2 Bq/l for the river Meuse at the Tailfer plant of the Brussels Water Supply Company, situated in the centre-south of the country. These results reflect the trajectory of the contaminated air masses above the Chernobyl area, which from April 29th on, were driven towards southern Germany. Then, the direction was changed into north-west heading towards the western part of Germany, East-Belgium, and the centre of The Netherlands (see Fig. 1) (ref. 10).

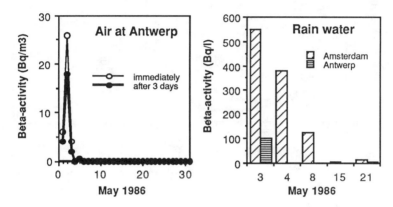

Fig. 2. Evolution of beta-activity in the air and in rain water in May 1986. (data of *Agfa-Gevaert* and *Gemeentewaterleidingen Amsterdam*)

The situation in the Antwerp drinking water followed the activity evolution in the raw water taken from the Albert Canal, which is a 130 km long canal, fed by the river Meuse at Liège and Maastricht. The 10 to 15 times higher activity level in the raw water with respect to normal, together with the direct effect of the precipitation on the treatment plants, caused the β-activity of the drinking water to increase to a maximum of 1.9 Bq/l on the 7th of May, which is almost twice the treshold value of 1 Bq/l recommended by the World Health Organisation.

On June 2nd, activity values still reached 0.5 Bq/l, whereas normal values are about 0.2 Bq/l. The extra radiation dose to the population, resulting from the ingestion of this contaminated drinking water, was small however, because of the fact that the exposure was very short. Moreover, the WHO limiting value was calculated for the hypothetic case of an exposure to the very toxic radionuclide ^{90}Sr, so that in this case, a more realistic higher value may be proposed, which takes into account the real composition of the radionuclide mixture.

As to the behaviour of β-emitting radionuclides in the different treatment plants, the following conclusions may be drawn. In the Notmeir-Walem Production Centre, the contamination level was reduced with 34% as an average over the period May 5th-26th. Whether this figure corresponds to the elimination efficiency of the treatment plants (coagulation with alum, rapid and slow sand filtration), remains an open question. It is true that the retention time of about 2 days is very short, but precipitation occured also on the uncovered buffer basins and slow sand filters, resulting in a higher activity than had been the case if contamination had been introduced exclusively with the raw water. Nevertheless, the given reduction percentage corresponds remarkably well with the mean value found over the period 1970-1980, which was 36% (K-40 inclusive).

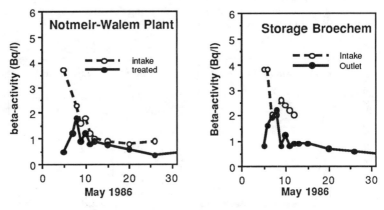

Fig. 3. Evolution of beta-activity in raw and treated water at the Notmeir-Walem treatment plant, and the Broechem storage reservoir of the Antwerp water supply company.

The presence of a storage reservoir of 4.5 million m³ capacity in the Broechem-Oelegem Production Centre had a positive effect on the contamination level, mainly because of the diluting effect upon the fall-out. Fig. 3 shows that, while the activity at the intake point decreased from almost 4 Bq/l on May 5th, to 2 Bq/l on May 12th, the values in the storage basin itself (surface layer) increased at first from 0.8 to 2.2 Bq/l, after which a level of 1 Bq/l was restored at May 15th, followed by a further decrease afterwards.

REMOVAL EFFICIENCIES IN DIFFERENT TREATMENT PLANTS
On the occasion of the Chernobyl incident, beta-radioactivity measurements were carried out by different water supply companies taking water from the rivers Meuse and Rhine in Belgium and The Netherlands. Data from the water supply companies of Amsterdam, Brussels (ref. 2), Rotterdam (2 plants), The Hague (ref. 11), North-Holland and from the water transportation company Rhine-Kennemerland (2 plants) are summarized in Table 2. Fig. 1 shows the location of the different plants. The results enable to estimate the over-all decontamination efficiency for β-emitters of the various treatment plants of concern, under normal working conditions, i.e. without any special decontamination measures. The (actvity based) removal efficiencies appear to range between 34 and 84% with an average value of about 50%.

The apparent scattering of results is due to differences between the analytical approach followed by the analyzing laboratories on the one hand, and between the conceptual characteristics of the treatment plants, as covered by the survey, on the other hand. Both types of characteristics are summarized in Table 3.

Some discrepancy may be caused in part by the fact that data on in- and outlet of the treatment plant proper, were not allways available : in cases 2 and 3a, the intake basin is included (retention time 6-8 weeks), causing an over-estimate of the efficiency. Infiltration into dune sands, as applied in plant 9 (retention time about 6 weeks), has a similar leveling effect. Also important is, whether the treatment plants are covered or uncovered. In case 4, the latter is true for the slow sand filters and in case 9 for the rapid filters, resulting in relatively low efficiencies. Given the larger surface area of slow sand filters, the impact of radionuclide deposition from the air is expected to be higher upon plant 4 than elsewehere, and this is confirmed by the results. This case corresponds to the allready discussed situation at *Antwerpse Waterwerken*.

Table 2. Summary of average removal efficiencies for Rhine or Meuse water based water supply systems in Belgium and The Netherlands after the Chernobyl accident.

plant	treatment description	period	% removal
1	coagulation (iron), filtration (covered). surface water intake/after transportation :	4-13 May	84%
2	intake basin, coagulation (iron; covered), filtration (covered). surface water intake/filter effluent :	4-13 May	72%
3	intake basin, coagulation (iron; covered), filtration (covered).		
	a. surface water intake/treated water :	4-13 May	73%
	b. raw/treated water :	10-13 May	50%
4	coagulation (alum), rapid filtration (covered), slow filtration (uncovered). raw/treated water :	7-26 May	34%
5	aeration (iron flocculation), activated carbon, rapid filtration (covered), slow filtration (covered). raw/treated water :	4-23 May	82%
6	coagulation (carbon, alum; covered), filtration (covered), ozone. surface water intake/treated water :	5-16 May	45%
7	coagulation (iron; covered), ozone, filtration (covered). raw/treated water :	6-27 May	54%*
8	coagulation (carbon, iron; covered), filtration (covered). raw/treated water :	6-27 May	50%*
9	dune infiltration, settling (after carbon dosage, aeration, rapid filtration (uncovered), slow filtration (covered).		
	a. raw/infiltrated water :	6 May - 5 Aug.	47%*
	b. infiltrated/treated water :	Idem	44%*
	c. raw/treated water :	Idem	71%*

* ^{40}K exclusive

In view of the dominant role of coagulation-flocculation, which technique is applied in all plants but one (case 9), similar decontamination efficiencies should be expected for all covered treatment plants without intake reservoir. In reality, four values of about 50% are found (cases 3b, 6, 7 and 8), and two of about 80% (cases 1 and 5). There is no obvious explanation for the discrepancy between the two groups. Probably, factors such as the part of precipitation in the untreated water (water depth), and the radionuclide composition play a role.

Because of the measurements being carried out by different laboratories, slight differences between analytical methods may be a source of unexplained variation in the removal efficiencies. The question whether the ^{131}I content is affected by pretreatment of the sample prior to the measurement proper, is particularly important, in view of the high contamination level with this radionuclide in precipitation water of May 1986. It appears that most activity data were obtained by counting with a G-M tube, which implies that samples were evaporated to dryness, causing an almost total loss of ^{131}I. Since this radionuclide is only poorly removed from water by conventional treatment (33% according to Masschelein et al. (ref. 2) , the exclusion of ^{131}I from the measurements will give rise to over-estimated over-all removal efficiencies. The effect however affected the results for all treatment plants in a similar way, so that the presented values still may be regarded as comparable.

Given the probably low part of ^{131}I in the activity data as resulting from the above described measurements, the time interval between sampling and measuring, which should be kept as short as possible when short living radionuclides are present, is not a critical factor for the present evaluation.

A further element in the discussion is the ^{40}K content which was excluded from the measurement data for plants 7 to 9 (residual activity). The influence of this factor may be quantified by calculating the activity expected from the potassium content of the raw water for these plants. Since the mean concentration level was 4 to 6 mg/l during May 1986, a corresponding activity level of 0.15 Bq/l results, which accounts for 10% of the residual activity in the raw water, and 30% of that in the treated water. The corrected removal efficiencies are 42%, 42% and 67% for cases 9a, 9b, and 9c respectively, indicating a slight over-estimation for the values in Table 2.

Table 3. Summary of beta-activity measurement and treatment plant characteristics.

plant	lab	K-40	filtr.	evap.	covered	storage	coag.-flocc.
1	5	+	-	100%	+	-	+
2	5	+	-	100%	+	+	+
3	5	+	-	100%	+	+	+
4	10	+	-	100%	±	-	+
5	5	+	-	100%	+	-	-
6	6	+	-	90%	+	-	+
7	7	-	+	95%	+	-	+
8	7	-	+	95%	+	-	+
9	9	-	+	90%	±	-	-

Finally, filtration of the sample is a last factor to be mentioned. Pre-filtration was carried out by labs 7 and 9, in combination with partial evaporation prior to liquid scintillation counting. Depending on the amount of suspended solids in the sample water, this step may introduce differences up to 40%. Since this affects essentially the raw water, removal efficiencies could be underestimated as a result of this procedure. In cases 7 to 9 however, the suspended matter content of the raw water was extremely low, i.e. <3 mg/l, so that filtration hardly could interfere.

CONCLUSIONS

The results of a full scale plant experiment by the water supply company of Antwerp, and an evaluation of beta-radioactivity measurements by Belgian and Dutch water supply companies following the nuclear accident at Chernobyl, confirm data from literature which show that elimination of radionuclides in conventional drinking water production plants, without special arrangements to improve decontamination efficiency, is moderate to poor. It must be concluded that advanced, but from a point of view of radionuclide removal still conventional water treatment, is not able to remove radionuclides with an efficiency of more than 50±20%. This is low as compared to removal efficiencies for conventional pollutants for which 90 tot 99% removal can be obtained. This conclusion should be kept in mind when evaluating health risks related to nuclear events. When calculating the radiation dose to the population through the pathway "surface water/drinking water", it is more safe to assume no reduction at all.

The Chernobyl event has focused the attention on the importance of monitoring radioactivity in relation to drinking water production. Water supply companies responded in two ways : either they started up measurement schemes carried out by their own laboratories, or they entered into agreements with other specialized bodies to monitor radioactivity in the water source and in the end-product, drinking water. Monitoring water however does not prevent it from getting contaminated, and since serious accidents with nuclear power plants cannot be excluded, it must be concluded that the existence of nuclear power plants represents a substantial threat to the continuity of drinking water supply, which can only be overcome by costly measures, such as interconnection of networks or diversifying the water resources, as part of emergency schemes.

ACKNOWLEDGEMENTS

The author wishes to thank the General Manager of *Antwerpse Waterwerken* for his permission to publish the results of this survey. He expresses his gratitude towards his Belgian and Dutch colleagues, members of the Working Party on Nuclear Power Plants of the Association of Water Companies, using Rhine or Meuse water for drinking water production, RIWA, in particular the Chairman, M. Oskam, for their support. The author is also indebted to MM. Hurtgen and Vynckier of the Research Centre for Nuclear Energy at Mol for their valuable advice in radiometry matters, and to M. Kirchmann of the same institution, for the stimulating discussions resulting in and from the radionuclide balance experiment.

REFERENCES

1. J.D. LOWRY and S.B. LOWRY. Radionuclides in drinking water. J. Amer. Water Works Assoc., 1988, July, 50-64.

2. W.J. MASSCHELEIN, R. GOOSSENS, A. DELVILLE, J. GENOT and R. HALLEUX. Enseignements relatifs aux performances d'une filière classique de traitement d'eau potable lors des retombées de l'accident de Tchernobyl. In: Isotope techniques in water resources development, Proceedings of an international symposium, IAEA, Vienna, 30 March-3 April 1987.

3. Report on the joint program of studies on the decontamination of radioactive wastes. Oak Ridge National Laboratory, ORNL-2557, TID-4500, 1954.

4. D. CLIFFORD, W. VIJJESWARAPU and S. SUBRAMANIAN. Evaluating various sorbents and membranes for removing radium from groundwater. J. Amer. Water Works Assoc., 1988, July, 94-140.

5. T.J. SORG. Methods for removing uranium from drinking water. J. Amer. Water Works Assoc., 1988, July, 105-111 .

6. J.D. LOWRY, W.F. BRUTSAERT, T. McENERNEY and C. MOLK. Point-of-entry removal of radon from drinking water. J. Amer. Water Works Assoc., 1987, April, 162-169.

7. E.H. AIETA, J.E. SINGLEY, A.R. TRUSSELL, K.W. THORBJARNARSON and M.J. McGUIRE. Radionuclides in drinking water. An overview. J. Amer. Water Works Assoc., 1987, April, 144-152 .

8. W.J. MASSCHELEIN, personal communication.

9. R. L. VALENTINE, T. S. MULHOLLAND and R. C. SPLINTER. Radium removal using sorption to filter sand. J. Amer. Water Works Assoc., 1987, April, 170-176.

10. E. DE DYCKER. Study of the meteorological conditions during the first two weeks following the Chernobyl accident. In : J. KRETZSCHMAR and R. BILLIAU, Eds.,The Chernobyl accident and its impact. Study Center for Nuclear Energy, Publications nr. 86.02, 1986.

11. B. HOOGCARSPEL. Tsjernobyl : een les voor de toekomst. H$_2$0, 1986, nr. 25, 610-614.

Discussion

Mr R. Clayton, *Crowther Clayton Associates*
The effort described in Papers 15 and 16 is a considerable one to deal
with what Dr Miller (Paper 11) described as a non-problem. The most
striking feature in these two papers is the similarity of the strategies
which are being adopted by Strathclyde and Paris. Both are developing
plans for an interconnected network which will allow water from any
one source to be delivered throughout the network. It was not clear
from Mr Chambers' presentation how much of his area will be on the
interconnected network. Apart from the islands, is it the intention that
the whole area will be interconnected? Is there any plan for a Scottish
water grid similar to the one proposed many years ago by the National
Water Resources Board for England?

Both Authors mentioned supplying water from a 'reserve' source; in
the case of Paris it was from 'raw water storage basins' and in the case of
Strathclyde it would be by way of containers delivered to households. In
the case of Paris, is this 'bankside storage' or will it be from fully covered
tanks such as water towers? Mr Chambers mentioned the need for very
substantial manpower in delivering water in containers; has he
considered the alternative of supplying small ion-exchange cartridges
which could be easily manufactured in quantity for a cost of around £10
and which would be capable of supplying 50-100 days' worth of
de-activated water for a household?

The most interesting part of Mr Chambers' paper is that dealing with
the plan for communications. We have already heard of the need for
better information for consumers but there remains the question of
plausibility. If the answer to consumers' questions on the quality of their
water is reassuring, they are doubtful because they believe that the
supplier would always try to reassure them regardless of the actual
quality in order to make life easier or to stop a panic. The only way the
consumer can be fully reassured is if an independent body, such as
Friends of the Earth, confirms the information. Does Strathclyde plan to
use a fully independent body to confirm or certify the information it
provides?

One of the most interesting aspects of Paper 16 is the pilot plant work
on the removal of radionuclides by the water treatment process. The
paper says nothing about the results; is there any preliminary

information on radionuclide removal? When is it anticipated that this work will be completed, and could we request that the results be published in the most widely circulated international technical journals?

The question of how the radioactive sludges from the treatment processes will be dealt with was mentioned but no strategy or solution was given. How do the authorities in Strathclyde and Paris intend to deal with such radioactive sludges?

Mr D.M. Leguy, *Seine Normandy Basin Financial Agency, France*
Radioactive sludges produced by waterworks which treat contaminated raw water should be considered as other nuclear waste. They should, in fact, have the same distribution as the contaminated soil around the affected reactor.

Mr G.M. Roberts, *Yorkshire Water*
Both Mr Leguy (Paper 14) and Mr Cadet (Paper 16) have referred to extensive works undertaken primarily to protect against the consequences of a major nuclear, or other polluting, incident. Given that France, in common with other EC countries, subscribes to the principle that 'the polluter pays', could I have comment on who should have, and who did, pay for this precautionary work, none of which would have been necessary were it not for the proposed power station at Nogent.

Mr D.M. Leguy
Electricité de France did not pay any of the substantial investment made by the water suppliers and the basin agency (interconnecting pipes etc.) but participated in the programme of studies and in the installation of monitoring equipment at the waterworks.

Mr R. Clayton, *Crowther Clayton Associates*
The new UK Secretary of State for the Environment, Chris Patten, recently appointed Professor David Pearce of London University as his special adviser on environmental economics. Professor Pearce recently prepared a report in which he proposed that all economic evaluations for new projects should include a cost for the use of environmental resources (a cost which is currently 'externalized' - i.e. passed on to others - rather than 'internalized'. This is not yet official policy but is a promising development in the politics and economics of the environment, and in the longer term it may well provide the answer to the question posed by Mr Roberts.

Mr G. Fraser, *Commission of the European Communities, Luxembourg*
In my own text (Paper 5), I have already described the practical problems, as I see them, involved in establishing maximum permissible concentrations for radioactive materials in drinking water on a European Community basis, and have suggested that in any case such limits might serve little purpose since, in practice, all levels in normal conditions are far below what might imply significant exposure of the individual consumer. If we are addressing reassurance rather than protection of the

consumer, however, perhaps reference could be made to the investigation levels (not limits) given in the World Health Organization guidelines. From this point of view, it would be interesting to know how often the guidelines have been exceeded.

Mr J. Tracey, *Manchester City Council*
I have two points to make on contingency measures in relation to nuclear power plants. Firstly, electricity generating companies do not contribute to the cost of contingency measures, the cost of these measures will not be reflected in the unit cost of electricity, which is the main selling point of nuclear power plants. The public perceives that unit cost calculations for nuclear power do not take into account all relevant costs (e.g. decommissioning costs). Secondly, water authorities in England, unlike local authorities, do not have directly elected members; therefore, it could be argued that they are not as accountable. What efforts are made by water authorities in England to consult the public and local authorities on contingency plans?

Mr R. Clayton, *Crowther Clayton Associates*
Mr Tracey asks who, in the absence of elected representatives in the new water supply companies in England, is responsible for overseeing the quality. The Water Act 1989 has created the post of Director-General of Water Services who now carries this responsibility.

Mr A. McCredie, *Central Scotland Water Development Board*
In Scotland before Chernobyl very little radiological monitoring of water supplies was carried out by water authorities and, consequently, very little information was available on the radiological quality of drinking waters or on the removal of radioactive isotopes by existing water treatment processes. Paper 19 gives information on the removal efficiencies for various radioactive isotopes measured at various water treatment works in Belgium and the Netherlands, and Paper 17 gives information on the removal rates achieved at the Tailfer water treatment works using radioactive tracers. Could the Authors supply any information on the concentration of radionuclides that can be expected in the washwater-recovery plants and sludge-handling facilities of the various works studied?

The removal process would appear to involve the adsorption of the radioactive material on to the particulate matter present in the water, which is then removed in varying degrees by the water treatment process employed. Paper 19 states that slow sand filters are not efficient at removing radionuclides. However, as slow sand filters are efficient at removing particulate matter, I should have thought that they would consequently be just as efficient at removing adsorbed radioactive material. Would Dr Van Craenenbroeck care to comment?

Paper 17 reports some very interesting work on the adsorption of radioactive caesium on sand. Two sands were studied with differing adsorption characteristics. Could the Authors explain what the difference was between the sands used, and whether they have carried out any further work in this area?

Paper 18 details the contingency plans formulated by the City of Karachi for dealing with a nuclear accident. In general, contingency or emergency plans, once made, should be tested or exercised. Have the authorities in Pakistan any plans to test the Karachi emergency relief plan? If so, what are they? Or is the probability of a nuclear accident so remote that it is considered not necessary to carry out such an exercise? I should welcome Professor Khan's views on the testing of emergency plans. In Paper 18 it is suggested that, during a nuclear emergency, radioactive waste may be disposed of by burning. Is this considered to be an adequate method of disposal in Pakistan?

Mr L.G. Murray, *Cumbria County Council*
I should like to respond to the point concerning exercise of nuclear plans in this country. In Cumbria, at least, officers of the principal emergency services, local authorities and central Government are thoroughly exercised - at present at least once, occasionally up to three times annually - in order to validate off-site emergency plans. The exercises are required and monitored by HM Nuclear Installations Inspectorate and inevitably result in some significant amendment to pre-planned procedures.

I should like to ask Professor Khan a question. In a well -constructed organization created to respond to a serious civil emergency, to what extent has provision been made to cope with intense press and media interest and, specifically, to ensure that one element of the organization does not contradict public advice -which may include safety of public water supplies - issued by another agency?

Mr Goossens, *Paper 17*
The maximum concentration factor of a trace element in the dry sludge at the Tailfer water treatment works is established to fluctuate between 3500 and 4600 (see reference 1).

The sand used in module 1 at the Tailfer plant was crushed silica and that of module 4 was sifted, calibrated sand of the river Meuse. Further investigation is still under way.

Dr Van Craenenbroeck, *Paper 19*
Slow sand filters do remove radionuclides from water, on the condition that suspended matter is present and that the radionuclides of concern are adsorbed on to these particles. If the slow filtration step is preceded by flocculation-(rapid) filtration, practically no solids are present in the slow filters influent, and, consequently, the additional removal efficiency at the level of these filters will be low. Under the fallout conditions after Chernobyl, the majority of radionuclides remained in solution after precipitation on the uncovered slow sand filters, so that, in theory, low efficiencies would be expected. This hypothesis could not be verified, however, as only overall efficiency rates are available.

Mr L.G. Murray, *Cumbria County Council*

Professor Fleming has exhorted us to address the difficulty of reconciling radiological protection advice with public perceptions of risk. My comments may not concern the weightier specific business of this conference, but I would be pleased to offer some general local authority perspectives concerning nuclear emergency planning and information to the public at regional or county level.

We have heard assertions that the independence of central Government and national agencies may be in doubt where some elements of the public are concerned. There have been proposals that local authorities can address this facet of public concern by engaging in what they would like to be seen as an independent audit of statutory and regulatory radiation-monitoring activities.

I would be seriously concerned that local authorities going down that road may actually further undermine public confidence by creating a potential for contradiction at a time when it is critically important that all agencies involved in mitigating the off-site consequences of a serious nuclear accident take steps to avoid contradicting one another and compounding public alarm. Dr Feates has asked why members of the public seem to question the integrity of central Government scientists, and we have heard several possible explanations for this phenomenon. I am not, however, convinced that analyses and prognoses made by local authorities will ultimately be held in any greater esteem than those which their proponents aim to replace. On a routine basis, in my experience, local authority radiation monitoring initiatives have served merely to confirm the integrity of conclusions already arrived at by the NRPB, the MAFF/DAFS, and the nuclear industry. To what extent, having done this, will the local authority be able to secure the confidence of people unconvinced by highly qualified and thoroughly well-equipped central government analysts? In any event, I suspect that some people will remain unconvinced by the independence of any organization, whether local or central, unless it sustains their own parochial points of view, particularly where that is diametrically opposed to official assertions of safety.

Local authorities do, however, have an important role to play, specifically in the circumstances of a serious nuclear accident, by complementing and supplementing the national data collection and public information activities described in Paper 6, where they are usefully equipped and have been properly accredited.

With the benefit of extensive and detailed local knowledge which is unavailable to central agencies, local authorities can do much to ensure that important information and advice from crisis managers is widely disseminated, and augmented, where necessary, by local perspectives arrived at after full consultation with all agencies at regional or county level; it is essential, however, that this is done on a pre-planned basis and that it takes full account of the implications of the accident for the safety of public water supplies.

If it is true that, to an extent, the problem of compliance arises from central advice issuing at too great a distance from the areas where it is sought and for which it is intended, then perhaps a properly constituted and appropriately equipped local organization can do much to offset public alarm, reinforce statements originating from central sources, and take some weight from the public information officers of key agencies such as water suppliers.

Mr D.M.V. Aspinwall, *Engineers for Nuclear Disarmament*
There has been inadequate discussion at the conference on what could constitute a nuclear event. Here are a few scenarios that are imaginable, and therefore possible, but which have not been mentioned.

One possibility is gross contamination of the Thames by an accident at the effluent treatment plants at Harwell or Aldermaston. This would affect the water supply to a large part of London which draws its water from the Thames.

Another possibility is an accident at the Trawsfyndd nuclear power station in North Wales. This could contaminate Lake Vyrnwy, which supplies water to Liverpool, or the Elan reservoirs, which supply Birmingham.

A third possibility is a major accident at the storage facilities for high level waste at Sellafield. The fallout resulting from such an accident could be equivalent to that occurring from the explosion of a significant number of hydrogen bombs. The subsequent gross pollution of the Lake District would result in the contamination of the lake which supplies Manchester with drinking water.

It should be noted that two of the above-mentioned sites are connected with the manufacture of nuclear weapons.

The other point I should like to make concerns monitoring programmes and mathematical models. We have heard a number of cautious attitudes expressed regarding the cost of these items and whether they were worthwhile. I believe that monitoring programmes and mathematical models are substantially underfunded and that there should be no quibble about the cost, in view of the vast sums of money that have been spent on the nuclear industry - both for weapons and for electricity generation - since 1940.

Mr R. Castle, *North West Water*
While is it generally accepted by the delegates at this conference that a nuclear accident is unlikely to produce widespread contamination of water supplies, it is important that radioactivity monitoring is carried out as part of a screening procedure to ensure that water supplies are free from natural radionuclides, most notably radon and radium. Radon in some groundwater supplies is, in my view, a far more significant radiological hazard than man-made radionuclides, which are usually only present at the millibequerel level.

Reference
1.   MASSCHELEIN W.J., GENOT J., DE VLEMINCK R. and GOBLET Cl. Sludge treatment in water treatment plants. Tribune du CEBEDEAU, No. 450, 34, 245-260.